THE LIFE OF THOMAS PAINE,

AUTHOR OF

"COMMON SENSE," "RIGHTS OF MAN," "AGE OF REASON,"
ETC., ETC.

WITH CRITICAL AND EXPLANATORY

OBSERVATIONS ON HIS WRITINGS.

BY G. VALE,

EDITOR OF "THE CITIZEN OF THE WORLD."

NEW YORK:
PUBLISHED BY THE AUTHOR,
CITIZEN OF THE WORLD OFFICE, NO. 1 BOWERY (CHATHAM SQUARE).

1853.

CONTENTS.

Preface, containing earlier Histories, Cheetham's Trial, Carver's Letter, &c. .... p. 3-14

PART I.

Mr. Paine, his birth, parentage, early life, education, religious impressions 16
Employment, arrives in London, goes to sea 17
Leaves the sea, his School-master's influence, settles at Sandwich, marries, removes to Margate, becomes Exciseman, is dismissed, Petitions 18
Goes to London, becomes a Teacher, and Student in Natural Philosophy, Astronomy, and Mathematics 19
His style, and attainments 20, 21
Re-appointed in the Excise, resides at Lewes, second marriage, social habits, early Poetry, his Letter on Excise Officers, habits, and reputation 22, 23
Becomes tobacconist, suffers in business, separates from his Wife, her property, after-conduct, religion, singular connubial fact 24, 25
His early Thoughts on Government, revisits London, obtains Franklin's friendship, leaves England for America, Reflections 26-28

PART II.

Mr. Paine, his arrival in America, brings letters from Franklin, edits "Pennsylvania Magazine;" his poetry, song on Wolfe, object in coming to America, connexion with Dr. Rush, his literary attainments, a beautiful extract 30-33
Publishes "Common Sense," its effects, gives up copy-right, enters the army as a volunteer 50-53
Publishes the "Crisis," an extract, Cheetham's account of its influence on the Trenton affair, 2d "Crisis," to Lord Howe, 3d "Crisis," appointed Secretary to the Committee on Foreign Affairs 54, 55
4th "Crisis," on the loss of the battle at Brandywine, salutary effects of this Crisis, 5th "Crisis" (to Lord Howe), on predatory war, distribution of forged bills 56
6th "Crisis," to Carlisle, Clinton, &c., in ridicule of 'rightful sovereign,' after the treaty with France, 7th "Crisis," to the People of England, resigns his office of Secretary 58, 59
Becomes Clerk to the Legislature of Pennsylvania, 8th "Crisis," address to the People of England, 9th "Crisis," after the loss of Charleston .. 60, 61
"Crisis Extraordinary" on taxes, proposes in a letter to Mr. Isard of South Carolina, a loan from France, accompanies Col. Laurens to France, effects a loan, intention to visit England, advice of Gen. Greene, obtains the despatches of an English packet, a French fleet, gives five hundred dollars in relief of the Treasury 62-64
10th "Crisis" after the capture of Cornwallis, a supernumerary "Crisis" to Sir Guy Carleton, letter to Lord Shelburne, 12th "Crisis," publication of "Public Good," his disinterestedness and pecuniary loss from Virginia .. 65-67
His letter to Abbe Raynal, Washington's regard for Mr. Paine's services 68, 69
Receives $3,000 from Congress, receives 500l. from Pennsylvania, receives from New York an estate at Rochelle, publishes "Dissertation on Government, do. on "Paper Money," commences a private subscription, when public failed 71-73

PART III.

Mr. Paine, his departure from America, object, reception in France, iron bridge, visits Sir Joseph Banks, his mother, publishes "Prospects on the Rubicon," connexion with Society of Arts, their meanness 75, 76
Assisted by Mr. Whiteside, leaves England for France, account of French Revolution 77
Replies to Burke, secretly opposed by Government, "Rights of Man," .. 94-96
Goes to France, danger, reply to Abbe Syeyes, returns to London, address at Thatched House, 2d part of "Rights of Man," Government offers to bribe or purchase the printer 97-100
Prosecuted, his letter, addresses against "Rights of Man" by corporations, &c., "Address to the Addressers" 101-106
Elected to the French Convention, treatment at Dover and Calais, elected for Abbeville, Beauvais, and Versailles, his trial and conviction, retailers prosecuted 107-109
A list of his publishers prosecuted, social life in London, opposition to the death of the King of France, hated by Marat and others, attacked by Capt. Grimstone 110-113
His life in Paris, expelled the Convention by a motion to expel foreigners, is imprisoned by a motion to imprison persons born in England, publishes "Age of Reason," Americans in Paris seek his release, coldness of Washington, and Morris the American Minister in France, writes 2d part of "Age of Reason," his letter to Monroe, and reply 114-118
Released from prison, visits Mr. Monroe, miraculous escape, invited to return to the Convention, publishes "Age of Reason," its principles, Llandaff's reply, the publisher Williams prosecuted 119-125
His speech on Boissy d'Anglas' constitution, adopted, convention terminated, Mr. Paine not re-elected, 2d part of "Age of Reason," "Dissertation on Government," "Agrarian Justice," English Finances, his letter to Washington, his letter to a lady at New York, and attachment to America 126, 127
"A Theophilanthropist," his letter on the 18th Fructidor, to Camille Jordan, Mr. Paine at one time unpopular in France, resides in Bonneville's family, resolves on leaving France 128-130
His moral and social Character in France 131-134
His treatment by historians and booksellers, his iron bridge, poetry, his attempt to return, and final return to America 136-140

PREFACE.

There are four lives of Mr. Thomas Paine now extant; but none in print in the United States. Francis Oldys, or a person under that name, wrote a life of Mr. Paine about the year 1792, while Mr. Paine was yet alive, and active in the progress of the French Revolution. This life was written in fact by George Chalmers, one of the clerks of the Board of Plantation, at the instigation of Lord Hawksbury, afterward Lord Liverpool, for which he gave him five hundred pounds. Mr. Chalmers acknowledged the authorship of this book. This we have never seen; it has sunk into oblivion; it partly served the political purpose for which it was written, but the enemies of Mr. Paine and the Rights of Man were too prudent to endorse its acknowledged calumnies, and identify themselves with this transaction.

Immediately after the death of Paine, Cheetham wrote his life in 1809. Cheetham was an Englishman and had been a zealous disciple of Paine, both in politics and religion; but he had retrogaded in politics, and deserted the principles of the democratic party; Paine had attacked him with his accustomed force, and thus converted him into a personal enemy. Mr. Cheetham at this time edited a party paper (the Citizen) in New York, and while he was yet smarting under the lash of Paine, heated by party politics, and fired with revenge, like the ass in the fable, he kicked, not indeed the dying, but the dead lion, by writing the life of his adversary. Cheetham, however, connected this with a scheme of interest; for, becoming the deadly enemy of democracy, and losing the support of his old friends (for he was turned out of the Tammany society), he was preparing to go to Europe, and enlist in support of the tory government in England, by publishing a paper opposed to Cobbett, who had just come out in opposition to the government; and Cheetham apparently meant this life of Paine as a passport to the British treasury favor: at least, such was the opinion of the intimate friend of Cheetham, Mr. Charles Christian, who gave this relation to Mr. John Fellows and others, whom we have seen, and from whom we have learned this fact. This life of Paine, the only one published in the United States, abounds in calumnies, and after a lapse of some years caused the production of two other lives, one by Clio Rickman, the intimate friend of Mr. Paine for many years, and another by Mr. W. T. Sherwin, both published in London. Mr. Rickman was an excellent, amiable man, of the quaker profession, with whom Mr. Paine lived both in England and France, at different periods, and with whom he kept up a constant correspondence. The life of Paine, however, by Mr. Rickman, is sullied by a little vanity; he is to Paine, what Boswell was to Johnson. We are indebted to Mr. Rickman for many facts on which we can rely; but with the best intentions he was not the man to do Mr. Paine justice.

The best life of Paine before published, is that of Sherwin; and from this life we shall freely extract. But Mr. Sherwin is incorrect on some points, and his whole work is so exclusively adapted to a London reader, that it is deteriorated for this market. Mr. Paine changed public opinion in favor of a republic at the time of the Revolution; his earliest energies were in favor of American liberty; it was here that his mighty powers were first developed, and here his political principles took root. His success in the United States brought him out in Europe; and his "Rights of Man," which shook the corrupt government of England, and endeared him to all France and every friend of liberty, was based upon his "Common Sense," which had concentrated public opinion in favor of a declaration of independence. And when the buds of liberty were nipped in England and France, to this country Mr. Paine retired, as his proper home, at the invitation of Jefferson, then the president, and avowedly the greatest and best statesman this country has known. And here, too, he died in peace, in a good old age, the firm and consistent friend of liberty. To this country, then, in a special manner belongs his life; here are his most numerous friends and personal acquaintances; it is here that the calumnies propagated by Cheetham may be effectually rebutted, by living witnesses yet in the sound possession of their faculties; and it is here that Paine can be identified with every *crisis* in the glorious Revolution which gave birth to this nation, which has set the glorious example of republicanism, whose principles are now progressing in the world. The want of a life thus identifying Mr. Paine with the glories of our Revolution, is our apology for our present undertaking.

The life of Paine by Cheetham has had a considerable influence; for though his calumnies are palpable, and his motives in publishing them apparent, he has given to them a degree of credibility by the free use of names, which the reader necessarily concludes are respectable references for the facts he has stated; fortunately, however, a public trial, in which he was convicted of libel, showed the shallow foundation on which his slander rested, and our acquaintance with some of the persons to whom he refers, enables us flatly to contradict these statements, and to denounce him on the very authority of many of his references as the utterer of gross falsehoods, to which he attached without their consent their names. With much ingenuity he relates a slander as a matter of fact, as if there were abundance of evidence, and apparently refers to the *only* source of this slander, as if this formed but a small part of his proof. Thus he declared Madame Bonneville to b... mistress of T. Paine, as if that fact were notorious; he produces no proof, but inserts a letter from Mr. W. Carver, written in anger, after a quarrel, in which such an insinuation is made, merely from the fact of that lady bringing her family to America, and leaving her husband in France. Madame Bonneville prosecuted Cheetham for this assertion, and Cheetham on that trial produced no other evidence than

Carver and his angry letter. His counsel admitted the falseness of the charge, and pleaded only the insinuation in Carver's letter as justifying Cheetham as an *historian* to repeat the slander.

This trial excited great interest at the time. The press generally reported it; and the brief facts with the counsel's speech have been preserved in a pamphlet form, from which pamphlet we shall give the introduction and a few extracts as pertinent to our object:—

[THE INTRODUCTION.]

"One James Cheetham, a man who had once been an editor of a republican paper in New York, had abandoned his past professions, and become the advocate of the British party in America. Among other means to serve them, he undertook to write the life of Thomas Paine, author of 'Common Sense,' 'Rights of Man,' &c., &c. In this biography, he introduced the name of Madame Bonneville, a virtuous and respectable lady, the wife of N. Bonneville of Paris. He charged her with prostitution; said Paine was her paramour, and that one of her sons had the features, countenance, and temper of Thomas Paine. For this atrocious attack on the character of Madame Bonneville, and outrage to her feelings, Mr. Cheetham was indicted for a libel, and on the 19th of June, 1810, his trial was brought on.

The counsel for the libeller took two grounds of defence:
1st. That the facts charged were true.
2d. That the defendant was an HISTORIAN, and, as such, had a right to publish what he had heard and believed, though it reflected on an innocent person.

The first position was, after a contemptible effort to support it, abandoned even by the libeller's counsel. They were ashamed of it themselves. Several ladies of the first distinction, whose daughters had been intrusted to the care of Madame Bonneville, to learn the French language, appeared in court, and attested to the unblemished character of this much-injured female.

The counsel for the libeller than had recourse to their last ground, and strenuously maintained the principle they had laid down. They perhaps felt confidence in the court, as it had, in an early stage of the trial, intimated an opinion favorable to the new and extravagant pretension, which set up a libeller under the title of an historian. Nor was this confidence misplaced. Mr. Recorder Hoffman directed the jury, that if they should be of opinion, that Mr. Cheetham had been informed of what he wrote, and believed it, he was justified, and that, though Madame Bonneville was an innocent woman, they were authorized, to acquit Mr. Cheetham. He also read the letter of a man, by the name of Carver, as a justification of the libeller, though his counsel had not mentioned it.

This monstrous doctrine, which leads to the prostration of private reputation, if not to the dissolution of civil society, was promptly rejected by the jury, although composed of men of different political sentiments, who returned in a few minutes a verdict of guilty.

The court, however, when the libeller came up the next day to receive his sentence, highly commended the book which contained the libellous publication, declared that it tended to serve the cause of religion, and imposed no other punishment on the libeller, than the payment of two hundred and fifty dollars, with a direction that the costs be taken out of it.

It is fit to remark, lest foreigners who are unacquainted with our political condition, should receive erroneous impressions, that Mr. Recorder Hoffman does not belong to what is called the republican party in America, but has been elevated to office by men in hostility to it, who obtained a temporary ascendency in the councils of the state."

EXTRACTS FROM MR. SAMPSON'S SPEECH ON THE TRIAL OF MR. JAMES CHEETHAM, FOR A LIBEL ON MRS. MARGARET BONNEVILLE, IN HIS LIFE OF THOMAS PAINE.

"In every other grief than that which this historian has inflicted on her the innocent find comfort; for innocence is in all other wrongs, against all other strokes of man's injustice or oppression, a sevenfold shield. Not so where woman's honor is assailed; suspicion there is worse than death itself. It is that for which alone the innocent wife of Cesar was repudiated. The man who dares attack it is of all other criminals the greatest. If he be not a traitor it is for this alone that he is worse. For many a man has suffered as a traitor, whom after-ages have revered and honored. But never was he who set his cloven-hoof upon a woman's honor worthy the name of man.

[Here the defendant rose and claimed the protection of the court, not so much with a desire to prevent the range of the ingenious counsel, as to prevent the utterance of personalities, that it would not be prudent perhaps to repeat out of court.

While the defendant was addressing the court, the counsel calmly advanced, and taking a pinch of snuff, modestly observed, that what he was doing was in court, and what was to be done out of court was not to be talked of here. Then pointing to the defendant, and casting a significant look upon him, he proceeded.]

This unrighteous man has, by this very movement of his choler, justified all that I can ever say. If he complains of personalities — he who is hardened in every gross abuse — he who lives reviling and reviled; who might construct himself a monument, with no other materials but those records to which he is a party, and in which he stands enrolled as an offender — if he cannot sit still to hear his accusation, but calls for the protection of the court against a counsel, whose duty it is to make his crimes appear — how does *she* deserve protection whom he has driven to the sad necessity of coming here to vindicate her honor from those personalities which he has lavished on her? Did not his opening counsel say before you that 'he could make the color fade upon this lady's cheek, and wish that she might be in court to hear him? regret that her own son was not here to testify against her?' Was not this monstrous personality? And when it is considered that before this very cause drew near its close, the other counsel of this same defendant rose and told you, that 'they admitted her character was spotless, and for that reason that no reproach was cast upon it, desire you to acquit their *innocent* client, who is a mere historian, who never could have malice, who was more ready to rectify his errors, than others to observe him.'

But it is well, and I am glad that I was interrupted; for the very evil genius that waits upon his life has here, for once, worked to an honest end. For while my voice was almost choked with crowding truths, struggling for utterance, and while the swell of honest indignation rose even to suffocation, he came forward and pointed my attention to that subject which first deserved rebuke.

I had said, that in the catalogue of crimes none could be found more base than his. Not treason, for the reasons I have given. Not murder; for he who murders life, murders all sorrow with it; but he has doomed this lady to days of sorrow, and to lingering death. The pirate meets his foe, or seeks his prey, where death and danger stare him in the face; and when he falls before the sword of justice, some sympathy may mingle with his shame, and men regret that one so brave in manly enterprise should fall so ignominiously. But here is an attack upon a woman far from her husband's side, from friends and home, whose infant sons are yet too tender to avenge their mother's wrongs. The forger who counterfeits some instrument to cheat you of your money, for that crime spins out his wretched days in hard captivity, in infamy and labor: will you compare his crime with that of one who, by his fabricated histories, pilfers from helpless woman the only precious jewel which she prizes—her more than life, her all—her spotless honor? That which the robber or the thief purloins may be retrieved, or may be spared; but not the worth of twenty thousand beings such as the libeller, were he worth twenty thousand times as much as ever he will be, reform how he may, would pay the twenty thousandth part of that which he has taken.

It is argued that everything should be intended in favor of this defendant, who has written so godly a work against the prince of deists, and for the holy gospel. I am sorry to hear such arguments advanced; they go almost to burlesque religion itself. He a man of God! He write for the love of God! His book a godly book! a vile, obscene, and filthy compilation, which bears throughout the character of rancorous malice, and tramples upon every Christian charity. Libel an innocent woman, lie and calumniate, for the sake of Christianity! If this be the only godly deed this man has done, I pray to Heaven to be more merciful to him than he has been to Mrs. Bonneville, and that for this very work of godliness he be not damned.

If you be Christian jurors punish him; for be assured of this, that twenty Paines, were twenty such just now upon this earth, could not conjointly do more harm to Christianity by their most violent efforts, than this man by defending it would do. If any one of wavering faith should hear that the best vindication of God's word was this most libellous and scandalous work, he never would be a Christian from that hour. Not every one that saith, Lord, Lord, shall enter the kingdom of heaven, but least of all he that makes the blessed name of God a cloak for malice and iniquity. He may be like those priests of whom we read in history, who, with the holy cross in the one hand and the bloody sabre in the other, commit atrocities at which nature shudders.

Where did he learn, that the God of mercy took delight in human sacrifices, and that, to do him honor, a woman's heart should palpitate upon a bloody altar? Has he ever read the word of God? or, this heavenly *historian*, does he know one letter of the gospel history? If he does, he is as blunt and dull in understanding, as he is dead to sensibility and delicacy. When a woman was brought before the author of the Christian religion, taken in the very fact of adultery, what did he say? He left behind him a specimen of tenderness ever memorable and divine. 'Let him,' he said to the fanatical and malignant rabble, 'let him who is innocent cast the first stone.'

And if this Christian *historian* had ever known or felt the benignant spirit of holy inspiration, would he not be sensible that he was not innocent? If he be innocent, then are tigers gentle.

There was a monastery where deadly crimes were expiated called La Trappe: when sinners entered it they made a terrible vow of everlasting silence, and from that awful moment never uttered a word, and daily with their nails dug their own graves. When the midnight bell tolled them to prayer, they left their solitary cells, and moved with noiseless step through gloomy cloisters and whispering aisles, with downcast look, turning their rosaries, but never spoke. Such is the penitence, such the everlasting silence that would become the ruthless slanderer of woman's honor. But he who acts the bully and the bravo, and calls himself the champion of high Heaven, what words can paint the horror he inspires! Then let us leave him.

My duty calls me now to recapitulate the testimony of all his witnesses. The first and principal is Mr. Carver. He, with uplifted hand, affirmed, by the ever-living God, the truth of what he testified — and what was that? His letter tells us all: that he and Paine had a dispute for money; and in their correspondence you may find the crimes and baseness they reciprocally urged against each other. Mr. Carver, whose vulgar scurrilous letter makes the chief buttress of this man's defence, the more to spite his adversaries, flings out some calumny against the lady. Carver himself admits, that when she got a sight of it she threatened to prosecute him for that very letter. Yet on no better ground has this audacious libeller defamed her reputation.

From the same source springs the infernal hint that little Thomas Bonneville had the countenance and features of Thomas Paine. In his little nose no doubt the *historian* could discern, by learned inspection, the germes of future blossoms, and gems that in due course of nature should come to this world's light.

Carver gives evidence of what *he heard* from Paine of Mrs. Bonneville, which he himself retailed to Cheetham; and Cheetham, rather than such sublime history should not shine forth to save poor sinners' souls, becomes his *historian* for the love of God, and gives them to the world as *history*. This is the history of this *historian* and his history!

I pushed him (Carver) farther, and he stated that *he and his wife* had often gone to Mr. Purdy's on the farm to visit Mrs. Bonneville. Then it was, that seeing the toils in which his honesty and decency had fallen, he tapered off by saying he never had seen the slightest indication of any meretricious or illicit commerce between Paine and Mrs. Bonneville; that they never were alone together, and that all the three children, the little godson Thomas and all, were *alike* the objects of Paine's care.

Here ends the black conspiracy and conjuration for the love of God. And now the sickened soul revives, and a bright scene appears: A group of matrons led by those hands which holy wedlock had joined to theirs for ever — heads of families, beloved, distinguished, full of respect and honor; in form so bright, in innocence so lovely; so pure in unsuspected truth, so proud in conscious worth and dignity; who never till that hour had crossed the threshold of a court of justice, or been where discord reigns; whose lips had never uttered other oaths than those which bound them by the willing ties of constancy and love; who, when the seraph-voice of piety called them down, first glided from their spheres upon the wings of heaven-born charity, and having done their mission, disappeared. But, oh! it was a holy sacrament when wife and husband twined their oaths together with such solemnity, such beaming truth, as when they made before the altar of their God that vow so full at once of joy and awe that linked their future destiny together and made them ever one. They would have told you of this lady's sorrows and her resignation, of her spotless conduct, of her merit; how they intrusted to her care and tutelage the jewels of their souls, the children of their hearts; with what reproachless truth; what anxious duty she answered to the trust; had not the rules of evidence and technical formalities of law cut short their story. Her general character was all they were allowed to testify. Their words were few, but like so many messages of grace or high commands from heaven.

The wives of your own bosoms are not more pure than this injured lady is proved, nay, more, *admitted* now to be. If they were stigmatized by an *historian*, what would you say of him, that he was innocent or guilty?

You have heard the witnesses for Mrs. Bonneville, and you may judge if this historian had inquired of them, instead of grubbing filth from every dunghill, how bright a name she would have deserved, who has been, nevertheless, doomed by this terrible man to misery.

If he had begged access to any of those high distinguished persons under whose roof she lived, whose children she had taught; of Mr. Emmett, who oppresses no one, but protects the innocent; or of Mr. Fulton, who knew her and her husband in their own country; if he had asked of Mr. Jarvis — that man of keen sagacity, of observation, with knowledge of mankind and of all the parties; if he had been satisfied with Mr. Hitt's word, rather than that of 'pious nurses and kind attending doctors,' and reverend teachers, who had disputes and lawsuits; he would have known what all but his mutinous genius now concedes. I have no cause of private malice against him, but quite the contrary. When he had any spark of character, he praised me more than ever I could merit, and I could not but thank him. When he had nothing good to give but his abuse, without offence or change in me, he gave me that with equal liberality, and I thanked him. If I could ask a favor of him now, it would be to abuse me more and more, and never let his malice go to the length of praising me: for although my friends who know me well might not despise me, yet in this community where I am little known, and still almost a stranger, I may not have formed sufficient character to stand against his praise, nor be entitled to so much indulgence that it should be believed that I could have his praise, and yet be honest."

This same Cheetham, the libeller of Madame Bonneville, and through her of Paine's memory, is the author of other calumnies on Paine. It is by him that the public have been informed that Paine was drunken and dirty in his person; and so industriously and faithfully have the clergy preached and circulated these calumnies, that we shall scarcely be believed in contradicting them on the very best evidences, his companions now alive, and in some cases the very men whom Cheetham impudently names as sources of his information. Thus, Mr. Jarvis, the celebrated painter, with whom Mr. Paine lived, informs us distinctly that Mr. Paine was neither dirty in his habits nor drunken: nay, he good-humoredly added that *he* always drank a great deal more than ever Paine did. Mr. John Fellows lived in the same house with Mr. Paine, above a twelvemonth, and was his intimate friend for many years after his return to this country, and never saw him but once even elevated with liquor, and then he had been to a dinner-party. We know more than twenty persons who were more or less acquainted with Mr. Paine, and not one of whom ever saw him in liquor. His habit appears to have been to take one glass of rum and water with sugar in it, after dinner, and another after supper. His limit at one period, when at Rochelle, was one quart of rum a week, for himself and friends, for Mr. Paine was rather penurious in his old age. This, and this alone, is the only moral fault we find in his character, and we wish to be his impartial historian. His manner of life at this time we get from Mr. Burger, a respectable watchmaker in New York, but then a clerk in the only store at Rochelle, who served Mr. Paine with his liquor, and waited upon him when sick, and drove him about the neighborhood at the request of his employer, and thus saw much of his social habits. This gentleman never saw Mr. Paine intoxicated. Carver, with whom Paine lived, but from whom he parted in anger, is the only man we know who has not spoken distinctly on that subject; and he remarks, that "Paine was like other men [at that period], he would sometimes take too much." But Carver had unfortunately committed himself on this subject in an angry letter, the same on which Cheetham based his libel. In fact, this letter is the groundwork for all Cheetham's calumnies. Mr. Grant Thorburn, a few years back, republished this letter in his "Forty Years' Residence," on which occasion Carver vindicates himself in one of his last publications, where he thus speaks of that letter:—

EXTRACT FROM "A BONE TO GNAW FOR GRANT THORBURN," BY W. CARVER.

"When I first read the life of Grant Thorburn, I made this remark, and wrote it on the cover of his book: 'I have read this life of Grant Thorburn. I presume a great part of which it is composed has no more connexion with his life than mine, or the pope of Rome's, to wit: the corresponding letters between Thomas Paine and myself, and those letters I have cut out of his book.' These letters were first printed by Cheetham without my consent for base purposes, after he became a tory and a hypocritical turncoat, like Grant Thorburn, who has now reprinted them for the same purpose. They were written by Paine and me in anger. Mr. Paine had boarded with me without any regular agreement, and we quarrelled about the bill, what has happened a thousand times to other people; he wrote angrily and I angrily replied. But the affair was amicably settled by Walter Morton and John Fellows; the latter is still living. I think some things Paine said of me were not in earnest, and I answered in anger: the letters should have been burnt. But Cheetham said many things of Paine that were not true, after he turned tory. I told him 'I believed that he had had his hand crossed with British gold.' Mr. Charles Christian was present; he said to Cheetham: 'That is a bold attack of Carver in your own house.' He replied and said: 'I know Carver; he will contradict a judge on the bench if he thinks him not right;' but he did not deny the charge. When Paine was on his deathbed, I wrote him the following letter. This shows what opinion I had of him; I think he was one of the greatest men that ever lived.

'DEAR SIR: I have heard that you are much indisposed in health, and that your mind, at present, is not reconciled to me. Be that as it may, I can assure you that, on my part, I bear no ill-will, but still remain your sincere well-wisher; and am still a zealous supporter and defender of the principles that you have advocated, believing they are founded on immortal truth and justice; therefore I think it a pity that you or myself should depart this life with envy in our hearts against each other — and I firmly believe that no difference would have taken place between us, had not some of those of your pretended friends endeavored to have caused a separation of friendship between us.

I, sir, want nothing of you or from you, but only that the ignorant and superstitious herd may not have it in their power to exclaim and say that Thomas Paine or Carver died without a reconciliation to each other. I have often told my friends, if I were on my dying bed, I should send for you, hoping that all our differences might be buried in oblivion before our bodies were buried in the grave, as I hope that my dying pillow may not be planted with thorns; I consider that time with me is short, and perhaps shorter with you. If I never should see you again in this world, I wish you all the consolation that your great mind is capable of enjoying, and that you may resign yourself with full confidence on your Maker, and leave a noble testimony to the world of the independency of your mind and honesty of your heart; and this, my friend, will produce to you more comfort than all the prayers of the priests in the Christian world.

Yours in friendship,
WM. CARVER.'"

Mr. Grant Thorburn, mentioned above, scarcely knew Mr. Paine, as Mr. Carver observes, nor does his conduct command respect.

Such are the men, who, admitting the truth of Mr. Paine's writings, seek to destroy their effects by the most puerile attack on his private character. Cheetham, Thorburn, and others, have repeated slanders suggested in an angry letter; the enemies of Paine, corrupt statesmen, and the clergy in particular, have so industriously circulated these slanders, as even to deceive the very friends of Mr. Paine. In commencing our inquiries we really thought the fact that Mr. Paine was a drunkard in old age was well established. In seeking, however, for the proofs of this, we arrive at a very different conclusion. In the course of this work we shall show the sources from which we have derived our information.

G. V.

LIFE OF THOMAS PAINE.

PART I.

Most men pursue personal happiness and their own greatness as worthy objects; but Mr. Paine labored for the greatness of the nation of which he was a member, and sought its nappiness; and in the pursuit of which he built up his own greatness and promoted his own happiness. Nothing will be clearer established by this record of his life than the fact now alluded to; and this fact marks him as peculiarly distinguished even among great and good men. We are not, however, about to write a eulogy; to enhance his virtues, or to suppress his faults, or vices. Paine was a part of human nature, and partook of its imperfections; and our purpose is fairly to represent him as he was; but the greater part of Mr. Paine's life was *public*, and as such we know of no man who had greater virtues or less vices. His natural life is distinctly marked into four periods: his history in England before he embarked for North America; his residence and exertions in this country during the revolutionary war; his return to Europe, and his exertions in France and England during the great French revolution and revolutionary war; and his final return and residence in the United States till his death. The first part will necessarily be the least interesting; his merits were only known to a few; but fortunately among those few was Dr. Franklin (by whose advice he visited this country). We have already noticed Sherwin's life of Paine, and as we find Paine's early life fairly delineated there, with some exceptions, we shall at once transcribe so much of that work as suits our purpose; correcting it where we find it necessary, and making such additions as we think proper from the abundant facts we have accumulated.

THE EARLY LIFE OF THOMAS PAINE.

"Thomas Paine, the subject of these memoirs, was born at Thetford, in the county of Norfolk, England, on the 29th of January, 1737. His parents were obscure as to birth, having nothing to depend upon, except what was derived from their own industry. His father, Joseph Paine, was a member of the society of quakers, a person of sober habits and good moral character: he obtained a decent, but humble livelihood by following his trade, which was that of a staymaker. The maiden name of his mother was Frances Cocke, the daughter of an attorney at Thetford, and a member of the established church. It was probably owing to the disagreement in the religious tenets of his parents that Paine was never baptized. He was, however, privately named, and through the pious care of his aunt, he was afterward confirmed by the bishop of Norwich.

At an early age, Paine was sent to the grammar-school at Thetford, where he was taught reading, writing, and accounts. Before he left this school, he likewise obtained a slight knowledge of the Latin tongue; but from the aversion or contempt which he subsequently acquired for the study of the dead languages, or from want of opportunity, it does not appear that they ever became the objects of settled attention.

It does not seem, or at least it is not known, that, during his boyhood, he exhibited any peculiar signs of that genius which was afterward to exalt him to the very pinnacle of political fame. But from a passage in the 'Age of Reason,' it is evident, that however matured in judgment he might be before he became a politician, his first impressions on the subject of religion were made at a very early period of his life.

Paine himself says: 'From the time I was capable of conceiving an idea, and acting upon it by reflection, I either doubted the truth of the Christian system, or thought it to be a strange affair; I scarcely knew which it was: but I well remember, when about seven or eight years of age, hearing a sermon read by a relation of mine, who was a great devotee of the church, upon the subject of what is called *redemption by the Son of God*. After the sermon was ended, I went into the garden, and as I was going down the garden steps (for I perfectly recollect the spot) I revolted at the recollection of what I had heard, and thought to myself that it was making God Almighty act like a passionate man that killed his son, when he could not revenge himself any other way; and as I was sure a man would be hanged that did such a thing, I could not see for what purpose they preached such sermons. This was not one of those kind of thoughts that had anything in it of childish levity; it was to me a serious reflection, arising from the idea I had, that God was too good to do such an action, and also too almighty to be under any necessity of doing it. I believe in the same manner to this moment; and I moreover believe, that any system of religion that has any thing in it that shocks the mind of a child, cannot be a true system.'—'*Age of Reason*,' Part I., p. 37.

At the age of thirteen he was taken from school by his father, who, unable from his circumstances to apprentice him to any other trade, employed him as an assistant in the business of staymaking. Whether he was ever bound apprentice does not appear, nor is it a matter of much consequence. The sedentary shopboard had few attractions for our author, and he left it the first opportunity. After remaining with his father about three years, he left his native town and proceeded to London, where he doubtless hoped to better his circumstances; conceiving, as many had done before him, that the metropolis was the only place where a youth can attain a proper knowledge of the world, and the only scene where natural talent can find an opportunity of displaying itself to the best advantage. His mind, which nature appears to have formed for enterprise, was of too aspiring a turn to be restricted to the limits of a provincial town, or to brook the idea of being confined for life to a business which would not only have cramped his genius, but which at best would have afforded him but a scanty livelihood. His prospects in London, however, do not seem to have been at first much more inviting than those he had left in the country. On his arrival, he found himself without either friends or money, and destitute of the means of procuring any, except by again having recourse to the business he had just deserted. He applied to a Mr. Morris, a staymaker, in Hanover Street, Long Acre, of whom he procured employment for some weeks. From London he went to Dover, where he worked at his business for a short time, with a Mr. Grace.

How long a time elapsed from the period of his leaving his father to his quitting Mr. Grace does not appear, nor, if known, would it be a matter of much interest. Probably, not more than two or three months. Finding himself baffled in the expectations he had formed on quitting his home, he left his second employer, and went on board the Terrible privateer, Captain Death. To a mind like his, which appears at the time we are speaking of, to have been ardent in the extreme, it is not surprising that the war which had just then been declared against France, afforded an abundant field of enterprising anticipation. Situated as he was, and feeling as he probably did, the army or the navy was his only choice, and he took the latter because it was nearest at hand. How long he remained on board the Terrible, has not been ascertained; but from his own account of the affair, the time must have been short. 'From this adventure,' says he, 'I was happily prevented by the affectionate and moral remonstrance of a good father, who, from his own habits of life, being of the quaker profession, must begin to look upon me as lost.'

Paine had been induced to go to sea from the impressions which the master of the school at Thetford had given him; who having been a chaplain on board a man-of-war, retained much of the enthusiasm of the sea service, and indirectly infused it into the most ardent of his scholars. This affair made a considerable impression at the time; but, like most of the impressions of youth, it soon wore away, and left his disposition for enterprise in much the same state as it was before the circumstance occurred. Shortly afterward, he entered on board the King of Prussia privateer, Captain Mendez; but as no account has been published of this transaction, except that given by himself, it does not appear how long he remained at sea, or what occurred to induce him to desert the naval profession altogether, and resume his own business.

In the year 1759, he settled at Sandwich as a master-staymaker. There he soon became acquainted with a young woman of the name of Mary Lambert, to whom he was married about the end of the same year. She was the daughter of an exciseman, and is said to have possessed considerable personal attractions.

His staymaking business not exactly answering his expectations, he removed with his wife to Margate, where she died in the year 1760. From Margate he went to London, and from London he again removed to Thetford.

Here he resolved upon relinquishing his business altogether. He had long wished for some employment more congenial to his turn of mind. At length, through the interference of Mr. Cocksedge, the recorder at Thetford, he obtained a situation in the excise. This was toward the end of 1763.

For some trifling fault he was dismissed from this situation, in something more than a year afterward. What the nature of that fault was, has never been satisfactorily explained; but those who are acquainted with the practices of the excise, must be well convinced that if the offence had been of any magnitude, he would never have been restored to the office, which was the case in about eleven months after his dismissal."

Mr. Paine, it appears, sent a petition to the board of excise begging to be restored to his situation. In the petition, Paine admits the justice of his dismissal, but uses the expression,

"No complaint of the least dishonesty or intemperance ever appeared against me." For what he was dismissed is not stated, and what is very remarkable, his enemies in the British government who must have known the cause of his dismissal, never made it public, although they sought to destroy him by every means. We consequently conclude that he was not criminal, or such an opportunity would not have been omitted. Those who have lived on the coast of England know that the *impartial* exercise of an exciseman's duty, will expose him to censure; for they will know that those who make and administer the laws are themselves concerned in smuggling. Clio Rickman, the friend of Paine, exposed a flagitious case of this kind, involving even the prime minister of England, which, from its peculiarity, we shall insert:—

"When Admiral Duncan rendezvoused in the Downs with his fleet on the eighth of January, 1806, the Spider (lugger), Daniel Falara, master, was sent to Guernsey to smuggle articles for the fleet, such as wine, spirits, hair-powder, playing-cards, tobacco, &c., for the supply of the different ships.
At her arrival in the Downs, the ships' boats flocked round her to unload her and her contraband cargo. A customhouse extra boat, commanded by William Wallace, seeing the lugger, followed and took her; in doing which he did his duty.
On his inspecting the smuggled articles with which she was laden, he found a number of cases directed to Admiral Duncan, the Right Honorable William Pitt, the heaven-born minister of England, and to the Right Honorable Henry Dundas, Walmer Castle. In a few days, Wallace, the master of the customhouse cutter, received orders from government to give the lugger and her smuggled cargo up, on penalty of being dismissed the service, and these cases of smuggled goods were afterward delivered at the prime minister's, Mr. Pitt's, at Walmer Castle."

At this very time, says Clio Rickman, there were *fourteen poor* persons in *one* jail in England for smuggling. From the surprising silence of Paine's enemies on the subject of his dismissal, we strongly suspect it was connected with something they did not want exposed.

"After his dismission he proceeded to London, where he became a teacher in an academy kept by Mr. Noble of Goodman's Fields. In this situation he remained until the period of his restoration to office. It is probable that it was during his stay in London at this period, he applied himself to the study of astronomy and natural philosophy, and that this is the time he alludes to, when he says, 'As soon as I was able I purchased a pair of globes, and attended the philosophical lectures of Martin and Ferguson, and became afterward acquainted with Dr. Bevis of the Society called the Royal Society, and an excellent astronomer.' Indeed, as he himself expresses it, the natural bent of his mind appears to have been to science, and though from his disadvantageous situation in life he necessarily met with many obstacles, it is evident from several of his productions, that he attained a great proficiency in mechanics, mathematics, and astronomy. It was from his being well grounded in the principles of science, during the earlier part of his life, that he afterward became such a powerful adept in reasoning; it was from the mathematical principles which had been engrafted on his mind while it was yet tender enough to receive the impressions of instruction, that he was subsequently enabled to write with such precision upon almost any subject, that he was enabled to reduce abstruseness to simplicity, to understand difficult subjects himself, and to render them intelligible to others."

The enemies of Mr. Paine have represented him as an ignorant, vulgar man, and his style coarse and rude, but imbued with strong good sense. His worst enemies allow him the latter qualities, except Cheetham; who, heated by party politics, and corrupted by expectancies from Britain, has outraged common sense by denying Paine *any* good qualities, while his own work abounds with proofs to the contrary. Paine's style was clear, forcible, and elegant: in our opinion, he is the best English writer we know. We never misunderstand him; and it is almost impossible to put the same thoughts in fewer or better chosen words than he has done. Those who have attacked his style, are themselves ignorant or vicious, with no literary character to lose. When the clergy have urged on their hearers the vulgarity of the style of Mr. Paine, it has always appeared to us that they have presumed on the ignorance of their hearers, or have themselves been the dupes of what they *wished* to believe: for Paine was decidedly a learned man, but self-taught, as indeed most learned men are; for the meager instruction of a school only gives the rudiments—the base—that on which the fabric must be raised. Paine's knowledge of the classics was indeed very limited; perhaps the mere elements obtained when a boy at the grammar-school; but even this gave him one important advantage: the little he did know enabled him rightly to estimate the value of Greek and Latin, which are of great *intrinsic* worth only in some cases, and of *none* to Mr. Paine in any of his pursuits or works; and when he stated that a Greek milkman knew more of Greek than the best Greek scholar in England, he lifted the veil which covered ignorance; although a scholar might know much of the grammar or philosophical construction of the language, which a Greek milkman might not. In his biblical criticisms, he showed that the *authorized English* Bible was not the Word of God; and thus he cut off all reference to ancient languages. His acquaintance with mathematics and natural philosophy was evidently extensive. His references to these subjects are frequent, and always pertinent; while there is no egotistical display of knowledge or learning; yet every learned man knows well the certainty of detecting ignorance in a man who, by references, assumes a knowledge of science which he does not possess. Paine grappled, too, with the higher branches of the mathematics, for he was acquainted with their application to mechanics and to bridges; and this latter is one of the most difficult subjects to which they are applied. It was not then a compliment that Paine was admitted a member of various learned societies in this country, France, and England. He had substantial claims to such a standing; and those who have attempted to degrade him on this subject, have taken a mean advantage of his unpopularity in the religious community, and of the ignorance and prejudices of that community against him. We have now in our possession a part of a letter in Paine's handwriting, on the difficult subject of *fortification*, in relation to New York, and which he treats in a scientific and masterly manner. The subject, too, has his own peculiarity, that of *utility* and being *well-timed;* for then it was a desideratum to fortify New York.

We return now to the narrative of events, and shall again make use of Sherwin's life, as containing an elegant narrative of the facts we wish to communicate. On Paine's petition to the board of excise, was written: "July 4th, 1766; to be restored on a proper vacancy." He was therefore restored; and leaving his scholastic pursuits, he returned again to the excise for several years.

"On his reappointment to the excise, our author immediately returned from London to Thetford, where he continued until the spring of 1768, when he was removed to Lewes, in Sussex. There he resided in the house of a person of the name of Ollive, a tobacconist. With him he remained upward of twelve months, when the former died, leaving a widow, a daughter, and several sons. Our author then left the family for a short time, but soon afterward returned, when he opened the shop on his own account. In consequence of this, and of his having previously lived under the same roof, he soon contracted an intimacy with Miss Ollive, the daughter of his former landlord, whom he married in the year 1771."

At this time Paine appears to have mingled a little politics with his pursuits; and he is reported to have written an electioneering ballad, and to have been paid for it: but we know of none but a *jeu d'esprit*, "*The Trial and Execution of the Farmer's Dog*," in ridicule of both parties, and therefore not likely to be paid for by any one; besides, Paine when better known, never made a profit of his political works, or even reserved a copyright. We therefore doubt that he was paid for such a service; although pay for honorable services, is by no means unreasonable.

In 1772 he wrote "The Case of the Excise Officers," a small pamphlet, on a very limited and unpopular subject: yet in this pamphlet Mr. Paine's style and principles are recognised.

"The same conciseness, clearness, and benevolence, which form such prominent features in the future productions of Paine, are distinguishable in almost every page of the pamphlet in question. Exclusive of the 'Introduction,' it is divided into two parts: 'The State of the Salary of the Officers of Excise;' and 'Thoughts on the Corruption of Principles, and on the Numerous Evils arising to the Revenue from the too great Poverty of the Officers of Excise.' In the introduction is stated the design of the excise officers, in all parts of the kingdom, to make an application to parliament to have the state of their salaries taken into consideration. The subject is then entered upon and discussed with all the energy and ability which might have been expected from a long-experienced advocate. The deductions that are made upon the exciseman's salary by unavoidable contingencies, and the danger to which his duty necessarily exposes him, are recapitulated in the most forcible manner. Under the second head, the policy of our author's object is insisted upon: he advises the government to render their officers honest by relieving their necessities; and the pamphlet concludes by enumerating the advantages that would be ensured by adopting the recommendation.

Of this pamphlet four thousand copies were printed by Mr. William Lee, of Lewes; but to what extent they were circulated I have not been able to learn. It would doubtless be read with pleasure and avidity by the class of men who were interested in the result; but whatever might be the distresses of the excisemen, it was not likely that they would meet with much sympathy or encouragement from the public. The nature of their occupation, and the unpleasant mode in which the duties of it are performed, have always rendered them objects of public odium; and however misdirected or useless such odium may be, it will ever continue an appendage to the character of those who collect this tyrannical impost. The public, therefore, viewed the complaints of the excisemen with indifference; and though considerable exertions were made by various individuals, as well as our author, there was no member to be found to bring the subject before parliament. The distresses of the officers, and the consequent depredations on the revenue, which our author had so ably pointed out, and so zealously endeavored to get removed, were not deemed of sufficient importance to merit parliamentary inquiry, and the proposal, like many other proposals for the removal of public evils, fell to the ground without investigation."

During Mr. Paine's residence at Lewes, he was held as a man of talents in the small circle of that town. His company was sought by men of greater affluence than himself. He was decidedly a good companion, whether engaged in amusements or debate. Paine at that time was fond of bowls, then a fashionable game: even Dr. Young, the elegant author of the Night Thoughts, was a member of a club, and attended a bowling-green. Paine in this amusement mingled with the best company in the place. He met, too, an evening club at Lewes in the principal tavern, for conversation and debate; and in that society, the best the town afforded, he carried the palm as a debater. While, however, he was thus social, he neither drank to excess, nor did he indulge in the vulgar habit of swearing, a habit he *never* contracted; and which, even in his latter days, he reproved in some of his intimate friends. This fact is confirmed to us by Mr. Jarvis, the celebrated painter, with whom Mr. Paine lived sometime before his death. This is worthy of note; for his enemies, foiled by his arguments, and not being able to attach to him crimes, have assumed faults and magnified them into vices. We have these facts from those who knew Paine at Lewes, and from those who knew the company he kept, and his habits. Carver, with whom Paine afterward lived in New York, was then an apprentice in the town, and used to saddle Mr. Paine's horse, and well remembers both him and his reputation. We know, too, the family of Rickman, who always resided in that neighborhood; and on their information and others we can rely.

"I have already observed, that on the marriage of our author with Miss Ollive, he commenced the business of a tobacconist and grocer, which he carried on in much the same method as his predecessor had done before him. This circumstance, as might have been anticipated, soon rendered him an object of suspicion in the eyes of the commissioners, and it is not improbable that the zeal which Paine had displayed in exposing the pernicious consequences of doling out so pitiful a provision to the active class of excisemen, while their betters were spending their days in ease and affluence, had rendered him an object of dislike among his superiors in office. The spirit of independence which he showed on all occasions, and which there is very little doubt he communicated in a considerable degree to those around him, was but little calculated to ensure the approbation of persons who regard implicit obedience as the test of merit, who look upon a proposal for reform as a step toward revolution, and the protection of abuses as the only mode of perpetuating the blessings of the English system of government. Considerable pains were taken to discover some flaw in the conduct of Paine; but so strictly had he performed his duty, that nothing of any consequence could be substantiated against him. His keeping a tobacconist's shop was, however, a sufficient pretext with those who wished to rid themselves of so troublesome a servant, and he was a second time dismissed from the excise in April, 1774."

At this period Paine became unfortunate in his business; perhaps he suffered from his social qualities, and a spirit of independence. His companions, we have already remarked, were generally in better circumstances than himself; and these sought his company for its intrinsic worth, for he was both instructive and amusing; and perhaps he incurred expenses and a loss of time, which he was unable to afford;

while a sanguine temper would still afford him hope, till his affairs were too bad to mend. His goods, at this period, were sold to pay his debts; and in the following month, May, 1774, he separated from his wife by mutual consent, and articles were signed on the 4th of June, by which she retained the little property she had brought him at marriage, and which was just sufficient to maintain her in a decent manner for the rest of her life. All the causes of this separation are not known. Mr. Paine uniformly spoke of his wife with kindness; and Clio Rickman informs us, in his life of Paine, that he frequently sent her money, without letting her know the source whence it came. She was afterward a professor of a sectarian religion in Cranbrook, Kent, and boarded in the house of a watchmaker, a member of the same church; his house was consequently visited by religious people, many of them with strong prejudices, and some very ignorant. These, after the publication of the "Age of Reason," would sometimes speak disrespectfully of Mr. Paine in her presence, when she uniformly left the room without a word. If, too, she was questioned on the subject of their separation, she did the same. We have these facts from those who resided with her. Our most intimate friend at one period, was a Mr. Bourne, a watchmaker in Rye, about eighteen miles from Cranbrook, England. This gentleman was apprenticed in the house where Mrs. Paine lived: he sat at the same table with her for years. We have these facts confirmed by other residents at Cranbrook. Thus nothing could be learned from her, except that though she differed from Mr. Paine on religious subjects, she could not bear to hear him spoken ill of. Paine, as we have before remarked, spoke respectfully of her; but if any person became inquisitive, he immediately answered rudely, that "his separation was a private affair." Clio Rickman asserts, and the most intimate friends of Mr. Paine support him, that Paine never cohabited with his second wife. Sherwin treats the subject as ridiculous; but Clio Rickman was a man of integrity, and he asserts that he has the documents showing this strange point, together with others, proving that this arose from no physical defects in Paine. When the question was plainly put to Mr. Paine by a friend of ours, he admitted this singular fact; but replied, "*I had a cause; it is no business of anybody.*" Singular, therefore, as this fact is, as both parties preserved a taciturnity on the subject, we have not the means of arriving at the truth. It was, as Paine said, a private affair; and we have not the means of withdrawing the veil, and have consequently no right to come to an uncharitable conclusion toward either party. We however infer that Paine had a cause; without which his wife ought to and would have exposed him, especially as she was surrounded by his bitter enemies.

Paine, while at Lewes, was a whig; and as such never thought of examining the first principles of government. A king, lords, and commons, were admitted as forming the best government by the admixture of the three sorts, royal, aristocratic, and democratic. As a whig, all he sought was the preservation of the supposed constitution; but a trifling expression from one of his companions, gave his thoughts a deeper range, and formed the basis of his "Common Sense" and " Rights of Man," which afterward so materially influenced the people in North America, France, and England. While sitting over some punch after a game at bowls, a Mr. Verral observed of Frederick, king of Prussia, that " he was the best fellow in the world for a king; he had so much of the devil in him." Simple and accidental as this observation was, it turned Paine's thoughts on the rights by which kings existed and governed, and thus led him into an examination of the inherent rights of the people; while the breaking up of his business, and separation from his wife, led him forward to the proper scene in which his talents and his principles could be properly estimated. Sherwin, speaking of this period, remarks:

" Our author was by this and prior events relieved from every tie which might be supposed to bind him to his country. Deprived of his home, and destitute of friends and employment, he had to commence life anew, and that without either credit or capital. His parents were become much advanced in years; their industry was no more than sufficient to procure a maintenance for themselves, and therefore Paine could not have derived, even if he had desired, any assistance from their kindness. The cheerless prospect which lay expanded before him, the misfortunes that had already befallen him, and the desolate situation in which he was then placed, must have impressed upon his mind the idea that to whatever country he went, it was impossible for his condition to become worse. In England there was no hope. Every change only brought an accumulation of fresh misfortunes. Borne down by poverty, and surrounded by difficulties of every description, his condition appears to have been that of a ruined, hopeless man.

In this situation many would have sat down discouraged without a struggle. But despair and dismay appear to have formed no part of Paine's character. He seems never to have sunk into the extreme of depression, or to have risen to that tumultuous gladness which so often accompanies the extreme of elevation. His mind appears never to have been crushed by defeat, or elated by success. The unshaken fortitude which can smile on disappointment and danger, and look serenely amidst the tumult of triumph, seems to have been the most prominent feature in his character.

"After the sale of his effects and the separation from his wife were concluded, our author again went to London. By what means he procured a living during his stay in the metropolis is unknown, but soon after his arrival he obtained an introduction to Dr. Franklin, who advised him to go to America. The doctor probably perceived in his interviews with Paine that he was a man possessed of abilities of no ordinary character, and this accounts for the readiness with which he furnished him with a letter of introduction to one of his most intimate friends in the United States. Our author was thus afforded an opportunity of beginning life again, and that at an age when his ardent and enterprising spirit must have been considerably tamed by the sharp lessons of adversity. He had as he himself observes, 'served an apprenticeship to life,' and it is more than probable that those sublime ideas on the subject of liberty which were afterward to raise his name so very high in the temple of fame, were produced by his early misfortunes.

> ' By wo the soul to daring action swells;
> By wo in plaintness patience it excels;
> From patience, prudent, clear experience springs,
> And traces knowledge through the cause of things!
> Thence hope is formed, thence fortitude, success,
> Renown—whate'er men covet and caress.'
> SAVAGE.

Poverty is certainly not the parent of genius, but it is unquestionably its best preceptor. The finest productions we have in the language have been written by men whose intellectual powers have forced their way into life under circumstances of the most abject penury. In most instances it has happened that the fire of genius has been long confined by the heavy black clouds of adversity, before it acquired sufficient strength to burst its boundary; and as the streaming lightning is more or less vivid in proportion to the density or lightness of the clouds which encompass it, so it has generally proved that the powers of a fine imagination have been more or less brilliant, in proportion to the poverty or plenty by which the possessor was surrounded. The enlivening wit of Congreve, the melting scenes of Otway, the rural tenderness and pathetic simplicity of Goldsmith, and the dignified ease and elegance of Thomson, would have been unknown to us, if these luminaries in the hemisphere of literature had been born in a state of affluence; for though the men might have lived with much more comfort to themselves than they did, it is very probable that the easy couch and plentiful board would have destroyed the inspiration which gave birth to their finest productions.

But to our author. He had by this time seen enough of the world to despise its follies, and he had witnessed too many of the bad effects of misgovernment in his native country to feel any affection for them, when directed against the country of which he was about to become a citizen. Dr. Franklin could not therefore have selected a man more likely to repay his kindness in vindicating the cause of the people, by whom he was deputed ambassador to England. Our author sailed from this country [England] toward the end of the year 1774, and arrived at Philadelphia about two months afterward."

We have thus briefly brought Mr. Paine to the close of the first period of his life; a period of no important interest to the public; and only valuable as qualifying him for the other periods, which belonged wholly to the public. His good sense was the work of nature; his acquired knowledge, whether of books or men, was the effect of study and observation; but to these was added experience, the result of accident; but admirably adapted to fit him for his future tasks, of which he could have no conception. We have seen him necessarily a mechanic, a sailor, a tradesman, an exciseman, a storekeeper, and a teacher, acquainted with London, and different sections of Great Britain; intimate with the corruptions and revenue of the country from his connexion with the excise; an author, a politician, and associating with various classes in the community; with a habit for observation and original thinking, and thus qualified to address a whole people on the subject of liberty. His father a quaker, his mother of the established church, and his wife and her friends dissenters, he could have but little religious prejudice. While accident, however painful to himself, which sent him to this country, unencumbered with either wife, family, or fortune, contributed highly to render him devoted to the people among whom he was about to reside, during their arduous struggle in support of liberty.

PART II.

FROM MR. PAINE'S ARRIVAL IN AMERICA TO THE END OF THE WAR OF INDEPENDENCE.

Mr. Paine having resolved to leave England, brought letters of recommendation from Dr. Franklin, then on an embassy from a northern state to the British government in London. Mr. Paine left England in the autumn of 1774, and arrived at Philadelphia in the latter part of the same year; and not in 1772, as Dr. Rush states. Sherwin correctly says:

"From this period to the day of his death, the abilities of Paine never lay dormant. Very shortly after his arrival in Philadelphia, he became acquainted with Mr. Aitkin, a respectable bookseller of that town. In January, 1775, Mr. Aitkin commenced the publication of the Pennsylvania Magazine, of which Paine became the editor. Many of the pieces in this publication are truly elegant. In these, as in most of his other writings, he is singularly happy in clothing an original boldness of thought with a peculiar beauty of diction. The article in which he treats of the hidden riches of the earth, and the diligence with which we ought to search after them, is a fine specimen of this rare combination. The well-known song on the death of General Wolfe, appeared in an early number of this magazine; and it is unquestionably one of the most beautiful productions of the sort in the English language. The ideas would have done honor to any of the poets of old, and the poetry is an example of the most polished versification. As this little piece is still much admired, even by those who disapprove of its author's political and religious notions, I here insert it, as transcribed from an original copy:

SONG ON THE DEATH OF GENERAL WOLFE.

'In a mouldering cave, where the wretched retreat,
  Britannia sat wasted with care:
She mourned for her Wolfe, and exclaimed against fate,
  And gave herself up to despair.
The walls of her cell she had sculptured around
  With the feats of her favorite son,
And even the dust, as it lay on the ground,
  Was engraved with some deeds he had done.

LINES ON THE DEATH OF WOLFE.

The sire of the gods, from his crystalline throne,
  Beheld the disconsolate dame,
And, moved with her tears, he sent Mercury down,
  And these were the tidings that came:
" Britannia, forbear, not a sigh or a tear,
  For thy Wolfe, so deservedly loved ;
Your tears shall be changed into triumphs of joy,
  For thy Wolfe is not dead, but removed.

The sons of the east, the proud giants of old,
  Have crept from their darksome abodes,
And this is the news, as in heaven it was told,
  They were marching to war with the gods.
A council was held in the chambers of Jove,
  And this was their final decree,
That Wolfe should be called to the armies above,
  And the charge was intrusted to me.

To the plains of Quebec with the orders I flew,
  He begged for a moment's delay ;
He cried, ' Oh forbear, let me victory hear,
  And then thy commands I'll obey.'
With a darksome thick film I encompassed his eyes,
  And bore him away in an urn ;
Lest the fondness he bore to his own native shore
  Should induce him again to return." '

In addition to the above, he wrote several other articles for the Pennsylvania Magazine, of considerable literary merit. These principally consist of a letter to the publisher on the utility of magazines in general ; 'Useful and Entertaining Hints on the Internal Riches of the Colonies ;' 'Reflections on the Death of Lord Clive ;' and 'New Anecdotes of Alexander the Great.' The 'Reflections on the Death of Lord Clive,' I have not seen, though I have been at considerable pains to procure them ; but I have been informed that they contain much originality of thought, and that they caused the work to be sought after with great avidity. He likewise wrote for the same publication an elegant little piece in the form of a poetical dialogue, between a snowdrop and a critic, in which the former is made to describe the variety and pleasure intended to be conveyed, to the public through the medium of the new work, in opposition to the cavilling objections of the latter. These productions are already in the possession of the public, and they serve to show the versatility of our author's disposition."

Dr. Rush, of Philadelphia, and formerly a member of that congress which declared these states independent, in his letter to Cheetham, says that Paine came to this country with the design of opening a school for the instruction of young ladies in branches of literature not then generally taught. Paine's introduction to Mr. Aitkin appears to have been through Dr. Franklin's recommendations. There Dr. Rush met him ; and afterward, being excited by an article in one of Mr. Aitkin's papers on the subject of the African slavery, he sought his acquaintance. And in that letter ascribes to *himself* suggesting to Paine the subject of his "Common Sense," and the title. That letter, though highly favorable to Paine, is certainly egotistical, which renders this suggestion doubtful; especially as the object of Cheetham in getting that letter written to him, as well as others from different persons, was obviously to pare off, if possible, any part of Paine's reputation. Dr. Rush was clearly incorrect in one of his dates; and distinctly marks his prejudice in conclusively stating, that he declined to see Paine on his last return to this country, on account of the principles avowed in his "Age of Reason." This observation, though intended by Dr. Rush to exalt himself at the expense of Mr. Paine, and as such is published by Cheetham, is, in fact, highly important. It satisfactorily accounts for many of Paine's early sycophants deserting him, without any dereliction of personal worth on his part.

Mr. Paine's acquaintance with Dr. Franklin; the object of his coming to this country (to introduce a higher scale of education than that in use); his first employment (engaged or hired to edit a new magazine, and other periodicals published by Aitkin); the success and reputation of those publications, and his acquaintance with Dr. Rush as a consequence of his reputation; the very idea of Dr. Rush suggesting to Mr. Paine the subject of a pamphlet to act on the people, whether true or false, together with the circumstances just noted, mark Mr. Paine as then possessing literary attainments in an eminent degree; and ought to have preserved him against the vulgar abuse with which so many of the clergy and his theological opponents have assailed him. This attack on his literary character, successful in an extraordinary degree, depended on the suppression of his works; the presumption of the ignorance of those works by the body of the party addressed; and on the assumption of the power of the clergy to prevent those works being read. It is remarkable, that Cheetham, dishonest in his purposes, and, comparatively with Paine, of small abilities, and very prejudiced and ignorant, makes also this charge, while he himself furnishes the most satisfactory proofs to the contrary. In Cheetham's life is to be found the song we have already inserted. He likewise furnishes the following beautiful extract from the pen of Paine, published in an early number of Aitkin's magazine, from which the style of Paine may be inferred in what is called polite literature.

"In one of his lucubrations, adverting to the riches of the earth, the diligence which is necessary to discover, and the labor to possess them, he thus elegantly invites us to industry and research:—

'Though nature is gay, polite, and generous abroad, she is sullen, rude, and niggardly at home. Return the visit, and she admits you with all the suspicion of a miser, and all the reluctance of an antiquated beauty retired to replenish her charms. Bred up in antideluvian notions, she has not yet acquired the European taste of receiving visitants in her dressing-room: she locks and bolts up her private recesses with extraordinary care, as if not only resolved to preserve her hoards, but to conceal her age, and hide the remains of a face that was young and lovely in the days of Adam. He that would view nature in her undress, and partake of her internal treasures, must proceed with the resolution of a robber, if not a ravisher. She gives no invitation to follow her to the cavern: the external earth makes no proclamation of the interior stores, but leaves to chance and industry the discovery of the whole. In such gifts as nature can annually recreate, she is noble and profuse, and entertains the whole world with the interest of her fortunes, but watches over the capital with the care of a miser. Her gold and jewels lie concealed in the earth in caves of utter darkness; the hoards of wealth, heaps upon heaps, mould in the chests, like the riches of a necromancer's cell. It must be very pleasant to an adventurous speculatist to make excursions into these Gothic regions; and in his travels he may possibly come to a cabinet locked up in some rocky vault, whose treasures shall reward his toil, and enable him to shine on his return as splendidly as nature herself.'"

Were Paine's works known and read, the slander about his vulgar style would necessarily be confuted, without the labor of an advocate; and we regret the necessity of exposing the meanness which would suggest such a course to suppress a theological opponent. We are happy to find that his bitter enemies should be compelled to resort to falsehood for such a purpose. This conduct on the part of his personal enemies, ought then to awaken suspicion that this is not the only false and malicious slander under which Paine has too long lain.

That a man who could write poetry so well should have written so little, is at once a mark of his good sense and strong resolution. Paine had remarked that poets were generally pretty triflers, and he suppressed a talent which he thought of little use to society. It is evident that Paine was not naturally fond of politics; he was led by circumstances, and a strong sense of justice and utility, into the course he took. The beauties of nature and the happiness of the human family occupied his mind. And the violence done to nature, and to human happiness by tyranny and superstition, together with the remarkable events of his day, deflected his course from the pursuits of peace, which he was so fitted to enjoy, into the more violent but useful course he did pursue. The man who could write the beautiful article we have just quoted, did not want the excitement of a storm or a revolution to give zest to life. Nothing could be more beautiful than either Paine's poetry or prose; he possesses not only strength and clearness, but a beauty of diction surpassed by no English writer we know: and if we wished to recommend a single model for fine English composition, we should certainly name Paine's writings as the best.

We find Mr. Paine so completely identified with every great point in the revolution, and of the independence of this country, that we cannot do justice to him without giving a brief but clear account of those events, and the circumstances which led to them. Indeed, some of the most important events to be related were actually created or produced by him. Other men have followed events; Paine actually created them.

Soon after the discovery of this continent colonies began to be planted in North America. During the last century the French held the north or Canada, and large portions of the south and west. The English had several colonies in the middle, while other Europeans had made small settlements. These colonies were little regarded at first; they were safety-valves for daring spirits who were discontented at home. The inhabitants formed an amalgamation, as they have done since, from every clime; but with the exception of those transported to these shores for their crimes, they were industrious and independent, the general characteristics of all voluntary emigrants. Colonies have always been regarded by the English government only as they profit the mother-country, or rather the party governing. In the first place large grants of territory were made by various English sovereigns, either as rewards to favorites, or for some services received, and these grants being made without a correct knowledge of the country or rights of the natives, they were frequently given with uncertain boundaries; which, as we shall presently see, was the remote cause of the American war of independence. When the colonists, by dint of their own industry, could raise a surplus of some produce, they became importers of manufactured goods, and as such an object of attention to the government of Great Britain. But the interference of the British government was for their own benefit. They appointed governors, always sycophants of power, to be paid by the colonists. And they regulated their trade so as to produce to Great Britain the greatest advantage. A liberal policy, the mutual benefit of both parties, has never yet been conceived and executed by any ministry. The very principles of the British government laid the seeds of discontent, and established two interests: the governor pursued his own and the interests of Britain, or rather what he thought the interests of the British government; while the assemblies formed by the people, and their *juries* (for British settlers claimed British rights and customs), naturally preferred the interests of the colonies.

In 1750, a company was formed in London called the Ohio company. They obtained a grant of six hundred thousand acres of land on the rivers Ohio and Mississippi. This grant was made without much regard to the Indian rights, and as it cut off the northern French territories from their southern and western, the French resisted it in practice. The trade of this company was chiefly carried on by the Virginians; but these traders were constantly annoyed by the French, who at last built a fort on the Ohio, and a French governor went so far as to order the seizure of every British subject found trading there. To counteract this the Virginians formed a troop with which to protect their traders, and in this troop Washington was employed as a volunteer in the year 1753, and in the winter of that year undertook an arduous embassy to the French commandant, through a district that could not then be travelled by a horse, and at this early period marked out spots eligible for forts, especially Fort Duquesne. The embassy failing, force was attempted, and Washington became lieutenant to Colonel Fry. The French fort became the theatre of war, which was alternately taken and retaken; during which petty battles Colonel Fry died and left Washington in command; and in this situation the general of the revolution gained some fame from a masterly retreat before a very superior force of regular French soldiers. When the British government heard of these transactions they resolved to profit by them, and to dispossess the French of some of their territories through the means and at the expense of the colonies. They directed the governors of the several states to form a union, and raise a force; and that these united governors, assisted by two members of their respective council, should direct the whole, and draw upon the British treasury for the necessary expenses, in the first instance, but to be reimbursed by a *tax laid on the colonies by the British parliament*. This is the origin of the question which led to the disputes between Great Britain and the colonies, which ultimately led to independence. Franklin was consulted on this subject by Governor Shirley, and he at once declared the principle of taxation by the British parliament, in which they were not represented, to be unconstitutional and unjust. And thus he, too, as early as 1754, was initiated into the principles and into the subjects on which he so much distinguished himself at a period twenty years later.

In 1755, the king of Great Britain, George II., sent out a large armament, Admiral Boscawen, to St. Lawrence, and General Braddock to Virginia, without a declaration of war, assuming that the French had *commenced* hostilities; and Washington became the aid-de-camp of Braddock. Braddock led his army into the field, relying chiefly on his veterans; nay, actually despising the militia of the country, and neglecting the experience of Washington. Near Fort Duquesne he was caught in an Indian defile, and subject to a species of warfare he was unaccustomed to; and in that battle he was slain. Washington extricated the army from its perilous situation, retreated to Philadelphia, and afterward defended the frontiers of Virginia with much ability. Pitt, afterward Lord Chatham, becoming minister in England, pushed the war with vigor; and sent out Lord Amherst, an excellent commander, assisted by Wolfe, General Forbes, and others. In 1758, Forbes took Fort Duquesne, while Wolfe lost his life at, but took Quebec; and in 1760 Amherst took Montreal; and in 1762, the whole of Canada and French North America was yielded to the English, except New Orleans and the adjacent province. At this period, and in the following year, the colonists were perfectly content. They did not expect Indian aggression when not supported by French power. They were satisfied with Britain imposing on them governors, as representatives of royalty, while they enjoyed their colonial assemblies, their trial by jury, and other British rights; they were in fact, satisfied British subjects, approving of king, lords, and commons, and, like other British subjects, boasted of their liberty and their matchless constitution; which they really thought, for the opinion was common, that this mixed government united all that was excellent in each; while the parts checking each other, suppressed all that was vicious in royalty, aristocracy, or democracy. They were afterward to be taught the fallacy of these opinions by Thomas Paine. At this period, 1763, they were politically divided, as in England, into whigs and tories; or those who assumed to defend or extend the popular part of the government, and those who leaned to the aristocratical part, and favored the restriction of representation to property qualifications, and privileged or self-elected corporations: but the whigs predominated. It is to this period, 1763, that the colonists constantly refer in the early part of their revolution, before the declaration of independence, as the situation to which they wished to be restored; and therefore it deserves particular attention. Parliamentary taxation had been named, but never enforced or acted upon; and in all their after-petitions all they ask, is the repeal of laws since 1763. "Place us," they repeatedly say, "in the situation in which we then were." No feeling of republicanism is perceived in their addresses; none in their public acts. Nothing of the kind was openly avowed by any of their leading men; and the individuals who did occasionally hint at such an event, were regarded as *ultras;* who, however correct in theory, held dangerous and impracticable doctrines: and these were the *national* feelings up to the very *eve* of the declaration of independence; just before which a change in the whole public sentiment was effected by the powerful pen of Thomas Paine, in his " Common Sense ;" before which publication the only object *avowed*, even by the great men of the age, and seriously sought after by the rest of the people, was to be placed in the situation of 1763; to be restored to royal favor, and to enjoy their old British *privileges* (not rights).

In 1764 commenced the British and colonial troubles. Mr. George Grenville had then become minister in Britain. He proposed to raise a revenue in the American colonies for the exclusive use of the British treasury. This was, of course, based upon the late expense of the war, borne by Great Britain, and in consonance with the scheme before noted, of future remuneration to the mother-country. About the same time that this measure was talked of, other obnoxious acts were attempted. In Massachusetts, the governor published in support of the ministry, and attempted to establish a religious test, by giving offices only to episcopalians: on which occasion the people sent agents to England. On March 10, 1764, the stamp act was *declared* (not acted upon); which made certain transactions unlawful if not recorded on stamped paper, paid for as a tax. Against this Virginia led the way by petition and remonstrance; Massachusetts passed legislative censures; and these two states took the lead in the whole of the preliminary contests and revolutionary war. The memorials were not received by parliament; but the parties were suffered to be heard by council. Dr. Franklin at this time was agent for Massachusetts. In 1765 the stamp act passed, and Boston went into mourning; manifested great public spirit; and her merchants agreed to import no goods till the unjust act should be repealed; while the lower classes committed some acts of violence. In Virginia a legislative action was had on it. Patrick Henry, then a young man, and scarcely acquainted with the rules of the assembly, waited for the action of some of the elder legislators; but finding them silent, or disposed to conciliate, he rose in his place, and proposed a series of resolutions, denouncing the stamp act as violations of their ancient charters, and destructive of British and American freedom, and disclaiming any other authority to enforce taxes than a general assembly. These resolutions, after considerable debate, were admitted, and served as a precedent for other states. The biographer of Patrick Henry, the late Mr. Wirt, relates, that after Mr. Henry's death, a sealed paper was found, directed to be read only when he had ceased to live. This paper contained the resolutions referred to, with remarks of Mr. Henry in his own handwriting. He observes: "The resolutions passed with a small majority; but the alarm spread throughout America. The ministerial party were overwhelmed: the great point of resistance to British taxation was universally established in the colonies. This brought on the war, which finally separated the two countries."

In every chain of events there are some links of more importance than others; nay, essential to that chain. It is evident that Patrick Henry thought so of these resolutions: it is equally evident that he himself looked forward to a separation of the two countries, and regarded these resolutions as important to that object; yet on the face of them they only claim what every Briton claims, and independence and republicanism are not even hinted. The time had not yet come for such sentiments to be broached; nor how it was to come was not then known, either to Patrick Henry or to any other patriot. The man who was destined to convert a nation by a few pages of "common sense," was then in obscurity; had just resigned staymaking for a paltry office in the English excise, and had never published an article: but the resolutions of Patrick Henry contributed to the crisis which brought Mr. Paine forward as an author; and as *such* we regard *him* as a chief link, too, in the chain of events which produced and consummated the revolution.

In this same year, 1765, one James Otis, in Massachusetts, proposed a congress to be held in New York. A committee was formed to arrange this. South Carolina was the first to yield to the suggestion. The various governors, alarmed, prorogued the assemblies of Virginia, North Carolina, and Georgia: but committees of correspondence were established in each state; and thus the nucleus of organized resistance was formed. On the day the stamp act was to take effect, Boston had the bells tolled; public meetings were held, and fast days appointed. Violence in some cases was used: and to wear *homespun* became respectable, as marking national principle. The violent opposition to the stamp act induced inquiry in London. Franklin was examined at the bar of the house; and the whigs generally wished the repeal of the obnoxious stamp act. In the house of lords it is remarkable, that the bishops first recommended force to be used to the Americans; and the king did not wish the repeal of the act. The law was, however, repealed; and such were the feelings of the American people, that they manifested the most rapturous joy; and actually adulated the British government for *not doing them so great an injustice* as to impose on them taxes without representation. In Virginia a *statue* was voted to the king. From Massachusetts votes of thanks were agreed upon to the Duke of Grafton and Mr. Pitt; while Boston, and other parts of the continent, illuminated; and rejoicings were everywhere heard. Well might Thomas Paine say, as he afterward did, in the "Crisis, No. VII.:" "I found the disposition of the people such, that they might be led by a thread and governed by a reed. Their attachment to Britain was obstinate; and it was at that time a kind of treason to speak against it. They disliked the ministry, but they esteemed the nation. Their ideas of grievance operated without resentment; and their single object was *reconciliation*."

The foolish ministers again opened the wound by wishing the states to remunerate those who had suffered by the acts of violence in resisting the stamp act. And in 1767, when Mr. Pitt, or Lord Chatham, had again come into power, but during his illness, an act was passed, "to restrain the legislative power in New York;" and soon after an act of perfidy awakened the jealousy and anger of the people; for some *troops* landed in Boston, alleging they were driven in *precisely* to that port by *stress of weather*. And in the same year, one Charles Townsend, in the English parliament, publicly announced a plan for taxing the Americans by the English parliament, *without* giving them offence; and this plan, thus foolishly announced, consisted in imposing a duty on glass, paint, tea, and paper, to be imported into the colonies; and to assist this notable scheme, a board of admiralty was imposed on the colonies, to be paid by the natives, and whose operations cramped the colonies for the supposed benefit of the mother-country. These measures roused the people, and again awaked the worst feelings. Boston took the lead, closely followed by other parts. The mob committed acts of violence; while the better sort were loud in petitioning and remonstrating. Lord Chatham, who had been ill, resigned; Townsend died; and Lord North succeeded as English chancellor of the exchequer, and afterward as prime minister: and to his *perseverance* in a wrong course, for the sake of consistency, England lost her colonies and America gained her independence. This, without merit to Lord North, is another important link in the chain which led to independence.

In this year the spirit of resistance was fostered by some tolerable essays from one John Dickenson, Esq., published in a Philadelphia paper; while the seizing of Hancock's sloop "Liberty," for smuggling, furnished the Bostonians the subject of a riot. To quell this, the governor, Bernard, sent for troops; and the respectable body of the people, at a large public meeting held at Faneuil Hall, proposed *arming in fear of French invasion*. This was undoubtedly a justifiable *ruse* to meet the duplicity of the English ministers, whose troops landed by alleged *stress* of weather at Boston: it shows, too, that the Bostonians meant to *fight* for their *liberty;* though independence was never named, nor evidently scarcely conceived of, except by a very few.

In 1769, Lord North, the English minister, obtained a good support both in the house of commons and in the house of lords; and he determined to *maintain* the *supremacy* of the English government in *all* things; and to prevent the effects of *native juries*, proposed trying civil officers, charged with murder or violence in the colonies, in support of the British government, in England. On this occasion all the *ports* agreed to suspend importations till this grievance should be removed.

In 1769, the opposition to the arbitrary measures of the British government was so great in the colonies, and so powerful the effect of the non-importation agreement, that the ministers agreed to discontinue all the duties, *except* that on *tea*; thus perseveringly preserving the principle of taxation without representation, while they gave up the greater part of the profit. The war, therefore, that succeeded was a war on *principle*, not amount, of taxation. On this occasion, Lord Chatham, who had partially recovered from his late illness, violently opposed the ministers. During this and the following year, the spirit of resistance increased, for the Americans were not to be duped by the repeal of taxes, while the principle or right of taxation was maintained. In Boston, where the presence of the soldiers was obnoxious, riots ensued; individual quarrels between soldiers and citizens became party quarrels; and three of the soldiers were killed by the ropemakers. In New York, the people erected liberty-poles, which the soldiers cut down. But the most powerful incitement to opposition came from the pen of McDougal, a Scotchman, who boldly charged the assembly with betraying the city and colony of New York, because they had discouraged the people and sanctioned the governor and the troops; not from attachment, but the necessity of supporting the laws. McDougal was thrown into prison, where he remained three months, and then dismissed without a trial. This fact shows the force of his writings, and we shall afterward find this man rendering essential service, for which the notoriety given him by this persecution qualified him.

In 1771, Rhode Island showed considerable excitement. Philadelphia refused to receive the taxed tea; New York and other places followed, and the vessels returned. But in Boston, where a quantity was assigned, some of the people dressed like Indians boarded the ships and threw three hundred and forty-two chests of tea into the sea. Yet, in this act, they only sought the liberties which the charters granted them; and in all their requests, they simply asked to be restored to the situation they were in in 1763. In all this violence the word independence was never pronounced.

In 1774, North, enraged at the conduct of the Bostonians, procured bills, closing their harbor and destroying their ancient charter and constitution; thus punishing a whole people and people *unborn* for the specific acts of some. Against this Lord Chatham protests; and Burke the Irish orator made a brilliant speech. The career of the latter is identified with Paine; for he afterward became a pensioner to the British government, and apologist for the Bourbon family, and the opponent of the French revolution, and his work on this subject produced Paine's celebrated "Rights of Man." Boston, when her harbors were about to be closed, appealed to other cities and states. Virginia, ever ready and firm in the cause of opposition to arbitrary measures, appointed through her legislature the day for closing Boston harbor (1st of June, 1774), as a day of *solemn fasting;* a measure always efficacious, for it enlists religious enthusiasm, and presents to the opponent a ghostly power, of immense force, which feels no blows. Cromwell, Mahomet, and Thomas à Becket, perfectly understood these tactics, and succeeded in their use. The governor dissolved the house in May, but the members formed an association, before even they had heard from Boston. They published, too, a manifesto, recommending that no East India produce be used, except saltpetre and spice. At New York, the parties were nearly equal; but the popularity of M'Dougal, the Scotchman before noticed, for his spirited writings, gave him a considerable influence, well supported as he was by Captain Sears. M'Dougal had both the honor to propose a second congress, the influence to get a committee for that purpose, and the address to carry this out, together with standing local committees: and this arrangement lasted till the declaration of independence. The various members to this congress, are the distinguished men, whose names are familiar to us as fathers of the revolution. This congress was generally appointed by the legislatures, and made legal, to effect which there were some previous secret meetings in Massachusetts. A committee had been appointed on the state of the province, which consisted of Samuel Adams, Joseph Warren, John Hancock, I. Cutting, Robert Treat Paine, and others. Before they reported they requested the doors might be shut; and then they proceeded to recommend a congress and an immediate decision. A spy of the governor affected a bowel complaint, and was suffered to depart; but neither he, nor the governor, nor his agent, was suffered to enter till the congress was confirmed; and the governor's dissolution of the assembly, made on the outside, was neither heard nor regarded. Virginia appointed Washington, Patrick Henry, &c., and declared herself ready to support Boston, but at the same time carefully instructed her delegates not to *break* with Britain; to support only their *British privileges*, or what they claimed as the *rights* of Englishmen. At this period, Rhode Island issued a motto, now familiar to our ears, but which at the same time is degraded by party politics, "United, we stand — divided, we fall." A motto, a song, a toast, or a pamphlet, will sometimes produce a unanimity, which much greater efforts have failed in. Georgia, of all the states, sent no deputies to this congress; but she, too, soon after, when the danger had not decreased, joined the union.

It should be remembered, that about this time, Mr. Thomas Paine, by the advice of Dr. Franklin, then in England, was embarking for North America. It is evident that Franklin had a design of benefiting his country by this recommendation, in the precise way in which Paine effected it; for Franklin soon followed Paine, and almost immediately offered to put into his hands the materials for the eventful history of the times. Paine at that time was actually engaged on his "Common Sense," and soon after sent him the first copy to surprise him by showing that he had anticipated his designs and wishes. These events throw a sort of halo about the characters of these two men, highly respectable to both. When Franklin knew Mr. Paine, he was in London, ruined in his fortune and prospects; of no literary reputation, but for one pamphlet, in which he pleaded the unpopular cause of the excisemen. He had then no distinguished acquaintances, to whom he was indebted for an introduction. Franklin was at this time a doctor, distinguished for his learning, philosophy, and above all for his common sense. He was an old man, pithy and sententious, acquainted with the manner of addressing the people, himself an author (and authors are tenacious), yet he becomes the friend of Paine, advises him to come to this country, gives him letters which procure him at once a literary engagement, and on his return almost immediately offers to put in his hands the materials for the history of the times; while Paine was but a foreigner of a few months standing. What, then, are our conclusions, but that Franklin had the genius to discover Paine's peculiar tact and talents, and that he had the address to second Paine's wishes in coming to this country, without acquainting Paine with all his motives, and thus indirectly to effect what he himself wished? But what means had Franklin to know Paine? His pamphlet on the excise must have been the only source by which his qualities as a writer could be known; but that pamphlet is characteristic, and Franklin's conclusion must have been correct that he who could employ such good sense, in so powerful a manner, on such a bad subject, could, on a better subject, effect much. Franklin must, too, have discovered the sound and correct judgment of Paine, by conversations, and he must have believed in the correctness of his principles and extent of his knowledge, before he could think of giving into his hands what his own countrymen thought himself (Franklin) so capable of. This conduct of Franklin, in preferring Paine to himself for this important object, while it reflects the greatest credit upon Paine's natural abilities, acquisitions, and moral virtues, redounds also to Franklin's glory. It is great men only that can afford to be generous; and Franklin in this preference marks a greatness of character, which never forsook him: while it marks also the calumniators of Paine, those who have attempted to present him to the public as a demoralized, vulgar, and illiterate man, as base unprincipled slanderers, whose calumnies are not the less venomous for proceeding frequently from reverend persons.

While Mr. Paine was preparing to leave his country, and during his voyage, events were ripening the crisis which should render his services valuable. Boston was distressed by a blockade; while the men, assisted even by the women, exercised themselves in arms. The governor of Boston had removed to Salem; but the spirit of the people brought him back. His proclamations availed nothing. Meetings were held: and we cannot but observe the imperfect notions of political justice and civil rights, when among their complaints, they charge on the British government as a crime their doing a portion of justice to the catholics of Canada: such is the force of prejudice, religious instruction, and early impressions. The Bostonians were now indeed cruelly treated; but they were upheld by all the states; and the congress was now assembled (the latter part of September, 1774): Patrick Henry first spoke, and gave a manly tone to the meeting: events had presented the subject; it was not a matter of choice. The first question necessarily was: "Shall we make common cause with Boston?" and after a month's delay, or of protracted discussions, the congress (on Oct. 6, 1774) resolved upon supporting Boston; still, however, praying a reconciliation. In their resolutions they declare themselves his majesty's loyal subjects: they declare they are Englishmen, and want only Englishmen's rights: and they especially demand to be *restored* to the situation they were in in 1763; that is, after the French war, in which the French lost Canada, and before Sir George Grenville's stamp act. After a variety of useful resolutions, and a declaration not to support the slave-trade, the formation of committees, and the establishment of provincial congresses, they dissolved; but resolved to meet again in May, 1775, in Philadelphia. This then was not a dissolution, but an adjournment of the congress, which afterward declared for independence. At this time Thomas Paine must have embarked from England; for he arrived at Philadelphia in the winter of 1774. The local congress formed two committees: one of safety, which provided a militia; and the other a committee of supplies, which provided for them, and other necessary expenses. A new parliament in England was much divided. The king, in his speech, was unfavorable to the colonies: Lord Chatham, and the greatest men in the ministry, in favor of them: while Lord North still attempted to intimidate the people by unjust acts. He proposed a bill to restrict the people of New England from fishing; and performed other irritating acts of tyranny. In the colonies the military seized on several collections of arms and stores: but the militia being sanctioned by the local congresses, retaliated; as these assemblies declared the supplies collected in forts necessary for the safety of the state: thus the people of Province, in New Hampshire, took the stores from Forts William and Maria. In Virginia Patrick Henry trained a company. At this period Paine had arrived, and was engaged on various periodicals by Mr. Aitkin, of Philadelphia; in which situation he necessarily became acquainted with the local politics; while, from his recent arrival, he knew also public feeling in Great Britain: and thus he was becoming matured for what he afterward so well effected. Dr. Franklin had, too, returned to the colonies, and took the place of another deputy in Congress; Thomas Jefferson, likewise, took the place of another member: and thus events gradually led on the cause of independence; while not a word on the subject was uttered, even by those who wished it; for they had no hopes of seeing the people unanimous, and really expected that any proposition of the kind would subdivide those struggling against the tyranny of the British government.

In April, 1775, an important event occurred. General Gage marched a few troops to Concord to seize some military stores. The people knew his design, and resolved on opposition. At Lexington a few militia were drawn up to watch his motions, but with strict orders not to molest him. These General Gage ordered to disperse; and after repeating his orders, fired on the body, and killed eight militiamen. The militia dispersed; but some of them returned the fire. The British colonel (Smith) now moved on to Concord; during which time the militia assembled in great numbers, resolved to harass the troops on their return. The stores were removed from Concord, except a little flour, which Col. Smith destroyed, and then commenced a retreat; but the British were met at every pass, and annoyed by secret foes along the whole road; and it is probable that the whole force of nine hundred men would have been destroyed, had not Lord Percy brought a re-enforcement to his rescue. In Virginia, about the same time, the king's troops seized on a quantity of powder; but being pursued by Patrick Henry, who suddenly raised five thousand men, the *value* of the powder was recovered. In Massachusetts an army was immediately raised, and the command given to Putnam, who had fought in the Canada war. This man, who was one of the best revolutionary generals, had to lay by his leather apron when he became a general. The provincial troops now seized on the military stores wherever they could; and thus the example of the king's troops afforded the first means of getting supplies. In this year Colonel Ethan Allen and Arnold not only took the stores, but the fort of Ticonderoga, by surprise. The British at this time were commanded by Howe, Clinton, and Burgoyne. An offer of pardon was made to those who would lay down their arms, excepting Samuel Adams and Hancock: this last, as a compliment to the distinction shown him by the British, was made president of the congress: but he was more remarkable for his wealth and courage than abilities. On the 15th of June, Washington received the chief command: he declined a salary, and only wished his expenses paid.

On the 16th of June, General Putnam ordered Colonel Prescott to take possession of Bunker's hill, with a thousand men. By some mistake Breed's hill was occupied instead; and the general himself assisted in throwing up a breastwork during the night. To dispossess the Americans of this post, the famous battle of Bunker's hill was fought; which, though lost by the Americans, was so honorable to them, that it served as a watchword during the war, and as a grateful monument since. The men accustomed to the rifle repeatedly repulsed the enemy by reserving their fire till the approaching column was very near, and offered marks to be shot at. This coolness was altogether unexpected from raw troops; and could it have been exercised in all subsequent engagements, the war which succeeded would have been of short duration. In the summer of 1775, an Irish regiment arrived to the assistance of the Americans; but as they were destitute of both arms and provisions, they were not at first very useful to the cause they came to serve. In July, Georgia sent deputies to congress; and in the same month congress published a declaration, earnestly desiring a reconciliation with Britain: they forwarded also a *most humble* petition to the king. The language of this petition is more humiliating than either the circumstances required, or the spirit of the people could suggest; and it was evidently drawn up to satisfy that class of people who always *hope* for the *best;* and who, on this occasion, *hoped* to obtain by begging, what others knew very well could only be obtained by courage. But these good meaning men would have been lost to the party had their wishes not been attended to. The action on this petition was afterward of great importance. In the meantime the congress did not trust to petitioning: they did something more substantial; they trained riflemen. In the south twelve volunteers travelled to Florida, and seized a vessel with fifteen thousand pounds of gunpowder in it; and giving the captain *bills* on congress, brought it off. In the south Lord Dunmore proposed to liberate the slaves, and arm them against their masters; but he either could not, or did not effect much in that way. In the north, an expedition was undertaken to Canada. St. John and Montreal were taken by Montgomery; but Colonel Allen was made prisoner, Montgomery was killed, and Arnold had his leg broken: the expedition was not finally successful. Letters of marque were also granted. On the other side, Lord Dunmore burned Norfolk, and threatened other places. At this period, late in the year 1775, Paine was engaged on his "Common Sense." About January, 1776, accounts were received that the petition forwarded to the king, from which so much was hoped by a part of the people, had been rejected; and *no answer* was deigned in reply. The same opportunities brought accounts of foreign troops (Hessians) being engaged to combat the colonies; and that a large armament was coming out. Mr. Penn had indeed been examined at the bar of the house of commons; and his examination proved that the colonists had then no thoughts of independence. They were now operated on by anger and fear: anger at the

contemptuous treatment of their petition; and fear for the
consequences of resistance, and at the force about to be
brought against them. Yet none talked of independence, but
a few of no weight in society; as none of the leaders would
risk their popularity in supporting what appeared hopeless:
yet Jefferson, Franklin, Patrick Henry, and others, evidently
wished independence: but this could only be supported by
the unanimity of the body of the people; and these did not
dare to dream of it. At this period of excitement, anger, and
fear, Paine published his "Common Sense;" and boldly proposed independence, as the *best* means to get out of the difficulties into which they had now plunged; and as an object
alone worth fighting for. This pamphlet effected wonders:
it overcame difficulties, apparently insurmountable, for it removed prejudices, generally a hopeless task: it convinced
the people that the British constitution was not the *best that
could be*, and that a government of kings, lords, and commons,
might not be the essence of all that is excellent in each; but
that the union might retain much that was bad in each: he
satisfied the people of the disadvantages of carrying on
war with a government whose authority was acknowledged:
and he opened to them the resources within their power, and
hinted at the possibility of getting foreign help as an independent nation. He produced, what his writings generally did
produce, a change of opinion. The pamphlet was read from
north to south; everybody talked about it; and each seemed
surprised that he had not had the same thoughts, so clear did
the propositions appear as explained in "Common Sense."
The boldness of the language, indeed, alarmed those who are
in the habit of understanding for other people: they had no
objection to it themselves, but they thought the people not
yet prepared for such opinions; and some ludicrous scenes
occurred. The people, indeed, were not prepared: they read
first from curiosity, and then became convinced. Paine absolutely produced the events he sought. He wanted a declaration of independence, and he *produced* the *wish* for it. Clio
Rickman observes, in a note on Cheetham's life of Paine,
that—

"When 'Common Sense' arrived at Albany the convention of New York was in session: General Scott, a leading member, alarmed at the boldness and novelty of its arguments, mentioned his fears to several of his distinguished colleagues, and suggested a private meeting in the evening for the purpose of writing an answer. They accordingly met, and Mr. M'Kesson read the pamphlet through. At first it was deemed both necessary and expedient to answer it immediately, but casting about for the necessary arguments they concluded to adjourn and meet again. In a few evenings they assembled, but so rapid was the change of opinion in the colonies at large in favor of independence, that they ultimately agreed not to oppose it."

When Mr. Paine saw the avidity with which his book was read, as he had not published for interest but principle, he generously gave the copyright to every state. His own observations on the subject are these:—

"Politics and self-interest have been so uniformly connected that the world from being so often deceived has a right to be suspicious of public characters. But with regard to myself, I am perfectly easy on this head. I did not at my first setting out in public life, nearly seventeen years ago, turn my thoughts to subjects of government from motives of interest; and my conduct from that moment to this proves the fact. I saw an opportunity in which I thought I could do some good, and I followed exactly what my heart dictated. I neither read books, nor studied other people's opinions—I thought for myself. The case was this:—
During the suspension of the old government in America, both prior to and at the breaking out of hostilities, I was struck with the order and decorum with which everything was conducted, and impressed with the idea that a little more than what society naturally performed was all the government that was necessary. On these principles I published the pamphlet 'Common Sense.'

The success it met with was beyond anything since the invention of printing. I gave the copyright up to every state in the Union, and the demand run to not less than one hundred thousand copies, and I continued the subject under the title of 'American Crisis,' till the complete establishment of the American revolution.'

The disinterested conduct of Mr. Paine, considering the enormous quantity that was sold, is a remarkable trait in his character, and one which should excite in the breast of every

American citizen a lively sense of gratitude. Paine, at this time, was yet a poor man. It would have been perfectly honorable in him to take the ordinary profit. That profit on "Common Sense" alone must have been enormously large, and a large profit could have been made on each number of the "Crisis;" and Paine, without the slightest imputation on his character, could have realized a handsome fortune, while he rendered a most important service to his adopted country. We know of no example of the kind; some rich men publish for principle, but we know of no poor man, who had the temptation of popularity to anything like the extent which Mr. Paine enjoyed by this publication, who gave to the public his copyright. He stands, therefore, alone, as a remarkable instance of great generosity and public spirit. Mr. Paine was never an extravagant man. While in public life, and in the enjoyment of a moderate competency, he lived like a gentleman in this country, in England, and in France: but when in retirement, both in France and in this country, at a late period of his life, when many of his former friends avoided an intimacy for fear of the unpopularity of his religious opinions, he then evidently became careless of appearances, and, though always well clothed, comfortably lodged, and possessed of the comforts of life, yet, in his old age, his style of living was mean. Yet what can we say of the meanness of a man, who thus nobly gives up thousands, glorying in the act, and persevering in it, in all his successive political and theological publications? The only answer is that he had not an extravagant taste, and this enabled him to be generous; while this taste, at variance with the taste of others in equal circumstances, will necessarily appear parsimonious. Had Paine been less parsimonious, he would probably have been less generous. His capability of living on a little, evidently suggested the idea that great riches were unnecessary in a private situation.

"The time was now arrived," says Sherwin, "when our author was to take an active as well as a decisive part in public affairs. The declaration of independence had removed the scene of political warfare from the closet to the camp, and it was now become necessary to try the strength of public patriotism by bringing it into the field of military operations. Warlike preparations were immediately set on foot by the Americans. Many individuals of respectability volunteered their services in support of their country's freedom, and among the foremost of them was Mr. Paine. In this capacity he was introduced to the friendship of the Marquis de la Fayette, who was likewise serving as a volunteer in the American army. The officers treated our author with every possible mark of respect; at their tables he was hailed as a welcome guest, and General Washington himself neglected no opportunity of showing the high opinion he entertained of his talents and integrity."

Cheetham, in spite of his prejudices, gives the following brief account of Paine's services at this time:—

"When 'Common Sense' was written, the friends of independence were not republicans. Paine's invectives against monarchy were intended against the monarchy of England, rather than against monarchy in general, and they were popular, in the degree to which the measures and designs of the British cabinet were odious. The question, when no alternative but colonial vassalage or national independence presented itself, was one merely of independence, for, as Mr. Adams truly remarked, the colonists had no wish but for the 'immemorial liberties of their ancestors.' To this may be added the observation of Dr. Franklin, that they could not even hope for a government under which they could enjoy liberties more precious.

On the fourth of July, 1776, congress declared the colonies 'free and independent states,' which was as soon after the publication of 'Common Sense,' Paine remarks, 'as the work could spread through such an extensive country.'

Paine now accompanied the army of independence as a sort of itinerant writer, of which his pen was an appendage almost as necessary and formidable as its cannon. Having no property, he fared as the army fared, and at the same expense, but to what mess he was attached·I have not been able to learn, although, from what I hear and know, it must, I think, though he was sometimes admitted into higher company, have been a subaltern one. When the colonists drooped he revived them with a 'Crisis.' The first of these numbers he published early in December, 1776. The object of it was good, the method excellent, and the language suited to the depressed spirits of the army, of public bodies, and of private citizens, cheering. Washington, defeated on Long Island, had retreated to New York, and been driven with great loss from Forts Washington and Lee. The gallant little army, overwhelmed with a rapid succession of misfortunes, was dwindling away, and all seemed to be over with the cause, when scarcely a blow had been struck. 'These,' said the 'Crisis,' 'are the times that try men's souls. The summer soldier and the sunshine patriot will, in this crisis, shrink from the service of his country; but he that stands it NOW, deserves the love and thanks of man and woman. Tyranny, like hell, is not easily conquered; yet we have this consolation with us, that the harder the conflict the more glorious the triumph : what we obtain too cheap we esteem too lightly.'

The number was read in the camp, to every corporal's guard, and in the army and out of it had more than the intended effect. The convention of New York, reduced by dispersion occasioned by alarm, to nine members, was rallied and reanimated. Militiamen, who, already tired of the war, were straggling from the army, returned. Hope succeeded to despair, cheerfulness to gloom, and firmness to irresolution. To the confidence which it inspired may be attributed much of the brilliant little affair which in the same month followed at Trenton."

The impression which this first number of the "Crisis" made on the public mind, is evident by the *very first* sentence being handed down already to two generations, as a sort of watchword : "These are the times that try men's souls ;" yet the dastardly enmity to Paine has suppressed the author. Thousands use this expression, while individuals only know the origin of it. Yet the fact of this expression being thus handed down even in spite of the personal prejudices against the man, clearly shows the impression this well-timed pamphlet must have made on the nation. The extract we have given scarcely shows the facts : the American army was dispirited ; they were even brought into contempt by their unsoldierlike appearance in comparison to the well-clothed, well-fed regulars, preceded by elegant bands of music. The militia whose time was up were returning in disgust; the army appeared disbanded. It was Paine's task to reinstate it, to place honor where it was deserved, and to convert the despairing, degraded, because despised soldier, into a warm patriot, and to convert a feeling of scorn into one of encouragement; and this task Paine admirably performed.

"The affair of Trenton elevating American confidence," as Cheetham remarks, "and breathing caution into the British army, Paine, in January, 1777, congratulated the 'free and independent states' in a second number of the 'Crisis.' It is addressed to Lord Howe, and ridicules his proclamation, 'commanding all congresses, committees, &c., to desist and cease from their treasonable doings.' Against the king and his purposes, it is full of invective, but of a sort rather popular than exquisite. Fortunately for the United States the British commander-in-chief dealt more in impotent proclamations, than in the efficacy of arms. Washington's retreat to Trenton was a compulsive one. He had not from choice and by military skill drawn the Hessians into the toil in which they were ensnared. I do not believe that even a number of the 'Crisis' could have saved the American army and cause from annihilation, if Howe had been an active and persevering, an enlightened and energetic commander. Washington's patience and care, his admirable coolness and prudence, although often, in the course of the war, provoked to battle by a thousand irritating circumstances, by internal faction, and by British sneers, saved America to freedom; while the idle dissipation of Howe, his devotion to licentious pleasures, his unmartial spirit and conduct, lost it to the crown.

On the nineteenth of April, 1777, he published, at Philadelphia, the third number of the 'Crisis.' As there had been no military operations from the capture of the Hessians at Trenton, it was devoted to an examination of occurrences since the declaration of independence, and to a repetition of the arguments which he had employed in 'Common Sense' in favor of independence."

At this time, or rather on the 17th of April, Mr. Paine was elected by congress secretary to the committee for foreign affairs. No man could be more suitable for this situation: and ably did he serve it. The duties of his office corresponded with that of the English secretary for foreign affairs. He stood in the same relation to the committee as that officer did to the cabinet. All foreign communications were addressed to Mr. Paine, and by him perused, and then laid before the committee by whose instructions he acted. In his foreign communications he assumed the same title which the British minister did who performed the same task. On this subject Cheetham is very spiteful, and supposes he did so from vanity; and insidiously mentions the amount of the paltry salary which Mr. Paine received, as a sort of presumptuous evidence that he ought not, with such a salary, to call himself "secretary for foreign affairs." But the fact is, it was policy in

Mr. Paine to do so: he wrote then in the style of an equal, and assumed a proper dignity useful to his adopted country.

In the early part of September, 1777, Sir William Howe and Cornwallis were pushing on the line of the Brandywine toward Philadelphia; and to satisfy the public mind, Washington was obliged to risk a battle. He did so, and lost the battle; but being ably assisted by La Fayette, and other French and Polish officers, he made good his retreat, without any very serious injury. On this occasion Paine published his fourth "Crisis;" short, but admirably adapted to the purpose; and the *morale* or confidence of the army increased, so that, could they have fought the battle over again, the soldiers would have done it.

While Washington was engaged with Howe and Cornwallis near Philadelphia, General Gates was watching the movements of Burgoyne, descending the Hudson; and fell upon him at Saratoga, where the militia simultaneously joined him; and Burgoyne, weakened by his march, and disappointed in the junction of the New York army with him in this neighborhood, was surrounded, and obliged to surrender. Howe, aware of this, and not being able to bring Washington to a general engagement, became predatory in his warfare: on which occasion Paine brought out his fifth "Crisis;" which, as Sherwin remarks—

"Was published at Lancaster, in Pennsylvania, March, 1778. It consists of a letter addressed to General Sir William Howe, and an 'Address to the Inhabitants of America.' The advantages gained by General Howe he considers of so trifling a nature, as rather to prove the impotence of his troops, than to show their ability to prosecute their object. He cites the retreat of the British as a confirmation of this conclusion. He ridicules, with considerable force, the vanity of attaching importance to titles, and the pretensions which Sir William had set forth to the esteem of the Americans. He is very severe on the mean and cowardly conduct of Sir William in distributing forged continental bills. If this charge were true, and the evidence given is too conclusive to admit of its being doubted, it is a most disgraceful circumstance to those employed in carrying on the war.* In the conduct of an army there are certain

---

* The only parallel to this proceeding that I have ever heard of, is the conduct of Pitt toward the French in 1795. It has been said that Mr. Pitt was the inventor of this cowardly species of warfare; but this the reader will perceive to

acts which we consider dishonorable, and which a commander who values his character will always be careful to prevent. These are not laid down by any law; because, when countries are at war with each other, law is totally out of the question: they depend on the disposition of a general and the discipline of his troops. But of all the low, drivelling practices that were ever resorted to by an army to distress a people with whom it was at war, the project of forging their bills is the most despicable. It is in a moral sense what assassination is in a physical sense; and ought never to be resorted to except as a measure of retaliation. It is, however, impossible to reprobate the practice in stronger terms than Paine has done in the publication before us. 'You, sir,' says he, in the address to Sir William, 'have abetted and patronised the forging and uttering counterfeit continental bills. In the same New York newspapers in which your own proclamation under your master's authority was published, offering or pretending to offer pardon and protection to the inhabitants of these states, there were repeated advertisements of counterfeit money for sale; and persons who have come officially from you, and under sanction of your flag, have been taken up in attempting to put them off. A conduct so basely mean in a public character is without precedent or pretence. Every nation on earth, whether friends or enemies, will join in condemning you. It is an incendiary war upon society, which nothing can excuse or palliate: an improvement upon beggarly villany; and shows an inbred wretchedness of heart, made up between the venomous malignity of a serpent, and the spiteful imbecility of an inferior reptile.' The severity of these reproaches finds an apology in the circumstances of the case; for though the language is harsh, it is nevertheless just; and the fault lies with the person who deserves, not with him who applies it.

There, perhaps, is not any species of composition which, in a few years, becomes so dry and insipid as disquisitions upon the politics of the day; and those writers who have been able to give to such a subject a permanent interest, must be allowed to possess talents of a superior description. The ability displayed by Paine in the productions before us, has conferred a lasting importance on events which, passing through the icy medium of distant history, would have met with but little attention. He makes us *feel* as well as *see* the objects he is writing upon; and though in some instances he does not attempt to give his language that high polish of which it is susceptible, yet we soon discover the intrinsic value of his sentiments, and we respect the rough exterior as an evidence of the

be an unfounded supposition. Not that I wish to deprive Mr. Pitt of any of the infamy of such an expedient. I merely mention it to show, that in one of his most dishonorable schemes he was no more than a common imitator.

author's sincerity, while a multitude of graces would only tend to bring his motives into suspicion.

The subsequent part of the letter to General Howe discovers a fund of thought, penetration, and feeling. Though I intend to be as brief as possible in making extracts from works which cannot be properly appreciated unless they are perused entire, yet the following is so prophetically true, that I cannot resist the temptation of quoting it:—

'There is something in meanness which excites a species of resentment that never subsides; and something in cruelty which stirs up the heart to the highest agony of human hatred. Britain has filled up both these characters till no addition can be made, and hath not reputation left with us to obtain credit for the slightest promise. The will of God hath parted us; and the deed is registered for eternity. When she shall be a spot scarcely visible among nations, America shall flourish, the favorite of Heaven, and the friend of mankind.'

If the implicit supporters of arbitrary power and orthodox despotism will not admit Paine to have prophesied from inspiration, it is to be hoped they will allow him to possess the merit of sound judgment and rational reflection. At all events, his calumniators cannot deny that the foregoing prediction is fast verging toward its fulfilment. Our author concludes No. V. with an address to the inhabitants of America. In this he exhorts them to fresh perseverance; and, after an elaborate description of the situation of the respective armies, he closes by proposing a plan for recruiting the American forces.

The sixth number of the 'Crisis' was published at Philadelphia, in October, 1778. The subject is a letter to the earl of Carlisle, General Clinton, and William Eden, Esq., British commissioners at New York. These gentlemen, in opposition to all the dictates of reason and experience, had issued a proclamation, calling upon the rebellious Americans to renew their allegiance to the king of Great Britain, whom they pompously described as the 'rightful sovereign' of America. The treaty which had recently been concluded between America and France, appears to have been the principal cause of this fresh display of folly. The pains which the poor commissioners were at to make themselves and their royal master appear ridiculous, were in strict conformity with the blundering policy which had given rise to their appointment; and their promises and pardons, their flattery and threats, were alike unavailing. The government of England, instead of being looked upon as an affectionate parent, was now regarded as an unnatural monster, who had sought to strangle her infant offspring. Even those who at first had been the most zealous friends of reconciliation, were by this time deprived of all their long-cherished hopes; for they clearly saw that a reunion with the British government would be the certain forerunner of the most abject slavery. The pretensions and offers of the commissioners were, therefore, either spurned as an insult to the people, or ridiculed as a silly display of imaginary power. And when to this state of things we add the previous capture of General Burgoyne, their situation becomes truly pitiable. With such materials to work upon, it is impossible that a man of any ability would write ill; and we therefore need not wonder that they furnished Paine with the groundwork of one of the best numbers of the 'Crisis.' As an analysis of this production would not tend in any degree to do justice to the writer's merits, I shall avoid making extracts from this as well as the subsequent numbers; recommending to the reader an attentive perusal of the whole, as the only mode of enabling himself to appreciate the talents, perseverance, and patriotism of the author.

The seventh number of the 'Crisis' was published at Philadelphia, Nov. 21, 1778. It consists of a letter to the people of England. The object of this number appears to have differed in some degree from that of its immediate predecessor: the one being written for the purpose of convincing the government, and the other of proving to the people the improbability of subduing America. The delusive hopes with which the ministry had amused the nation, the disgrace which must attend the hitherto invincible armies of England, and the wickedness of any man in even wishing those armies to be successful, are exposed with an ability which must have been most severely felt by the enemies, and warmly applauded by the friends of independence. The number likewise contains some excellent reflections on the subject of national honor and the mischievous effects of national vanity.

In January, 1779, our author resigned his situation of secretary for foreign affairs. This resignation was in consequence of a disagreement which had taken place between the congress and Mr. Paine, respecting a person of the name of Silas Deane. In the early part of the war, it appears that this man had been employed by the committee for foreign affairs as an agent in France, for the purpose of obtaining supplies, either as a loan from the French government, or, if he failed in this, to purchase them as regular merchandise. Without waiting the issue of his separate mission, he was soon after nominated with Dr. Franklin and Mr. Lee, who proceeded to the court of Louis for the same purpose. The French monarch, more perhaps from his hostility to the English government, than from any attachment to the American cause, gladly acceded to the request; and the supplies were immediately furnished from the king's arsenal. As France was then to all appearance upon amicable terms with England, a pledge was given by the American commissioners that the grant should remain a secret. The supplies were accordingly shipped in the name of a Mr. Beaumarchais, and consigned to an imaginary house in the United States. Deane, taking advantage of the secresy which had been promised by the commissioners, presented a claim for compensation in behalf of himself and Beaumarchais; thinking, perhaps, that the auditing committee would prefer a compliance with his fraudulent demand, rather than expose their ally, the king of France, to a rupture with England. At first there appeared an inclination to comply with his request; and Mr. Paine, perceiving this, and knowing the circumstances of the case, resolved on laying the transaction before the public. He accordingly wrote for the newspapers several essays, under the title of 'Common Sense to the Public on Mr. Deane's Affairs.' In these he exposed, without ceremony, the dishonest designs of Deane. The business, in consequence, soon became a subject of general conversation: the demand was rejected by the auditing committee, and Deane himself soon afterward absconded to England.

For this piece of service to the Americans our author was thanked and applauded by the body of the people; but by this time a party had begun to form itself, whose principles, if not the reverse of independence, were the reverse of republicanism. These men, as individuals, had long envied the popularity of Mr. Paine, but from their want of means to check or control it, they had hitherto remained silent. An opportunity was now offered for venting their spleen. Mr. Paine, in expressing his indignation against the claims of Mr. Deane, had mentioned one or two circumstances that had come to his knowledge in consequence of his office; a plan was immediately formed for depriving him of his situation; and, accordingly, a motion was made by one of the members for an order to bring him before the congress. Mr. Paine readily attended; and on being asked whether the articles in question were written by him, he replied that they were. He was then directed to withdraw. As soon as he had left the house, a member arose and moved: 'That Thomas Paine be discharged from the office of secretary to the committee for foreign affairs;' but the motion was lost upon a division. Mr. Paine then wrote to congress, requesting that he might be heard in his defence, and Mr. Laurens made a motion for that purpose, which was negatived. The next day he sent in his resignation, concluding with these words: 'As I cannot, consistently with my character as a freeman, submit to be censured unheard; therefore, to preserve that character and maintain that right, I think it my duty to resign the office of secretary to the committee for foreign affairs; and I do hereby resign the same.'

This conduct on the part of the congress may, in some degree, be attributed to a desire to quiet the fears of the French ambassador, who had become very dissatisfied, in consequence of its being known to the world that the supplies were a present from his master. To silence his apprehensions, and preserve the friendship of the French court, they treated Paine with ingratitude. This they acknowledged at a future period by a grant; of which we shall have occasion to speak in its proper place.

Our author was now deprived of the means of obtaining a livelihood; and not being disposed to render his literary labors subservient to his personal wants, he engaged himself as clerk to Mr. Biddle, an attorney at Philadelphia.

Mr. Paine's dispute with the congress produced no change in his patriotism. On every occasion he continued to display the same degree of independence and resolution which had produced his first animated efforts in favor of the republican cause. Neither personal altercation, nor pecuniary embarrassments, had any effect upon his principles. He had enlisted himself as a volunteer in the American cause; and he vindicated her rights under every change of circumstance, with the unabated ardor of a freeman.

Soon after the resignation of his secretaryship, our author was chosen clerk of the legislature of Pennsylvania. This appointment is a proof that, though he had some enemies, he had many friends; and that the insidious insinuations of the former had not been enabled to weaken the attachment of the latter.

In March, 1780, Mr. Paine published the eighth number of the 'Crisis.' The subject of this is a second address to the people of England. It is written much in the same style as the one which preceded it. From all that had taken place, it was apparent that America was beyond the reach of conquest; and seeing this, he very properly asks the English people what their motive was in protracting a contest which appeared to be fraught with nothing but self-destruction. He dwells with great emphasis on the calamities of war; and represents the people of England as ignorant of any of its effects, except that of taxation. He could not have had a better opportunity of depicting the miseries of military contention; and the portrait he has drawn is as natural as life.

In June following, he published at Philadelphia the ninth number of the 'Crisis.' This seems to have been written for the purpose of consoling the Americans for the loss of Charlestown, which had recently fallen into the hands of the British. He reasons with considerable force and ingenuity on the insignificance of such a conquest; and consoles his readers by reflecting that similar misfortunes were unavoidable during a state of local warfare; and that they were in some measure advantageous, inasmuch as, without endangering the real safety of the country, they were sufficiently injurious to prevent its being lulled into the lap of false security.

In the beginning of October, 1780, our author published, at Philadelphia, a long discussion on the subject of taxes, under the title of 'A Crisis Extraordinary.' He draws a comparison between the extent of taxation in the respective countries of England and America: he shows, from calculation, that the former exceed the latter in more than a tenfold degree; and concludes by recommending the plan of congress; that of funding its paper, and issuing a new coinage as a substitute. Notwithstanding the determined hostility of the Americans toward the English, their army was considerably oppressed for want of pecuniary means; and to this cause, more than to any other, we may attribute the apparent hardiness of their operations about this period. In the course of his reflections, he takes an opportunity of repeating his former arguments against the tyranny, folly, and avarice of the English government: he treats the difficulties of the country as affairs of a temporary character, which a little privation and perseverance would speedily remove.

While those financial discussions were pending, the congress resolved upon attempting a more effectual plan for removing the public embarrassments, than could be derived from any application of the internal resources of the states. Mr. Paine drew up a letter to Count Vergennes, stating the difficulties in which the country was placed; and concluding with a request that France would, either as a subsidy, or as a loan, supply the United States with a million sterling, and continue that supply annually during the war. This letter Mr. Paine showed first to M. Marbois, the French minister's secretary. He objected to the application by observing, that 'a million sent out of a nation exhausted it more than ten millions spent in it.' Our author was not to be baffled in his design by this rebuff; and he accordingly presented his scheme to Mr. Isard, member for South Carolina. This gentleman readily agreed to bring the subject before congress; which he did very shortly afterward. The congress, after a very short discussion, acceded to the proposal; and a mission to the court of France was resolved upon immediately.

Colonel Laurens, son of the late president of congress, was appointed to negotiate the affair; and, at his anxious solicitation, Mr. Paine accompanied him to Paris. They sailed in February, 1781, and arrived in France the following month. Their mission was attended with more success than was expected. They obtained six millions of livres as a present, and ten millions as a loan, borrowed in Holland on the security of France. They sailed from Brest at the beginning of June, and arrived at Boston in August; having under their charge two millions and a half in silver, exclusive of a ship and brig laden with clothing and military stores.

From the account which Mr. Paine gives of himself, it appears that he had, some time previous to this, formed a design of coming over to England, for the purpose of exposing to the people the folly and perversity of their rulers. 'I was,' he observes, ' strongly impressed with the idea, that if I could get over to England without being known, and only remain in safety till I could get out a publication, that I could open the eyes of the country with respect to the madness and stupidity of its government.'* He would have carried his intention into effect almost immediately, but for the advice of his friend General Greene; who, it appears, fully approved of the plan: but the affair of Arnold and Andre happening shortly afterward, the general altered his mind, and wrote very pressingly to Mr. Paine to dissuade him from his design. With some reluctance he consented to adopt the general's advice; both parties conceiving that his personal safety would be greatly endangered by any attempt at that time to carry his scheme into practice.

During our author's voyage to France with Col. Laurens, another event occurred which confirmed the propriety and practicability of this project. An English packet, from Falmouth to New York, was taken by a French privateer; and, owing to an artful stratagem of the French captain, the government despatches in the packet were secured and brought on board his vessel. They were sent to Paris to the French minister, Count Vergennes; who, after reading them, presented them to Col. Laurens and Mr. Paine, to be conveyed to America for the information and use of congress.

What the contents of these despatches were is not known; but it appears that they afforded Mr. Paine a better opportunity of judging of the perfidy and intrigue of the English cabinet than could have been done by any other means. This circumstance renewed his former plan respecting the British government; but Colonel Laurens being unwilling to return alone, Mr. Paine was induced to postpone its execution to a more favorable opportunity."

Previous to this period the French had declared in favor of the United States. The campaign of 1778 was arranged in Paris, and a French army and fleet co-operated with Washington; yet, after the capture of Burgoyne no decisive action was fought till the capture of Cornwallis in 1780. The war for several years was chiefly predatory in the south, and

* 'Rights of Man,' Part II., p. 70.

General Howe, Cornwallis, and the traitor Arnold, laid waste the states of South Carolina, North Carolina, and Georgia; but their troops were continually harassed by the activity and skill of the American general, Greene, who from a blacksmith became one of the best generals in the service of the states. During this year (1780), the finances were in the most wretched state; the paper-money depreciated to a most alarming extent, and it was evidently impossible to raise the supplies by taxes. Washington's private accounts to the congress clearly revealed the miserable state of the army, while their published accounts deceived the enemy. Mr. Paine, by his "Common Sense," had previously produced the declaration of independence, and the unanimity of the people. The "Crisis," published as we have seen from time to time, preserved that unanimity, and in a great measure regulated the tone of public feeling. But Mr. Paine was not backward in his personal services: on one occasion when with the army, he formed a plan to destroy a part of the enemy's shipping, and offered to conduct the enterprise. This he explains in one number of the "Crisis," and shows that his object was not merely to effect a loss to the English, but to abate their pride in the strength of their navy, and to encourage the spirits of the people, who thought the British ships-of-war impregnable. When the finances were in the worst state, before Mr. Paine went to France, and when Washington feared the immediate dissolution of the army for want of pay and necessaries, Mr. Paine began a private subscription with five hundred dollars, all the money he could then raise, including his salary as secretary. The subscriptions on this occasion reached the large amount of three hundred thousand pounds; and this fund converted into a bank supplied the immediate wants of the government, and enabled Washington to commence the preparation to encompass and subdue Cornwallis, and thus bring an end to the war. These preparations were facilitated by a knowledge of the success of Colonel Laurens's mission to France, assisted by Mr. Paine: and the supplies actually arriving while Washington's army was manœuvring for the last great exploit, had, probably a considerable effect on the success of those manœuvres. This was evidently the opinion of Mr. Paine. New York was in possession of the enemy, the headquarters of Clinton. The anxious solicitude of Washington was to recover this city. Washington's plans were apparently all directed to this object; and the chief attention of Clinton consequently bent on the retention of that place. Cornwallis was then at Yorktown, Va., on the Susquehannah. The French fleet, by pretending to fly, drew out the English fleet till a re-enforcement entered the Chesapeake, and then returned to take and keep possession of that bay. Troops marching from the south did not alarm Clinton; re-enforcements from the west he was perhaps ignorant of; and the troops progressing down the Hudson from the north he supposed destined to join Washington near New York. When these collections of troops were all within a few days' march of the Susquehannah and Yorktown, Washington suddenly turned his own force in that direction. Clinton thought it a ruse, and remained inactive and thus was Cornwallis suddenly surrounded, in every direction, by sea and land, by the regulars, their auxiliaries, the French and Poles, and by the militia. Cornwallis, unprepared for a siege, surrendered before he could be relieved by Clinton; and thus a virtual end was put to the war, for till peace was restored, the British merely kept possession of New York, and one or two other stations, holding in subjection only the parts actually occupied by their armies. Just before this brilliant affair Mr. Paine arrived from France, bringing with him two millions of livres in cash and other supplies, forming the loading of a brig and a ship. Mr. Paine was instrumental in procuring these supplies, as he was better known (from the reputation of his writings) than Col. Laurens, who for that reason had desired his company. Whether these supplies were actually used to facilitate Washington's masterly movements we do not know, but as they were known to be coming, they gave the government and Washington a credit which they would not otherwise have enjoyed. Money and credit are the sinews of war, and are as necessary to success as unanimity. Paine has the merit of contributing to both in a very high degree. We shall quote again from Sherwin, the most accurate of Mr. Paine's biographers.

"In March, 1782, Mr. Paine published at Philadelphia the tenth number of the 'Crisis.' The king of England, probably with a view of keeping the people in good humor with the expenses of the war, had delivered a speech at the recent opening of parliament in which the Americans were abused, and the English flattered, without any regard to truth or propriety. On this document our author delivers his opinion in terms of the severest reprobation. He satirizes the pretensions of the king to the title of sovereign of a free people, and draws an interesting parallel between the hardships of the Americans and those they would have suffered had the British been victorious. He concludes the number with an address to the people of America on the financial affairs of the states.

In May, 1782, he published at Philadelphia the eleventh number of the 'Crisis:' 'On the present State of News.' It had been conjectured and rumored that the object of the British cabinet was to detach France from America, for the purpose of making a separate peace with the former, in order that she might be enabled to bring her whole force against the independence of the latter. However absurd and dishonorable such an attempt might appear, it would have been no more than a continuance of the policy which had induced the ministry to persist so long in a war where there was neither hope to encourage nor principle to sanction their conduct. The present number appears to have been written with a view to inform the public that such a design had been contemplated by the British court, and that want of means alone had prevented it from being carried into execution.

In the same month, Mr. Paine published a supernumerary 'Crisis,' consisting of a letter to Sir Guy Carleton. This is a most forcible appeal to the English general respecting the barbarous murder of Captain Huddy, by a refugee of the name of Lippincot. Captain Huddy, of the Jersey militia, with a small party of Americans, had been attacked and taken prisoner by an armed force in the pay of the British, and carried into New York. About three weeks afterward he was taken down to the water-side, put in a boat, and brought again upon the Jersey shore, where he was atrociously murdered, under the direction of the refugee before mentioned. General Washington, determined that such an act should not pass without punishment, directed that lots should be cast by the British prisoners, for the purpose of selecting a victim in return for the murder of Captain Huddy. The lot fell upon Captain Asgill; and Mr. Paine's letter to Sir Guy Carleton, was written with a view to induce him to give up the murderer, and save the life of a brave and innocent officer. It does not appear that this request was ever complied with; and Asgill, after suffering all the suspense, misery, and despair, which naturally attend such a situation, was at last pardoned through the humanity of the American general.

In October, 1782, our author published, at Philadelphia, a letter to Lord Shelburne (afterward marquis of Lansdowne): this has since been classed as the twelfth number of the 'Crisis.' It is throughout an excellent production. The policy of concluding a peace with America, and acknowledging her independence, had on several occasions been discussed; but Lord Shelburne, unable to discover the propriety of the measure, and acting under the influence of that silly vanity which forms so noble an attribute of the freeborn Englishman, had declared that 'the sun of Great Britain would set whenever she acknowledged the independence of America.' The sentiment contained in this declaration is treated with a poignant satire, which must have been severely felt by the party with whom it originated.

The war was now fast drawing toward a conclusion, and America was about to enjoy the benefits of the liberty for which she had so long and so ardently contended. The British cabinet was at length convinced of the total impossibility of conquering the Americans; and the operations of the English declined in proportion as this conviction became more general. A definite treaty of peace was set on foot at Paris toward the end of the year 1782, and concluded a few months afterward. The triumphant situation of America—the grand and glorious effect of her courage and constancy, is admirably described by Mr. Paine in the last number of the 'Crisis.' He congratulates the country on the happy conclusion of 'the times that tried men's souls:' he dwells with pleasure on the fair character which America had established among the nations of the world; and observes with truth, that she need never be ashamed to tell her birth, or relate the stages by which she rose to empire. Shortly after the publication of this piece, Mr. Paine wrote a reply to a pamphlet by Lord Sheffield, on the subject of American commerce. This is classed with our author's previous productions as a supernumerary 'Crisis.'

To have preserved an exact chronological order, we ought to have noticed two other pamphlets, written by him some time previous to the cessation of hostilities. The first of these is entitled 'Public Good;' being an examination of the claim of Virginia to the vacant western territory. The method in which the case is investigated, discovers all the acuteness and ability which might be expected from the author; but as the subject is not *now* a matter of interest, even to the American reader, it is not here necessary to enter into the discussion. There is, however, one circumstance connected with the performance which ought not to be omitted, as it serves to show the disinterested character of Mr. Paine, and his determination to publish his opinions unbiased and unshackled, even though they should militate against his own private interests. The part which our author espoused in the dispute was in *opposition* to the claim of Virginia, though it was well known to him at the time that a proposition was pending before the assembly of that state, for granting him a pecuniary compensation for his writings in favor of independence. Before the publication of 'Public Good,' the majority of the members were decidedly in favor of the grant; but on the appearance of the pamphlet, they suddenly changed sides, and the motion was lost by a single vote! Such is the reward of ingenuous patriotism and a love of truth! With facts like this before us, we may cease to wonder that so many seemingly disinterested individuals, in every age and country, are continually drawn into the vortex of sycophancy and apostacy.

In 1782, he published a letter to the Abbe Raynal. The object of this letter was to clear up the mistakes, and expose the errors into which the abbe had fallen in his history of the American revolution. Among other things the abbe had asserted that none of those energetic causes, which had produced so many revolutions upon the globe, had existed in North America; that neither religion nor laws had there been outraged; that the blood of martyrs had not streamed from scaffolds; that morals had not been insulted; that neither manners, customs, habits, nor any other object dear to nations, had there been the sport of ridicule; and that the only question was, whether the mother-country had or had not a right to lay a small tax upon the colonies. To correct and refute such misrepresentations as these, a reference to facts was barely necessary. They were almost too palpable to require a confutation; and the popular character of the abbe in the literary world alone accounts for their obtaining a currency. That such a warm and enlightened friend of humanity and freedom, as the Abbe Raynal, should be mistaken in his ideas of the American revolution, is at first astonishing; but men who from their cradles have been surrounded by despotism, and who have only contemplated the blessings of liberty as a distant though delightful vision, are incapable of forming an opinion on so great an event. A long habit of beholding the acts of tyranny almost unfits the mind for the contemplation of any other object; and to this, more than to any other cause, must be attributed the mistaken conjectures and disordered statements of the Abbe Raynal.

From a comparison between some of the abbe's observations and those contained in 'Common Sense,' on the subject of society and government, it appears that the abbe had borrowed very freely from the latter. Some of his remarks are a literal transcript, with the exception of a few words. Among other things which he had misstated, was the account of the affair at Trenton, which I have already had occasion to notice. The abbe had described this as a mere accidental occurrence, falling, as he says, 'within the wide empire of chance.' This was a very unjust and ungenerous reflection. The highest praise was due to the American general and his troops, as the reader will perceive by turning to the account of the action; and it is to be regretted that such a distinguished writer as the Abbe Raynal should have been misled on the subject, for no person could have done it more justice.

After exposing the abbe's errors and misrepresentations, Mr. Paine indulges himself in a variety of philosophical reflections. The following description of prejudice is so replete with originality and beauty, that I cannot forbear quoting it:—

'There is something exceedingly curious in the constitution and operation of prejudice. It has the singular ability of accommodating itself to all the possible varieties of the human mind. Some passions and vices are but thinly scattered among mankind, and find only here and there a fitness of reception. But prejudice, like the spider, makes everywhere its home. It has neither taste nor choice of place, and all that it requires is room. There is scarcely a situation, except fire and water, in which the spider will not live. So, let the mind be as naked as the walls of an empty and forsaken tenement, gloomy as a dungeon, or ornamented with the richest abilities of thinking; let it be hot, cold, dark, or light, lonely or inhabited, still prejudice, if undisturbed, will fill it with cobwebs, and live, like the spider, where there seems nothing to live on. If the one prepares her food by poisoning it to her palate and her use, the other does the same; and as several of our passions are strongly characterized by the animal world, prejudice may be denominated the spider of the mind.'

The spirit of universal philanthropy which formed so conspicuous a feature in Mr. Paine's character, the powerful effect of his writings in favor of independence, and the talent which he possessed for philosophical and mechanical discussion, rendered his society a valuable acquisition. Of his friendship with Dr. Franklin, and several other distinguished individuals, we have already had occasion to speak; and of the esteem in which his services and character were held by General Washington, we have several very unequivocal proofs in his conduct toward the end of the war. Soon after the definitive treaty of peace was concluded, the general took up his quarters at Rocky Hill, in the neighborhood of Princeton (where the congress was then sitting), for the purpose of resigning his commission. There he was informed that Mr. Paine had retired to Bordentown, where he had a small property. Conceiving, probably, that Mr. Paine's circumstances were not in the most flourishing condition, he very kindly wrote to him the following letter:—

'ROCKY HILL, *Sept.* 10, 1783.

I have learned, since I have been at this place, that you are at Bordentown. Whether for the sake of retirement or economy, I know not. Be it for either, for both, or whatever it may, if you will come to this place and partake with me, I shall be exceedingly happy to see you at it.

Your presence may remind congress of your past services to this country; and if it is in my power to impress them, command my best exertions with freedom, as they will be rendered cheerfully by one who entertains a lively sense of the importance of your works, and who, with much pleasure, subscribes himself

Your sincere friend,

G. WASHINGTON.'

Mr. Paine was urged by several of his friends to make an application to congress for a compensation for his revolutionary writings; but this he uniformly refused to do. That the man who had been the means of first rousing the country to a declaration of independence, and whose writings had afterward very materially contributed to the attainment of the object, was deserving of remuneration, no one could deny; but Mr. Paine's services in this respect being entirely of a voluntary nature, he could not consent to petition the congress for a pecuniary recompense. His writings, however meritorious and serviceable they might have been (and the most illiberal of his calumniators do not deny that their effects were great and universal), were dictated by the pure principles of disinterested patriotism, and he could not degrade their character by converting them into a medium of sordid emolument.

I am well aware of the attempts which have been made to show that Mr. Paine's patriotism was not of that disinterested nature here described, and when we see that these attempts are founded upon the resolutions of congress itself, it is not surprising that they should have been attended with some success among the weaker part of mankind. A short explanation will, however, do away with the impressions which such reports are calculated to produce. Before offering any observations on the subject, we will first insert the resolutions as extracted from the journals of congress:—

'FRIDAY, *August* 26, 1785.—On the report of a committee, consisting of Mr. Gerry, Mr. Petit, and Mr. King, to whom was referred a letter of the 13th from Thomas Paine:—

Resolved, That the early, unsolicited, and continued labors of Mr. Thomas Paine, in explaining and enforcing the principles of the late revolution, by ingenious and timely publications upon the nature of liberty and civil government, have been well received by the citizens of these states, and merit the approbation of congress, and that in consideration of these services and the benefits produced thereby, Mr. Paine is entitled to a liberal gratification from the United States.'

'MONDAY, *October* 3, 1785.—On the report of a committee, consisting of Mr. Gerry, Mr. Howell, and Mr. Long, to whom were referred sundry letters from Mr. Thomas Paine, and a report on his letter of the 13th of September:—

Resolved, That the board of treasury take order for paying to Mr. Thomas Paine the sum of three thousand dollars, for the considerations mentioned in the resolution of the 26th of August last.'

That the congress granted, and that Mr Paine received, the three thousand dollars above mentioned, are facts beyond dispute. The only error is in the wording of the two resolutions, which makes the grant appear the reverse of what it really was. The case was this: the salary which Mr. Paine received as secretary to the committee for foreign affairs was very small, being only eight hundred dollars a year, and the depreciation which took place in consequence of the immense and repeated issues of paper-money, reduced even this to less than a fifth of its nominal value. Mr. Paine, aware of the difficulties in which the congress were placed, forebore to harass them with any applications for money during the war, but after it was closed he addressed to them a letter requesting that they would make up the depreciation, with some other incidental expenses which he had been at in the discharge of his official duties. The letter was referred to a committee, of which Mr. Gerry was chairman. This gentleman came to Mr. Paine and informed him that 'the committee had consulted upon the subject, that they intended to bring in a handsome report, but they thought it best not to take any notice of Deane's affair or Mr. Paine's salary.'—'They will indemnify you,' said he, 'without it. The case is, there are some motions on the journals of congress for censuring you with respect to Deane's affair, which cannot now be recalled, because they have been printed. We will, therefore, bring in a report that will supersede them, without mentioning the purport of your letter.'

The grant was therefore an indemnity to Mr. Paine for the depreciation in his salary as secretary of the committee, and the reason for couching it in the terms above quoted, was to shield the congress from a confession of the injustice they had done our author for his conduct during the disputes about the claims of Silas Deane. It was no more than he had a right to expect, and those who granted it had not much reason to boast of their liberality, in performing what was merely an act of pecuniary justice. So much for the grant of three thousand dollars, the false language in which it is clothed, and the malevolent insinuations which it has given rise to.

But though Mr. Paine had resolved not to make any application to the congress on the score of his literary labors, he had several friends in the provincial assemblies who were determined that his exertions should not pass unrewarded. I have already spoken of the proposition that was made to the assembly of Virginia for this purpose, and the cause of its failure. Similar motions were brought before the legislature of Pennsylvania and the assembly of New York; the former of which gave him £500, and the latter the confiscated estate of a Mr. Frederick Devoe, a royalist. This estate, situated at New Rochelle, consisting of more than three hundred acres of land in a high state of cultivation, with a spacious and elegant stone-house, beside extensive out-buildings, was a valuable acquisition; and the readiness with which it was granted, is a proof of the high estimation in which Mr. Paine's services were held by one of the most opulent and powerful states in the Union.

In 1786, he published at Philadelphia, his 'Dissertations on Government,' 'The Affairs of the Bank,' and 'Paper-Money.' The bank alluded to was the one which had been established some years before, under the name of the 'Bank of North America.' Whatever opinion may be entertained of these institutions in general, it is evident that the one in question had been of considerable service to the Americans during the most eventful period of their struggle for independence; to say the least, it was therefore entitled to their gratitude. But when men find themselves in a state of ease and security, they are too apt to forget the means by which they obtained these advantages; and the bank, without any regard to its past services, was attacked as an establishment at variance with every principle of private security and public freedom. In the pamphlet before us Mr. Paine gives an elaborate and interesting account of the rise and progress of the institution; and as he was one of the first promoters of the scheme, a short account of it here will not be altogether unnecessary, although it will involve some repetition.

The beginning of the year 1780 was a very distressing season for the Americans. The people, though not conquered, were depressed; the soldiers, though not driven from the field, were destitute of resources, and such was their condition, that General Washington was, for a considerable time, in the daily dread of a general mutiny. In this state of affairs he addressed a letter to the Pennsylvania assembly, describing in the strongest terms the nature of his situation. At that period Mr. Paine was clerk of the assembly, and, as a part of his duty, he was requested to read the letter. When this was done, he informs us, 'a despairing silence pervaded the house.' No one ventured to speak for a considerable time. At length one of the members arose and said: 'If the account in that letter is a true state of things, and we are in the situation there represented, it appears to me in vain to contend the matter any longer. We may as well give up at first as at last.' Another of the members, more cheerful than the last, rose and expressed his hope that the house would not be overcome by despair; that the only way to get over the difficulty was by exertion; and a motion for adjournment being made, the assembly separated without coming to any conclusion.

America was, indeed, at this period, in a most critical situation. There now appeared no chance of retrieving her affairs by taxation, for the people were already overburdened, and the only mode that presented itself was that of a voluntary subscription. There was no time to be lost; and, as a beginning, Mr. Paine, immediately on his return from the house, drew the salary due to him as clerk of the assembly, and enclosed five hundred dollars in a letter to Mr. M'Clenaghan, proposing to him to commence a subscription, as the only means of alleviating the wants of the army. This gentleman showed the proposal to several others who fully approved of it: a subscription was commenced, and after being attended with considerable success, the subscribers formed themselves into a bank, which soon answered all the purposes for which it was intended. In 1782, the subscribers were legally incorporated under the title of the 'Bank of North America,' which they held, with advantage to the public.'

Mr. Paine is clear in his opinion on paper-money: but he regards this bank as one of *necessity* in its origin, and of great service to the country during the latter part of the war, when the irredeemable notes issued by the government had lost their value by depreciation. Mr. Paine could not forget the services of the bank; and hence he defended it efficiently against this attack, which he considered rude and unnecessary: yet he explicitly condemns the *charter*, which was made *perpetual*. This was the last public act of Mr. Paine previous to his departure for Europe.

Thus we arrive at the conclusion of the second period of Mr. Paine's life. At this time he enjoyed the highest popularity, and, as we have seen, the friendship of the most enlightened patriots of the age. Mr. Paine was as much esteemed in his private life as in his public. He was a welcome visiter to the tables of the most distinguished citizens: his manners and habits were those of a gentleman, which rendered him agreeable, not only to the master of the family, but to the mistress also. He was full of anecdote, extremely social, and always mixed goodnature with his reflections. At a later period, in prospect of a dinner-party, Horne Tooke remarked, that " he would venture to say that the best thing would be said by Mr. Paine." Indeed, his conversational powers were as distinguished as his tact for writing. An old lady, now a boardinghouse-keeper in Cedar street, remembers, when a girl, visiting Mr. Paine just after the war, when he took possession of his house and farm at New Rochelle, and gave a village-fete on the occasion; she then only knew him as "Common Sense," and supposed that was his name. On that day he had something to say to everybody, and young as she was she received a portion of his attention; while he sat in the shade and assisted in the labor of the feast, by cutting or breaking sugar to be used in some agreeable liquids by his guests. Mr. Paine was then, if not handsome, a fine, agreeable looking man.

Those disposed to censure Mr. Paine, find a subject in the affair of Deane: they say nothing can excuse his betrayal of the public secrets of office, even though it was for the benefit of the people, to resist an unjust claim on the public, and to expose a public robber. In this affair we must, however, remember, that when France wished the secret kept she was not at war with England; but that when Paine made the exposure France was at open war with England. Still, we are not disposed to defend the act; while we acquit him of every moral impropriety. We think, with Sterne, in the case of Corporal Trim, who had disobeyed orders in the performance of an act of humanity, when he makes Uncle Toby say, "You did very right as a man, but very wrong as a soldier." Mr. Paine was placed in a position where he had the choice of two evils: in his choice he sacrificed himself for the benefit of the country. A man, less generous, would have taken care of himself at all hazards.

PART III.

FROM MR. PAINE'S DEPARTURE FROM AMERICA IN 1787 TO HIS FINAL RETURN IN 1802, EMBRACING THE PERIOD OF THE FRENCH REVOLUTION AND DURATION OF THE FRENCH REPUBLIC.

"We are now," says Sherwin, "to follow Mr. Paine to a different scene from that in which he had been a prominent performer for nearly thirteen years. His desire of attacking the English government on the spot where its principles were still in full operation, had suffered no change or abatement, and as America no longer stood in need of his services, he resolved on putting his project into execution as soon as possible. In April, 1787, he set sail from the United States for France, and arrived in Paris after a short passage. His knowledge of mechanics and natural philosophy had before his departure procured him the honor of being admitted a member of the American Philosophical society; he was likewise appointed master of arts by the university of Philadelphia. These academic honors, though not of much consequence in themselves, were the means of introducing him to several of the most scientific men in France, and soon after his arrival he exhibited to the Academy of Sciences in Paris, the model of an iron bridge which had occupied much of his leisure time during his residence in America. This ingenious and useful production received the most unqualified approbation of the academy, and it is but justice to Mr. Paine to observe, that his recommendations on this subject have been sanctioned and adopted by some of the most enlightened characters of the present age. Among those who have given their opinion on the subject, we ought to notice Sir Joseph Banks, who, in a letter to a friend in America, published some years ago, says: 'I expect many similar improvements from your countrymen, who think with vigor, and are in a great measure free from those shackles of theory which are impressed on the minds of our people, even before they are capable of exerting their mental faculties to advantage.'

From Paris Mr. Paine proceeded to London, where he arrived on the third of September. Before the end of that month he went to Thetford to see his mother, who by this time was borne down by age and penury. His father, it appears, had died during his absence; and he hastened to the place of his birth to relieve the wants of his surviving parent. He led a recluse sort of life at Thetford for several weeks, being principally occupied in writing a pamphlet on the state of the nation, under the title of 'Prospects on the Rubicon.' This was published in London, toward the end of the year 1787. The purport of the work is an investigation of the causes and consequences of the politics expected to be agitated at the approaching meeting of parliament. A great variety of subjects are introduced, not only on government in general, but on what is usually termed political economy. The principal portion of it is occupied with a discussion on the then unsettled state of the affairs of Holland, and a comparison between the population, revenues, wealth, and general condition of France and England. The French revolution was at this period beginning to bud forth, a spirit of inquiry was diffusing itself over the land, while in England the people were sunk into a state of torpid lethargy. 'The people of France,' Mr. Paine observes, 'were beginning to think for themselves, and the people of England were resigning up the prerogative of thinking.'

During the year 1788, Mr. Paine was principally occupied in building his bridge. For this purpose he went to Rotherham in Yorkshire, in order that he might have an opportunity of superintending the castings of iron, which were executed under the direction of his ingenious friend, Mr. Walker, the proprietor of the foundry at that place. For a copious account of the success which attended this project, the reader is referred to the author's letter to Sir George Staunton. This gentleman, who it appears possessed talent enough to appreciate the value of the performance, sent the letter to the Society of Arts, &c., in the Adelphi: its contents were deservedly regarded by the members of the society as a subject worthy of their notice, and it was unanimously determined that the letter should be published in their 'Transactions;' but the moment the first part of 'Rights of Man' made its appearance, this determination was reversed, and the votaries and advocates of science became the voluntary tools of despotism. How thoroughly despicable must the minds of those men be, who could be gratified by such an act of pitiful meanness!

Mr. Paine had been at considerable expense in the erection of his bridge, which was principally defrayed by a Mr. Whiteside, an American merchant. Of our author's connexions with this gentleman I have not been able to obtain any particulars which may be relied upon; but the probability is, that Mr. Paine had consigned over to him some of his property in America, and on the strength of this consideration had drawn upon him for money whenever he had wanted it. Be this as it may, it is certain he had overdrawn his account to a considcrable extent, and Whiteside becoming a bankrupt soon afterward, the assignees arrested him for the balance. From this disagreeable situation he was in a short time released by the kindness of two American merchants, who agreed to become his bail, Mr. Paine paying down a considerable portion of the money, which by this time he had received from America, and giving his promissory note for the remainder.

The situation of France was by this period become a matter of great interest to all Europe, and as Mr. Paine was in confidential intercourse with the chief authors of the great scenes which were taking place, he hastened over to Paris, that he might have the pleasure of witnessing the downfall of Bourbon despotism."

Mr. Paine's disinterested exertions in the cause both of French and English liberty can best be understood by taking a clear view of the French revolution; and as Mr. Paine has himself given us the best concise history of that event, we shall offer no apology for its introduction here. Our extract is taken from the "Rights of Man," a work which we must presently introduce as the principal political publication of Mr. Paine. In this work he quotes an expression of Mr. Burke, that, "All circumstances taken together, the French revolution is the most astonishing that has hitherto happened in the world." Mr. Paine then remarks:—

"As wise men are astonished at foolish things, and other people at wise ones, I know not on which ground to account for Mr. Burke's astonishment; but certain it is that he does not understand the French revolution. It has apparently burst forth like a creation from a chaos, but it is no more than the consequence of mental revolution previously existing in France. The mind of the nation had changed beforehand, and a new order of things has naturally followed a new order of thoughts. I will here, as concisely as I can, trace out the growth of the French revolution, and mark the circumstances that have contributed to produce it.

The despotism of Louis XIV. united with the gayety of his court, and the gaudy ostentation of his character, had so humbled, and at the same time so fascinated the mind of France, that the people appear to have lost all sense of their own dignity, in contemplating that of their grand monarch: and the whole reign of Louis XV., remarkable only for weakness and effeminacy, made no other alteration than that of spreading a sort of lethargy over the nation, from which it showed no disposition to rise.

The only signs which appeared of the spirit of liberty during those periods, are to be found in the writings of the French philosophers. Montesquieu, president of the parliament of Bourdeaux, went as far as a writer under a despotic government could well proceed: and being obliged to divide himself between principle and prudence, his mind often appears under a veil, and we ought to give him credit for more than he has expressed.

Voltaire, who was both the flatterer and satirist of despotism, took another line. His forte lay in exposing and ridiculing the superstitions which priestcraft, united with statecraft, had interwoven with governments. It was not from the purity of his principles, or his love of mankind (for satire and philanthropy are not naturally concordant), but from his strong capacity of seeing folly in its true shape, and his irresistible propensity to expose it, that he made those attacks. They were, however, as formidable as if the motives had been virtuous; and he merits the thanks rather than the esteem of mankind.

On the contrary, we find in the writings of Rousseau and Abbe Raynal, a loveliness of sentiment in favor of liberty, that excites respect, and elevates the human faculties; yet having raised this animation, they do not direct its operations, but leave the mind in love with an object, without describing the means of possessing it.

The writings of Quisne, Turgot, and the friends of those authors, are of a serious kind; but they labored under the same disadvantage with Montesquieu; their writings abound with moral maxims of government, but are rather directed to economize and reform the administration of the government, than the government itself.

But all those writings and many others had their weight; and by the different manner in which they treated the subject of government—Montesquieu by his judgment and knowledge of laws, Voltaire by his wit, Rousseau and Raynal by their animation, and Quisne and Turgot by their moral maxims and systems of economy—readers of every class met with something to their taste, and a spirit of political inquiry began to diffuse itself through the nation at the time the dispute between England and the then colonies of America broke out.

In the war which France afterward engaged in, it is very well known that the nation appeared to be beforehand with the French ministry. Each of them had its views; but those views were directed to different objects; the one sought liberty and the other retaliation on England. The French officers and soldiers who after this went to America, were eventually placed in the school of freedom, and learned the practice as well as the principles of it by heart.

As it was impossible to separate the military events which

took place in America from the principles of the American revolution, the publication of those events in France necessarily connected themselves with the principles that produced them. Many of the facts were in themselves principles; such as the declaration of American independence, and the treaty of alliance between France and America, which recognised the natural rights of man, and justified resistance to oppression.

The then minister of France, Count Vergennes, was not the friend of America; and it is both justice and gratitude to say that it was the queen of France who gave the cause of America a fashion at the French court. Count Vergennes was the personal and social friend of Dr. Franklin; and the doctor had obtained, by his sensible gracefulness, a sort of influence over him, but with respect to principles, Count Vergennes was a despot.

The situation of Dr. Franklin as minister from America to France should be taken into the chain of circumstances. A diplomatic character is the narrowest sphere of society that man can act in. It forbids intercourse by a reciprocity of suspicion; and a diplomatist is a sort of unconnected atom, continually repelling and repelled. But this was not the case with Dr. Franklin; he was not the diplomatist of a court, but of *man*. His character as a philosopher had been long established, and his circle of society in France was universal.

Count Vergennes resisted for a considerable time the publication of the American constitutions in France, translated into the French language; but even in this he was obliged to give way to public opinion, and a sort of propriety in admitting to appear what he had undertaken to defend. The American constitutions were to liberty what a grammar is to language: they define its parts of speech, and practically construct them into syntax.

The peculiar situation of the then Marquis de la Fayette is another link in the great chain. He served in America as an American officer, under a commission of congress, and by the universality of his acquaintance, was in close friendship with the civil government of America as well as with the military line. He spoke the language of the country, entered into the discussions on the principles of government, and was always a welcome friend at any election.

When the war closed, a vast reinforcement to the cause of liberty spread itself over France, by the return of the French officers and soldiers. A knowledge of the practice was then joined to the theory; and all that was wanting to give it real existence, was opportunity. Man cannot, properly speaking, make circumstances for his purpose, but he always has it in his power to improve them when they occur: and this was the case in France.

M. Neckar was displaced in May, 1781; and by the ill management of the finances afterward, and particularly during the extravagant administration of M. Calonne, the revenue of France, which was nearly twenty-four millions sterling per year, was become unequal to the expenditures, not because the revenue had decreased, but because the expenses had increased, and this was the circumstance which the nation laid hold of to bring forward a revolution. The English minister, Mr. Pitt, has frequently alluded to the state of the French finances in his budgets, without understanding the subject. Had the French parliaments been as ready to register edicts for new taxes, as an English parliament is to grant them, there had been no derangement in the finances, nor yet any revolution; but this will better explain itself as I proceed.

It will be necessary here to show how taxes were formerly raised in France. The king, or rather the court or ministry, acting under the use of that name, framed the edicts for taxes at their own discretion, and sent them to the parliaments to be registered; for, until they were registered by the parliaments, they were not operative. Disputes had long existed between the court and the parliament with respect to the extent of the parliament's authority on this head. The court insisted that the authority of parliament went no farther than to remonstrate or show reasons against the tax, reserving to itself the right of determining whether the reasons were well or ill founded; and in consequence thereof, either to withdraw the edict as a matter of choice, or to order it to be registered as a matter of authority. The parliaments on their parts insisted, that they had not only a right to remonstrate, but to reject; and on this ground they were always supported by the nation.

But to return to the order of my narrative: M. Calonne wanted money; and as he knew the sturdy disposition of the parliaments with respect to new taxes, he ingeniously sought either to approach them by a more gentle means than that of direct authority, or to get over their heads by a manœvre; and for this purpose he revived the project of assembling a body of men from the several provinces, under the style of an 'assembly of the notables,' or men of note, who met in 1787, and were either to recommend taxes to the parliaments or to act as a parliament themselves. An assembly under this name had been called in 1687.

As we are to view this as the first practical step toward the revolution, it will be proper to enter into some particulars respecting it. The assembly of the notables has in some places been mistaken for the states-general, but was wholly a different body; the states-general being always by election. The persons who composed the assembly of the notables were all nominated by the king, and consisted of one hundred and forty members. But as M. Calonne could not depend upon a majority of this assembly in his favor, he very ingeniously arranged them in such a manner as to make forty-four a majority of one hundred and forty. To effect this, he disposed of them into seven separate committees of twenty members each. Every general question was to be decided, not by a majority of persons, but by a majority of committees; and, as eleven votes would make a majority in a committee, and four committees a majority of seven, M. Calonne had good reason to conclude, that as forty-four would determine any general question, he could not be outvoted. But all his plans deceived him, and in the event became his overthrow.

The then Marquis de la Fayette was placed in the second committee, of which Count d'Artois was president; and as money matters was the object, it naturally brought into view every circumstance connected with it. M. de la Fayette made a verbal charge against Calonne, for selling crown-land to the amount of two millions of livres, in a manner that appeared to be unknown to the king. The Count d'Artois (as if to intimidate, for the bastile was then in being) asked the marquis if he would render the charge in writing. He replied that he would. The Count d'Artois did not demand it, but brought a message from the king to that purport. M. de la Fayette then delivered in his charge in writing, to be given to the king, undertaking to support it. No farther proceedings were had, upon this affair but M. Calonne was soon after dismissed by the king, and went to England.

As M de la Fayette, from the experience he had had in America, was better acquainted with the science of civil government than the generality of the members who composed the assembly of the notables could then be, the brunt of the business fell considerably to his share. The plan of those who had a constitution in view was to contend with the court on the ground of taxes, and some of them openly professed their object. Disputes frequently arose between Count d'Artois and M. de la Fayette upon various subjects. With respect to the arrears already incurred, the latter proposed to remedy them, by accommodating the expenses to the revenue, instead of the revenue to the expenses; and as objects of reform, he proposed to abolish the bastile, and all the state-prisons throughout the nation (the keeping of which was attended with great expense) and to suppress *lettres de cachet;* but those matters were not then much attended to; and with respect to *lettres de cachet, a majority of the nobles appeared to be in favor of them.*

On the subject of supplying the treasury by new taxes, the assembly declined taking the matter on themselves, concurring in the opinion that they had not authority. In a debate on the subject, M. de la Fayette said, that raising money by taxes could only be done by a national assembly, freely elected by the people, and acting as their representatives. 'Do you mean,' said the Count d'Artois, 'the states-general?' M. de la Fayette replied that he did. 'Will you,' said the Count d'Artois, 'sign what you say, to be given to the king?' The other replied that he not only would do this, but that he he would go farther, and say, that the effectual mode would be, for the king to agree to the establishment of a constitution.

As one of the plans had thus failed, that of getting the assembly to act as a parliament, the other came into view, that of recommending. On this subject, the assembly agreed to recommend two new taxes to be enregistered by the parliament, the one a stamp-act, and the other a territorial tax, or sort of land tax. The two have been estimated at about five millions sterling per annum. We have now to turn our attention to the parliaments, on whom the business was again devolving.

The archbishop of Thoulouse (since archbishop of Sens, and now a cardinal) was appointed to the administration of the finances, soon after the dismission of Calonne. He was also made prime minister, an officer that did not always exist in France. When this office did not exist, the chief of each of the principal departments transacted business immediately with the king; but when a prime minister was appointed, they did business only with him. The archbishop arrived to more state authority than any minister since the Duke de Choiseuil, and the nation was strongly disposed in his favor; but by a line of conduct scarcely to be accounted for, he perverted every opportunity, turned out a despot, and sunk into disgrace, and a cardinal.

The assembly of the notables having broke up, the new minister sent the edicts for the two new taxes recommended by the assembly to the parliaments, to be enregistered. They of course came first before the parliament of Paris, who returned for answer, that, *with such a revenue as the nation then supported, the name of taxes ought not to be mentioned, but for the purpose of reducing them,* and threw both the edicts out.*

On this refusal, the parliament was ordered to Versailles, where, in the usual form, the king held, what under the old government was called a bed of justice: and the two edicts were enregistered in presence of the parliament, by an order of state. On this, the parliament immediately returned to Paris, renewed their session in form, and ordered the enregistering to be struck out, declaring that everything done at Versailles was illegal. All the members of parliament were then served with *lettres de cachet,* and exiled to Trois; but as they

---

* When the English minister, Mr. Pitt, mentions the French finances again in the English parliament, it would be well that he noticed this as an example.

continued as inflexible in exile as before, and as vengeance did not supply the place of taxes, they were after a short time recalled to Paris.

The edicts were again tendered to them, and the Count d'Artois undertook to act as representative for the king. For this purpose, he came from Versailles to Paris, in a train of procession; and the parliament was assembled to receive him. But show and parade had lost their influence in France; and whatever ideas of importance he might set off with, he had to return with those of mortification and disappointment. On alighting from his carriage to ascend the steps of the parliament-house, the crowd (which was numerously collected) threw out trite expressions, saying: 'This is Monsieur d'Artois, who wants more of our money to spend.' The marked disapprobation which he saw, impressed him with apprehensions; and the word *aux arms* (*to arms*) was given out by the officer of the guard who attended him. It was so loudly vociferated, that it echoed through the avenues of the house, and produced a temporary confusion: I was then standing in one of the apartments through which he had to pass, and could not avoid reflecting how wretched is the condition of a disrespected man.

He endeavored to impress the parliament by great words, and opened his authority by saying: 'The king our lord and master.' The parliament received him very coolly, and with their usual determination not to register the taxes; and in this manner the interview ended.

After this a new subject took place; in the various debates and contests that arose between the court and the parliaments on the subject of taxes, the parliament of Paris at last declared, that although it had been customary for parliaments to enregister edicts for taxes as a matter of convenience, the right belonged only to the states-general; and that, therefore, the parliaments could no longer with propriety continue to debate on what it had not authority to act. The king, after this, came to Paris, and held a meeting with the parliament, in which he continued from ten in the morning till about six in the evening; and, in a manner that appeared to proceed from him, as if unconsulted upon with the cabinet or ministry, gave his word to the parliament that the states-general should be convened.

But after this, another scene arose, on a ground different from all the former. The minister and the cabinet were averse to calling the states-general: they well knew, that if the states-general were assembled, that themselves must fall; and as the king had not mentioned *any time*, they hit on a project calculated to elude, without appearing to oppose.

For this purpose, the court set about making a sort of constitution itself: it was principally the work of M. Lamoignon, keeper of the seals, who afterward shot himself. The arrangement consisted in establishing a body under the name of a *cour pleniere*, or full court, in which were invested all the power that the government might have occasion to make use of. The persons composing this court to be nominated by the king; the contended right of taxation was given up on the part of the king, and a new criminal code of laws, and law proceedings, was substituted in the room of the former. The thing, in many points, contained better principles than those upon which the government had hitherto been administered; but, with respect to the *cour pleniere*, it was no other than a medium through which despotism was to pass, without appearing to act directly from itself.

The cabinet had high expectations from their new contrivance. The persons who were to compose the *cour pleniere* were already nominated; and as it was necessary to carry a fair appearance, many of the best characters in the nation were appointed among the number. It was to commence on the eighth of May, 1788: but an opposition arose to it, on two grounds—the one as to principle, the other as to form.

On the ground of principle it was contended, that government had not a right to alter itself; and that if the practice was once admitted, it would grow into a principle, and be made a precedent for any future alterations the government might wish to establish; that the right of altering the government was a national right, and not a right of government. And on the ground of form, it was contended that the *cour pleniere* was nothing more than a large cabinet.

The then Dukes de la Rochefoucault, Luxembourg, de Noailles, and many others, refused to accept the nomination, and strenuously opposed the whole plan. When the edict for establishing this new court was sent to the parliaments to be enregistered, and put into execution, they resisted also. The parliament of Paris not only refused, but denied the authority; and the contest renewed itself between the parliament and the cabinet more strongly than ever. While the parliament was sitting in debate on this subject, the ministry ordered a regiment of soldiers to surround the house, and form a blockade. The members sent out for beds and provision, and lived as in a besieged citadel; and as this had no effect, the commanding officer was ordered to enter the parliament-house and seize them, which he did, and some of the principal members were shut up in different prisons. About the same time a deputation of persons arrived from the province of Britanny, to remonstrate against the establishment of the *cour pleniere*, and those the archbishop sent to the bastile. But the spirit of the nation was not to be overcome; and it was so fully sensible of the strong ground it had taken, that of withholding taxes, that it contented itself with keeping up a sort of quiet resistance, which effectually overthrew all the plans at that time formed against it. The project of the *cour pleniere* was at last obliged to be given up, and the prime minister not long afterward followed its fate: and M. Neckar was recalled into office.

The attempt to establish the *cour pleniere* had an effect upon the nation which was not anticipated. It was a sort of new form of government, that insensibly served to put the old one out of sight, and to unhinge it from the superstitious authority of antiquity. It was government dethroning government; and the old one, by attempting to make a new one, made a chasm.

The failure of this scheme renewed the subject of convening the states-general; and this gave rise to a new series of politics. There was no settled form for convening the states-general: all that it positively meant was a deputation from what was then called the clergy, the nobility, and the commons; but their numbers, or their proportions, had not always been the same. They had been convened only on extraordinary occasions, the last of which was in 1614; their numbers were then in equal proportions, and they voted by orders.

It could not well escape the sagacity of M. Neckar, that the mode of 1614 would answer neither the purpose of the then government, nor of the nation. As matters were at that time circumstanced, it would have been too contentious to argue upon anything. The debates would have been endless upon privileges and exemptions, in which neither the wants of the government, nor the wishes of the nation for a constitution, would have been attended to. But as he did not choose to take the decision upon himself, he summoned again the *assembly of the notables*, and referred it to them. This body was in general interested in the decision, being chiefly of the aristocracy and the high-paid clergy; and they decided in favor of the mode of 1614. This decision was against the sense of the nation, and also against the wishes of the court; for the aristocracy opposed itself to both, and contended for privileges independent of either. The subject was then taken up by the parliament, who recommended that the number of the commons should be equal to the other two; and that they should all sit in one house and vote in one body. The number finally determined on was twelve hundred: six hundred were to be chosen by the commons (and this was less than their proportion ought to have been when their worth and consequence are considered on a national scale), three hundred by the clergy, and three hundred by the aristocracy; but with respect to the mode of assembling themselves, whether together or apart, or the manner in which they should vote, those matters were referred.*

---

* Mr. Burke (and I must take the liberty of telling him that he is unacquainted with French affairs), speaking upon this subject says, 'The first thing that

The election that followed was not a contested election, but an animated one. The candidates were not men but principles. Societies were formed in Paris, and committees of correspondence and communication established throughout the nation, for the purpose of enlightening the people, and explaining to them the principles of civil government; and so orderly was the election conducted, that it did not give rise even to the rumor of tumult.

The states-general were to meet at Versailles in April, 1789, but did not assemble till May. They situated themselves in three separate chambers, or rather the clergy and the aristocracy withdrew each into a separate chamber. The majority of the aristocracy claimed what they called the privilege of voting as a separate body, and of giving their consent or their negative in that manner; and many of the bishops and the high-beneficed clergy claimed the same privilege on the part of their order.

The *tiers etat* (as they were called) disowned any knowledge of artificial orders and artificial privileges; and they were not only resolute on this point, but somewhat disdainful. They began to consider aristocracy as a kind of fungus growing out of the corruption of society, that could not be admitted even as a branch of it; and from the disposition the aristocracy had shown, by upholding *lettres de cachet*, and in sundry other instances, it was manifest that no constitution could be formed by admitting men in any other character than as national men.

After various altercations on this head, the *tiers etat*, or commons (as they were then called), declared themselves (on a motion made for that purpose by the Abbe Sieyes) 'THE REPRESENTATIVES OF THE NATION; *and that the two orders could be considered but as deputies of corporations, and could only have a deliberative voice but when they assembled in a national*

struck me in calling the states-general was a great departure from the ancient course;' and he soon after says, 'From the moment I read the list, I saw distinctly, and very nearly as it has happened, all that was to follow.' Mr. Burke certainly did not see all that was to follow. I have endeavored to impress him, as well before as after the states-general met, that there would be a *revolution*; but was not able to make him see it, neither would he believe it. How, then, he could distinctly see all the parts, when the whole was out of sight, is beyond my comprehension. And with respect to the 'departure from the ancient course,' beside the natural weakness of the remark, it shows that he is unacquainted with circumstances. The departure was necessary, from the experience had upon it, that the ancient course was a bad one. The states-general of 1614 were called at the commencement of the civil war in the minority of Louis XIII.; but by the clash of arranging them by orders, they increased the confusion they were called to compose. The author of *l'Intrigue du Cabinet* (Intrigue of the Cabinet), who wrote before any revolution was thought of in France, speaking of the states-general of 1614 says: 'They held the public in suspense five months; and by the questions agitated therein, and the heat with which they were put, it appears that the great (*les grandes*) thought more to satisfy their particular passions than to procure the good of the nation; and the whole time passed away in altercations, ceremonies, and parade.'—'*l'Intrigue du Cabinet*,' vol. i., p. 329.

character with the national representatives.' This proceeding extinguished the style of *etats generaux*, or states-general, and erected it into the style it now bears, that of *l'assemble nationale*, or national assembly.

This motion was not made in a precipitate manner: it was the result of cool deliberation, and concerted between the national representatives and the patriotic members of the two chambers, who saw into the folly, mischief, and injustice of artificial privileged distinctions. It was become evident that no constitution, worthy of being called by that name, could be established on anything less than a national ground. The aristocracy had hitherto opposed the despotism of the court, and affected the language of patriotism; but it opposed it as its rival (as the English barons opposed King John); and it now opposed the nation from the same motives.

On carrying this motion the national representatives, as had been concerted, sent an invitation to the two chambers, to unite with them in a national character, and proceed to business. A majority of the clergy, chiefly of the parish-priests, withdrew from the clerical chamber and joined the nation; and forty-five from the other chamber joined in like manner. There is a sort of secret history belonging to this last circumstance, which is necessary to its explanation: it was not judged prudent that all the patriotic members of the chamber, styling itself the nobles, should quit it at once; and in consequence of this arrangement, they drew off by degrees, always leaving some, as well to reason the case, as to watch the suspected. In a little time the numbers increased from forty-five to eighty, and soon after to a greater number; which, with a majority of the clergy, and the whole of the national representatives, put the malcontents in a very diminutive condition.

The king, who, very different to the general class called by that name, is a man of a good heart, showed himself disposed to recommend a union of the three chambers, on the ground the national assembly had taken; but the malcontents exerted themselves to prevent it, and began now to have another project in view. Their numbers consisted of a majority of the aristocratical chamber, and a minority of the clerical chamber, chiefly of bishops and high-beneficed clergy; and these men were determined to put everything to issue, as well by strength as by stratagem. They had no objection to a constitution; but it must be such a one as themselves should dictate, and suited to their own views and particular situations. On the other hand, the nation disowned knowing anything of them but as citizens, and was determined to shut out all such upstart pretensions. The more aristocracy appeared, the more it was despised; there was a visible imbecility and want of intellect in the majority, a sort of *je ne sais quoi*, that while it affected to be more than citizen was less than man. It lost ground more from contempt than from hatred; and was rather jeered at as an ass than dreaded as a lion. This is the general character of aristocracy, or what are called nobles or nobility, or rather no-ability, in all countries.

The plan of the malcontents consisted now of two things; either to deliberate and vote by chambers (or orders), more especially on all questions respecting a constitution (by which the aristocratical chamber would have had a negative on any article of the constitution), or, in case they could not accomplish this object, to overthrow the national assembly entirely.

To effect one or the other of these objects, they began now to cultivate a friendship with the despotism they had hitherto attempted to rival, and the Count d'Artois became their chief. The king (who has since declared himself deceived into their measures) held, according to the old form, *a bed of justice*, in which he accorded to the deliberation and vote *par tete* (by head) upon several objects; but reserved the deliberation and vote, upon all questions respecting a constitution, to the three chambers separately. This declaration of the king was made against the advice of M. Neckar, who now began to perceive that he was growing out of fashion at court, and that another minister was in contemplation.

As the form of sitting in separate chambers was yet apparently kept up, though essentially destroyed, the national representatives, immediately after this declaration of the king, resorted to their own chambers to consult on a protest against it; and the minority of the chamber (calling itself the nobles) who had joined the national cause, retired to a private house to consult in like manner. The malcontents had by this time concerted their measures with the court, which count d'Artois undertook to conduct: and as they saw, from the discontent which the declaration excited, and the opposition making against it, that they could not obtain a control over the intended constitution by a separate vote, they prepared themselves for their final object; that of conspiring against the national assembly and overthrowing it.

The next morning the door of the chamber of the national assembly was shut against them, and guarded by troops, and the members were refused admittance. On this they withdrew to a tennis-ground, in the neighborhood of Versailles, as the most convenient place they could find; and, after renewing their session, took an oath never to separate from each other under any circumstances whatever, death excepted, until they had established a constitution. As the experiment of shutting up the house had no other effect than that of producing a closer connexion in the members, it was opened again the next day, and the public business recommenced in the usual place.

We are now to have in view the forming of 'the new ministry, which was to accomplish the overthrow of the national assembly. But as force would be necessary, orders were issued to assemble thirty thousand troops, the command of which was given to Broglio, one of the new-intended ministry, who was recalled from the country for this purpose. But as some management was necessary to keep this plan concealed till the moment it should be ready for execution, it is to this policy that a declaration made by Count d'Artois must be attributed, and which is here proper to be introduced.

It could not but occur that while the malcontents continued to resort to their chambers separate from the national assembly, that more jealousy would be excited than if they were mixed with it, and that the plot might be suspected: but as they had taken their ground, and now wanted a pretence for quitting it, it was necessary that one should be devised. This was effectually accomplished by a declaration made by Count d'Artois, that '*if they took not a part in the national assembly, the life of the king would be endangered ;*' on which they quitted their chambers and mixed with the assembly in one body.

At the time this declaration was made, it was generally treated as a piece of absurdity in Count d'Artois, and calculated merely to relieve the outstanding members of the two chambers from the diminutive situation they were put in; and if nothing more had followed this conclusion would have been good. But as things best explain themselves by their events, this apparent union was only a cover to the machinations that were secretly going on; and the declaration accommodated itself to answer that purpose. In a little time the national assembly found itself surrounded by troops, and thousands daily arriving. On this a very strong declaration was made by the national assembly to the king, remonstrating on the impropriety of the measure, and demanding the reason. The king, who was not in the secret of this business, as himself afterward declared, gave substantially for answer, that he had no other object in view than to preserve public tranquillity, which appeared to be much disturbed.

But in a few days from this time the plot unravelled itself. M. Neckar and the ministry were displaced, and a new one formed of the enemies of the revolution ; and Broglio, with between twenty-five and thirty thousand foreign troops, was arrived to support them. The mask was now thrown off, and matters were come to a crisis. The event was, that in the space of three days the new ministry and their abettors found it prudent to fly the nation ; the bastile was taken, and Broglio and his foreign troops dispersed, as is already related in a former part of this work."

We shall now introduce Mr. Paine's description of the taking of the bastile, and then proceed with his life, or his connexion with these events and their consequences.

"The mind can hardly picture to itself a more tremendous scene than which the city of Paris exhibited at the time of taking the bastile, and for two days before and after, nor conceive the possibility of its quieting so soon. At a distance, this transaction has appeared only as an act of heroism standing on itself: and the close political connexion it had with the revolution is lost in the brilliancy of the achievement. But we are to consider it as the strength of the parties, brought man to man, and contending for the issue. The bastile was to be either the prize or the prison of the assailants. The downfall of it included the idea of the downfall of despotism; and this compounded image was become as figuratively united, as Bunyan's Doubting Castle and giant Despair.

The national assembly before and at the time of taking the bastile, was sitting at Versailles, twelve miles distant from Paris. About a week before the rising of the Parisians and their taking the bastile, it was discovered that a plot was forming, at the head of which was the Count d'Artois, the king's youngest brother, for demolishing the national assembly, seizing its members, and thereby crushing, by a *coup de main*, all hopes and prospects of forming a free government. For the sake of humanity, as well as of freedom, it is well this plan did not succeed. Examples are not wanting to show how dreadfully vindictive and cruel are all old governments, when they are successful against what they call a revolt.

This plan must have been some time in contemplation; because, in order to carry it into execution, it was necessary to collect a large military force round Paris, and to cut off the communication between that city and the national assembly at Versailles. The troops destined for this service were chiefly the foreign troops in the pay of France, and who, for this particular purpose, were drawn from the distant provinces where they were then stationed. When they were collected, to the amount of between twenty-five and thirty thousand, it was judged time to put the plan into execution. The ministry who were then in office, and who were friendly to the revolution, were instantly dismissed, and a new ministry formed of those who had concerted the project:—among whom was Count de Broglio, and to his share was given the command of those troops. The character of this man, as described to me in a letter which I communicated to Mr. Burke before he began to write his book, and from an authority which Mr. Burke well knows was good, was that of 'a high-flying aristocrat, cool, and capable of every mischief.'

While these matters were agitating, the national assembly stood in the most perilous and critical situation that a body of men can be supposed to act in. They were the devoted victims, and they knew it. They had the hearts and wishes of their country on their side, but military authority they had none. The guards of Broglio surrounded the hall where the assembly sat, ready, at the word of command, to seize their persons, as had been done the year before to the parliament in Paris. Had the national assembly deserted their trust, or had they exhibited signs of weakness or fear, their enemies had been encouraged, and the country depressed. When the situation they stood in, the cause they were engaged in, and the crisis then ready to burst which should determine their personal and political fate, and that of their country, and probably of Europe, are taken into one view, none but a heart callous with prejudice, or corrupted by dependance, can avoid interesting itself in their success.

The archbishop of Vienne was at this time president of the national assembly; a person too old to undergo the scene that a few days, or a few hours, might bring forth. A man of more activity, and bolder fortitude, was necessary; and the national assembly chose (under the form of vice-president, for the presidency still rested in the archbishop) M. de la Fayette; and this is the only instance of a vice-president being chosen. It was at the moment this storm was pending, July 11, that a declaration of rights was brought forward by M. de la Fayette, and is the same which is before alluded to. It was hastily drawn up, and makes only a part of a more extensive declaration of rights, agreed upon and adopted afterward by the national assembly. The particular reason for bringing it forward at this moment (M. de la Fayette has since informed me) was, that if the national assembly should fall in the threatened destruction that then surrounded it, some trace of its principles might have a chance of surviving the wreck.

Everything was now drawing to a crisis. The event was freedom or slavery. On one side an army of nearly thirty thousand men; on the other an unarmed body of citizens, for the citizens of Paris on whom the national assembly must then immediately depend, were as unarmed and undisciplined as the citizens of London are now. The French guards had given strong symptoms of their being attached to the national cause; but their numbers were small, not a tenth part of the force which Broglio commanded, and their officers were in the interest of Broglio.

Matters being now ripe for execution, the new ministry made their appearance in office. The reader will carry in his mind, that the bastile was taken the 14th of July: the point of time I am now speaking to, is the 12th. As soon as the news of the change of the ministry reached Paris in the afternoon, all the play-houses and places of entertainment, shops and houses, were shut up. The change of ministry was considered as the prelude of hostilities, and the opinion was rightly founded.

The foreign troops began to advance toward the city. The Prince de Lambesc, who commanded a body of German cavalry, approached by the palace of Louis XV. which connects itself with some of the streets. In his march he insulted and struck an old man with his sword. The French are remarkable for their respect to old age, and the insolence with which it appeared to be done, uniting with the general fermentation they were in, produced a powerful effect, and a cry of '*To arms! to arms!*' spread itself in a moment over the whole city.

Arms they had none, nor scarcely any who knew the use of them; but desperate resolution, when every hope is at stake, supplies, for a while, the want of arms. Near where the Prince de Lambesc was drawn up, were large piles of stones collected for building the new bridge, and with these the people attacked the cavalry. A party of the French guards, upon hearing the firing, rushed from their quarters and joined the people; and night coming on, the cavalry retreated.

The streets of Paris, being narrow, are favorable for defence; and the loftiness of the houses, consisting of many stories, from which great annoyance might be given, secured them against nocturnal enterprises; and the night was spent in providing themselves with every sort of weapon they could make or procure: guns, swords, blacksmith's hammers, carpenters' axes, iron crows, pikes, halberds, pitchforks, spits, clubs, &c.

The incredible numbers with which they assembled the next morning, and the still more incredible resolution they exhibited, embarrassed and astonished their enemies. Little did the new ministry expect such a salute. Accustomed to slavery themselves, they had no idea that liberty was capable of such inspiration, or that a body of unarmed citizens would dare to face the military force of thirty thousand men. Every moment of this day was employed in collecting arms, concerting plans, and arranging themselves in the best order which such an instantaneous movement could afford. Broglio continued lying round the city, but made no farther advances this day, and the succeeding night passed with as much tranquillity as such a scene could possibly produce.

But the defence only was not the object of the citizens. They had a cause at stake, on which depended their freedom or their slavery. They every moment expected an attack, or to hear of one made on the national assembly; and in such a situation, the most prompt measures are sometimes the best. The object that now presented itself, was the bastile; and the *eclat* of carrying such a fortress in the face of such an army, could not fail to strike terror into the new ministry, who had scarcely yet had time to meet. By some intercepted correspondence this morning, it was discovered that the mayor of Paris, M. de Flessels, who appeared to be in their interest, was betraying them; and from this discovery there remained no doubt that Broglio would reinforce the bastile the ensuing evening. It was therefore necessary to attack it that day; but before this could be done, it was first necessary to procure a better supply of arms than they were then possessed of.

There was, adjoining to the city, a large magazine of arms deposited at the hospital of the invalids, which the citizens summoned to surrender; and as the place was not defensible, nor attempted much defence, they soon succeeded. Thus supplied, they marched to attack the bastile; a vast mixed multitude of all ages and of all degrees, and armed with all sorts of weapons. Imagination would fail of describing to itself the appearance of such a procession, and of the anxiety for the events which a few hours or a few minutes might produce. What plans the ministry was forming, were as unknown to the people within the city, as what the citizens were doing was unknown to them; and what movements Broglio might make for the support or relief of the place, were to the citizens equally unknown. All was mystery and hazard.

That the bastile was attacked with an enthusiasm of heroism, such only as the highest animation of liberty could inspire, and carried in the space of a few hours, is an event which the world is fully possessed of. I am not undertaking a detail of the attack, but bringing into view the conspiracy against the nation which provoked it, and which fell with the bastile. The prison to which the new ministry were dooming the national assembly, in addition to its being the high altar and castle of despotism, became the proper object to begin with. This enterprise broke up the new ministry, who began now to fly from the ruin they had prepared for others. The troops of Broglio dispersed, and himself fled also."

The taking of the bastile by a mob has astonished most persons acquainted with that fortress, and especially military men, who know the obstacle to such an undertaking, nor was it generally understood how the moat was passed, or the drawbridge let down. We learn, however, from Robert Dale Owen, who had the information from La Fayette, that the chain of the draw-bridge was struck by a well-aimed cannon-ball, or perhaps by a chain-shot, and the chain or chains being thus broken, the bridge fell, the mob rushed over, and effected the rest by gallantry. Sherwin thus speaks on this subject:—

"The destruction of the bastile, and the universal diffusion of republican principles throughout the French empire, had rendered that country a singular object of terror to the English government. The mass of the nation saw with pleasure the dawn of French liberty, while the majority of their rulers beheld it as a treasonable invasion of the divine rights of monarchy. They dreaded the spirit of inquiry which it was calculated to diffuse, and they feared that the government of England, matchless and enviable as it was represented, would gain no credit by passing through the ordeal of national discussion. The first important attack that was made upon the principles of the French revolution was by Mr. Burke at the opening of parliament, 1790. This was followed by an advertisement in several of the newspapers, stating that he intended shortly to publish his opinions on the subject in the form of a pamphlet. The friends of liberty in this country were astonished at the sudden change in the politics of Mr. Burke, as he had, for several years previous, and particularly during the American war, been considered as a most eloquent and sincere advocate of public freedom. But it was shortly discovered that he had received a pension of three thousand pounds a year, and this sufficiently explained the grounds of his apostacy. At the period of his parliamentry attack on the French revolution, he corresponded with Mr. Paine, and so totally unexpected was his conduct, that the latter had written to him from Paris but a few weeks before, to inform him how prosperously matters were going on. When the advertisement was published announcing Mr. Burke's 'Reflections,' Mr. Paine promised the friends of the French revolution that he would answer the work whenever it appeared. He left France in November, 1790, having been an attentive observer, if not an active adviser, of the important proceedings which had taken place during the preceding twelve months. Mr. Burke's book appeared soon after his arrival. The popularity of the author as a literary character, the exertions of the government and its agents in all parts of the country, the flowery and impassioned language in which the historical and declamatory parts of the book were clothed, and the repeated delays which had retarded its appearance, and, consequently, increased the anxiety of the public, all conspired to give the work an interest, which its profligacy of principle and perversity of sentiment were insufficient to overcome. The mass of his readers were captivated by his eloquence, and but a few took the trouble to reflect on the distorted facts, the real falsehoods, and the egregious absurdities, with which the book abounded.

Mr. Paine lost no time in preparing his answer to the work. In less than three months he produced the first part of 'Rights of Man,' in which he had combated and confuted the greater portion of Mr. Burke's doctrines. The work was printed in February, 1791, for Mr. Johnson, of St. Paul's Church Yard, but on looking it over he discovered some passages which he conceived were liable to be prosecuted, and he declined the publication. This refusal, which was altogether unexpected, occasioned a month's delay. After some difficulty, a publisher was at length found in Mr. Jordan, at No. 166, Fleet street, and the work was brought out on the 13th of March, 1791.

This publication had a two-fold object in view;—firstly, that of rousing the attention of the people of England to the defects and abuses of their own system of government; and secondly, that of refuting the falsehoods and exaggerations in Mr. Burke's 'Reflections.' Among other doctrines equally devoid of principle, Mr. Burke had published a commentary on the proceedings of the parliament of 1688, in which he had argued that the people of England were bound by the declaration of the said parliament, who had consented 'to submit themselves, their heirs and posterities for ever,' to the heirs and posterity of William and Mary. Mr. Paine argues, that whatever right the parliament might have to submit *themselves*, they had not, and could not, have any right to enter into any agreement or contract respecting the government of *posterity*, for, says he, 'every age and generation must be as free to act for itself *in all cases*, as the age and generation which preceded it." A more self-evident position than this could not have been advanced, and the reflections naturally arising from it were quite sufficient to overturn the absurd conclusions which Mr. Burke had drawn from his omnipotent parliament of 1688.

Our author then proceeds to refute his misrepresentations relative to the French revolution, and the causes of it. He enters into an elaborate detail of the events immediately preceding the overthrow of the ancient despotism, and of the consequences which it was calculated to produce. In speaking of the destruction of the bastile, and of Mr. Burke's silence on the subject, he thus beautifully expresses himself: "Not one glance of compassion, not one commiserating reflection, that I can find throughout his book, has he bestowed on those who lingered out the most wretched of lives—a life without hope in the most miserable of prisons. It is painful to behold a man employing his talents to corrupt himself. Nature has been kinder to Mr. Burke than he is to her. He is not affected by the reality of distress touching his heart, but by the showy resemblance of it striking his imagination. He pities the plumage, but forgets the dying bird. Accustomed to kiss the aristocratic hand that hath purloined him from himself, he degenerates into a composition of art, and the genuine soul of nature forsakes him. His hero or his heroine must be a tragedy victim expiring in show, and not the real prisoner of misery sliding into death in the silence of a dungeon.' Mr. Paine reasons very deeply on the subject of rights, and the origin of government, in opposition to the dogmatical assertions and high-sounding declamation of his antagonist, and concludes his argument with a comparison between the constitutions of England and France, as the latter then stood under the authority of the national assembly. He ridicules the vanity of titles, and the policy of hereditary governors, and vindicates the conduct of the national assembly in abolishing the one, and neutralizing the authority of the other.

It has been urged against the work before us, that the author had neglected to arrange his matter methodically. But it should be recollected, that he was compelled to follow the track of his opponent, which, as Mr. Paine very truly observes, was a complete 'wilderness of rhapsodies.' It was therefore impossible to preserve that order which in any other work would be considered essentially requisite. It may, however, be safely asserted, that the author's meaning is always clear, that his facts are always correctly stated, and that his arguments are incontrovertible. With respect to the merits of the work as a composition, its immense circulation and immediate effect in exciting an inquiry into the abuses of the English government, will answer for this part of the subject. Perhaps there never was a period in which the people of that country were less disposed to attend to the discussion of politics than at the time Mr. Paine's pamphlet made its appearance: they had been so often amused, and so often deceived, by men who pretended to advocate their rights, that they were disgusted with the subject, and the apostacy of Mr. Burke was a confirmation of their sentiments. But the principles contained in the 'Rights of Man,' opened an entirely new field of argument and inquiry, and the thinking part of the people began to view the right of political reform, not as a boon to be expected or desired from the government, but as a power which the nation alone had the authority to exercise.

About the middle of May Mr. Paine again went to France. Soon after his arrival the king fled from Paris. On this occasion he observed to his friend Mr. Christie: 'You see the absurdity of monarchical governments. Here will be a whole nation disturbed by the folly of one man.' When the king returned to Paris, Mr. Paine was, from an accidental circumstance, in considerable danger of losing his life. An immense concourse of persons of all classes had assembled to witness the event. Among the crowd was Mr. Paine. An officer proclaimed the order of the national assembly, that all should be silent and covered. In an instant all hats were on. Mr. Paine, however, had lost his cockade, the emblem of liberty and equality. The multitude observing that he remained uncovered, supposed that he was one of their enemies, and a cry instantly arose, '*Aristocrat! Aristocrat! a la lanterne! a la lanterne!*' He was desired by those who stood near him to put on his hat, and it was sometime before the people could be satisfied by explanation.

The Abbe Syeyes, who had been one of the principal authors of the new constitution, being alarmed at the partial excesses which had been committed by the populace, and falsely attributing them to the propagation of republican principles, avowed his intention of defending the monarchical against the democratical system of government. Mr. Paine readily accepted the challenge, and offered, in the short space of fifty pages, to controvert all the arguments which the abbe could bring forward in defence of his proposition. The latter prudently declined the contest, and thus the matter ended.

On the thirteenth July, 1791, he returned to London, but it was not thought prudent that he should attend the public celebration of the French revolution, which was to take place on the following day. He was, however, present at the meeting which was held at the Thatched-House tavern, on the twentieth of August following. Of the address and declaration which issued from this meeting, and which was at first attributed to Mr. Horne Tooke, Mr. Paine was the author. A second meeting was intended to have been held at the same place, for a similar purpose, but the proprietor of the tavern was so much alarmed at the clamors of the government party, that he was under the necessity of informing Mr. Horne Tooke and his friends that he could not receive them.

Mr. Paine was now very much engaged in preparing the second part of the 'Rights of Man' for the press. In the meantime the ministry had received information that the work would shortly appear, and they resolved on getting it suppressed if possible. Having ascertained the name of the printer, they employed* him to endeavor to purchase the copyright of the second, together with the future copyright of the first part of the 'Rights of Man.' He began first by offering a hundred guineas, then five hundred, and at length a thousand; but Mr. Paine told him, that he 'would never put it in the power of any printer or publisher to suppress or alter a work of his, by making him master of the copy, or give him the

---

* I am aware that the circumstance of Mr. Chapman's being employed by government, has been denied by the partisans of the administration. But from the evidence which he gave on the trial, there is every reason to conclude that he was commissioned by the ministry or their immediate agents. He there states, that he refused to go on with the printing of the work from the fear of its being prosecuted. Is it probable that any man would be so extremely foolish as to offer a thousand guineas for the copyright of a book which he dare not sell, unless he had some prospect in doing it distinct from the profit that was to be derived from the publication? The case is too clear to require farther commentary.

right of selling it to any minister, or to any other person, or to treat as a mere matter of traffic that which he intended should operate as a principle."

Finding that Mr. Paine was not to be bribed by pecuniary offers, the ministry next attempted to impede, since they could not suppress, the publication of the work, and in this they partially succeeded. Among other things, it contained several propositions relative to a reduction of the public taxes. It was intended to have appeared on the day of the meeting of parliament, but when the printer found it was not to be purchased, he suddenly stopped in the middle of the work, and informed Mr. Paine that he would not proceed with the remainder on any consideration. Another printer, therefore, became necessary, and this occasioned a delay of a fortnight. From the circumstances, elsewhere stated, there is every reason to conclude that the proof-sheets were regularly sent to the cabinet, and that the small addition to the pay of the soldiers, as well as several proposals for reducing the taxes brought forward by Mr. Pitt at the opening of parliament, were done for no other object than that of making it appear that Mr. Paine's plan was merely an improvement on that of the minister. But even in this paltry purpose the parties in power were defeated, by the exposure of the circumstances in the appendix to the work.

The 'Rights of Man, part the second, combining principle and practice, was published by Mr. Jordan, of Fleet street, on the sixteenth of February, 1792. Exclusive of a dedication to M. de la Fayette, a preface and an introduction, it is divided into five chapters: chapter 1, on Society and Civilization; 2, on the Origin of the present old Governments; 3, on the old and new Systems of Government; 4, on Constitutions; 5, Ways and Means of reforming the Political Condition of Europe, interspersed with Miscellaneous Observations.

The second part is, strictly speaking, a continuation of the first. The general design of the work appears to have been an investigation of the abuses of the English government; an examination of the hereditary and representative systems; to which are added, a variety of propositions for meliorating the condition of the nation. In going over this work, it is difficult to decide whether the ability or benevolence of the writer is the most deserving of our admiration. The most abstruse and difficult subjects in the science of politics are rendered intelligible and interesting, and the abuses which had been accumulating for ages, and which antiquity seemed to have rendered sacred and venerable, are examined with a degree of boldness, which is wholly without precedent or parallel. The generality of those who had previously written on the subject of government, appear to have drawn their principles from existing systems, and all that they had attempted to effect, was the correction of a few exterior abuses, without daring to invade the assumed rights of the establishment itself. But our author's attack was quite of a different nature: he not only deprecated the practice, but he condemned the principle; he not only declared his contempt for the monarch, but his detestation of the monarchy. He had studied the science of politics in the school of human nature, and he spoke as he felt, without reverencing, or even referring to the subtleties of the sophists who had gone before him.

One of the great objects of the work was to do away with the delusive notion, that the members of the system ought to be expected to reform themselves. 'There does not,' says he, 'exist within such governments, sufficient stamina whereon to ingraft reformation.' 'The right of reform is in the nation, in its original character, and the constitutional method would be by a general convention elected for the purpose.' He likewise reasons with much energy in the first as well as the second part of the work against the prevalent opinions, with respect to the mixed system of government. 'A nation is not a body, the figure of which is to be represented by the human body, but is like a body contained within a circle, having a common centre, in which every radius meets, and that centre is formed by representation. To connect representation with what is called monarchy, is eccentric government. Representation is of itself the delegated monarchy of a nation, and cannot debase itself by dividing it with another.' Indeed, it requires very little reflection to discover the impossibility of uniting democracy with monarchy or aristocracy, for any beneficial purpose. The union may exist in appearance, but it never can take place in fact. The dignified pride of republicanism disowns the base connexion.

It is impossible to form an exact estimate of the number of copies which were circulated of the first and second parts of the 'Rights of Man,' but at a very moderate calculation there was at least a hundred thousand of each. When Mr. Paine saw the great interest which it excited, he thought the best mode of promulgating its principles, would be to give up the copyright in favor of the public, which he did about two months after the appearance of the second part. The probability of a revolution now became a subject of general discussion. The nation was divided into two numerous and powerful classes, the one consisting of the ignorant and the majority of the wealthy, arranged under the banners of civil and religious tyranny, and declaring their attachment to all that was superstitious in the church, and all that was despotic in the state—while the other, more numerous and less dependant, more enlightened though less opulent, being convinced that the government in its existing state, was the cause of the greater part of the misery with which the country was afflicted, were determined to let slip no opportunity of shaking off the load of oppression. That the different branches of government were in a state of the completest trepidation, is a fact that admits of no question, and that many of the most intelligent men of all parties expected a revolution, is equally indisputable. It is recorded of a certain ancient philosopher, who lived under a capricious tyrant, that he used every morning, when he awoke, to feel whether his head was on his shoulders; and the state of the English people at length became so unsettled, and the stability of the government so problematical, that the king and his ministry might almost consider themselves in as precarious a situation.

On the first appearance of the 'Rights of Man,' the ministry saw that it inculcated truths which they could not controvert, that it contained plans which, if adopted, would benefit at least nine tenths of the community, and that its principles were the reverse of the existing system of government ; they therefore judged that the most politic method would be to treat the work with contempt, to represent it as a foolish and insignificant performance, unworthy of their notice, and undeserving of the attention of the public. But they soon found the inefficacy of this mode of treatment ; the more contempt they showed, the more the book was read and approved of. Finding, therefore, that their declarations of contempt were as unsuccessful as their project of buying up the work, they determined upon prosecuting the author and publisher. Mr. Paine was not at all surprised at this resolution of the ministry ; indeed, he had anticipated it on the publication of the second part of the work, and to remove any doubt as to his intention of defending the principles which he had so effectually inculcated, he addressed the following letter to his publisher :—

'FEBRUARY 16, 1792.

SIR : Should any person, under the sanction of any kind of authority, inquire of you respecting the author and publisher of the "Rights of Man," you will please to mention me as the author and publisher of that work, and show to such person this letter. I will as soon as I am made acquainted with it, appear and answer for the work personally.

Your humble servant,
THOMAS PAINE.

MR. JORDAN,
No. 166 Fleet Street.'

The first intimation which Mr. Paine received of the intentions of the ministry, was on the 14th of May, 1792. He was then at Bromley in Kent, upon which he came immediately to town ; on his arrival, he found that Mr. Jordan had that evening been served with a summons to appear at the court of King's Bench on the Monday following, but for what purpose was not stated. Conceiving it to be on account of the work, he appointed a meeting with Mr. Jordan, on the next morning, when he provided a solicitor, and took the expense of the defence on himself. But Mr. Jordan, it appears, had too much regard for his person to hazard its safety on the event of a prosecution, and he compromised the affair with the solicitor of the treasury, by agreeing to appear in court and plead guilty. This arrangement answered the purpose of both parties—that of Jordan in liberating him from the risk of a prosecution, and that of the ministry, since his plea of guilty amounted in some measure to a condemnation of the work.

The following letter from Mr. Paine to Sir Archibald Macdonald, the then attorney-general, will serve to confirm this statement:—

'Sir: Though I have some reason for believing that you were not the original promoter or encourager of the prosecution commenced against the work entitled 'Rights of Man,' either as that prosecution is intended to affect the author, the publisher, or the public; yet as you appear the official person therein, I address this letter to you, not as Sir Archibald Macdonald, but as attorney-general.

You began by a prosecution against the publisher, Jordan, and the reason assigned by Mr. Secretary Dundas, in the house of commons, in the debate on the proclamation, May 25, for taking that measure, was, he said, because Mr. Paine could not be found, or words to that effect. Mr. Paine, sir, so far from secreting himself, never went a step out of his way, nor in the least instance varied from his usual conduct, to avoid any measure you might choose to adopt with respect to him. It is on the purity of his heart, and the universal utility of the principles and plans which his writings contain, that he rests the issue; and he will not dishonor it by any kind of subterfuge. The apartments which he occupied at the time of writing the work last winter, he has continued to occupy to the present hour, and the solicitors of the prosecution knew where to find him; of which there is a proof in their own office as far back as the 21st of May, and also in the office of my own attorney.

But admitting, for the sake of the case, that the reason for proceeding against the publisher was, as Mr. Dundas stated, that Mr. Paine could not be found, that reason can now exist no longer.

The instant that I was informed that an information was preparing to be filed against me, as the author of, I believe, one of the most useful books ever offered to mankind, I directed my attorney to put in an appearance; and as I shall meet the prosecution fully and fairly, and with a good and upright conscience, I have a right to expect that no act of littleness, will be made use of on the part of the prosecution toward influencing the future issue with respect to the author. This expression may, perhaps, appear obscure to you, but I am in the possession of some matters which serve to show that the action against the publisher is not intended to be a *real* action. If, therefore, any persons concerned in the prosecution have found their cause so weak as to make it appear convenient to them to enter into a negotiation with the publisher, whether for the purpose of his submitting to a verdict, and to make use of the verdict so obtained as a circumstance, by way of precedent, on a future trial against myself; or for any other purpose not fully made known to me; if, I say, I have cause to suspect this to be the case, I shall most certainly withdraw the defence I should otherwise have made, or promoted, on his (the publisher's) behalf, and leave the negotiators to themselves, and shall reserve the whole of the defence for the *real* trial.

But, sir, for the purpose of conducting this matter with at least that appearance of fairness and openness that shall justify itself before the public, whose cause it really is (for it is the right of public discussion and investigation that is questioned), I have to propose to you to cease the prosecution against the publisher; and as the reason or pretext can no longer exist for continuing it against him because Mr. Paine could not be found, that you would direct the whole process against me, with whom the prosecuting party will not find it possible to enter into any private negotiation.

I will do the cause full justice, as well for the sake of the nation, as for my own reputation.

Another reason for discontinuing the process against the publisher is, because it can amount to nothing. First, because a jury in London cannot decide upon the fact of publishing beyond the limits of the jurisdiction of London, and therefore the work may be republished over and over again in every county in the nation, and every case must have a separate process; and by the time that three or four hundred prosecutions have been had, the eyes of the nation will then be fully open to see that the work in question contains a plan the best calculated to root out all the abuses of government, and to lessen the taxes of the nation upward of *six millions annually*.

Secondly, because though the gentlemen of London may be very expert in understanding their particular professions and occupations, and how to make business contracts with government beneficial to themselves as individuals, the rest of the nation may not be disposed to consider them sufficiently qualified nor authorized to determine for the whole nation on plans of reform, and on systems and principles of government. This would be in effect to erect a jury into a national convention, instead of electing a convention, and to lay a precedent for the probable tyranny of juries, under the pretence of supporting their rights.

That the possibility always exists of packing juries will not be denied; and, therefore, in all cases where government is the prosecutor, more especially in those where the right of public discussion and investigation of principles and systems of government is attempted to be suppressed by a verdict, or in those where the object of the work that is prosecuted is the reform of abuse and the abolition of sinecure places and pensions, in all these cases the verdict of a jury will itself become a subject of discussion; and, therefore, it furnishes an additional reason for discontinuing the prosecution against the publisher, more especially as it is not a secret that there has been a negotiation with him for secret purposes, and for proceeding against me only. I shall make a much stronger defence than what I believe the treasury solicitor's agreement with him will permit him to do.

I believe that Mr. Burke, finding himself defeated, and not being able to make any answer to the "Rights of Man," has been one of the promoters of this prosecution; and I shall return the compliment to him by showing, in a future publication, that he has been a masked pensioner at fifteen hundred pounds per annum for about ten years.

Thus it is that the public money is wasted, and the dread of public investigation is produced.

I am, sir,
Your obedient humble servant,
Thomas Paine.

Sir A. Macdonald, *Attorney-General.*'

The business being thus settled with respect to Jordan, and he consenting to give up the documents in his possession relative to the 'Rights of Man,' in order to facilitate their means of proceeding against the author, they commenced their prosecution against the latter on the twenty-first of May. On the same day, they issued their celebrated proclamation against what they were pleased to term 'seditious writings.' The authors of this document preserved a careful silence as to the specific object of their alarms, but it was easy to discover that their intention was to cry down the 'Rights of Man,' and to influence the verdict of the jury which was to try the author. Another expedient was likewise resorted to—that of procuring addresses in favor of the existing system of government from the corporations, rotten boroughs, and other places under the influence of the ministry. Nothing could be more despicable than these addresses,* and nothing more glaring than the con-

---

* As a contrast to these contemptible and fulsome specimens of servility, I subjoin the following:—
 'At a meeting of the Manchester Constitutional Society, held this day, it was unanimously resolved—
 That the thanks of this society are due to Mr. Thomas Paine, for the publica-

duct of their promoters, who were chiefly persons directly or indirectly interested in the support of public abuses: but despicable as they were, they served in some measure the purtion of his "Second Part of the Rights of Man, combining Principle and Practice," a work of the highest importance to every nation under heaven; but particularly to this, as containing excellent and practical plans for an immediate and considerable reduction of the public expenditure; for the prevention of wars; for the extension of our manufactures and commerce; for the education of the young; for the comfortable support of the aged; for the better maintenance of the poor of every description; and, finally, for lessening, greatly, and without delay, the enormous load of taxes under which this country at present labors.

That this society congratulate their countrymen at large, on the influence which Mr. Paine's publications appear to have had, in procuring the repeal of some oppressive taxes in the present session of parliament; and they hope that this adoption of a small part of Mr. Paine's ideas, *will be followed by the most strenuous exertions to accomplish a complete reform in the present inadequate state of the representation of the people*, and that the other great plans of public benefit, which Mr. Paine has so powerfully recommended, will be speedily carried into effect.   THOMAS WALKER, *President.*
March 13, 1792.'   SAMUEL JACKSON, *Secretary.*

Sheffield Society for Constitutional Information.

'This society, composed chiefly of the manufacturers of Sheffield, began about four months ago, and is already increased to nearly *two thousand* members, and is daily increasing, exclusive of the adjacent towns and villages who are forming themselves into similar societies.

Considering, as we do, that the want of knowledge and information in the general mass of the people, has exposed them to numberless impositions and abuses, the exertions of this society are directed to the acquirement of useful knowledge, and to spread the same as far as our endeavors and abilities can extend.

We declare that we have derived more true knowledge from the two works of Mr. Thomas Paine, entitled "Rights of Man," parts the first and second, than from any author on the subject. The practice as well as the principle of government is laid down, in those works, in a manner so clear and irresistibly convincing, that this society do hereby resolve to give their thanks to Mr. Paine for his two said publications, entitled "Rights of Man," parts first and second.

Resolved unanimously, That the thanks of this society be given to Mr. Paine, for the affectionate concern he has shown in his second work in behalf of the poor, the infant, and the aged; who, notwithstanding the opulence which blesses other parts of the community, are, by the grievous weight of taxes, rendered the miserable victims of poverty and wretchedness.

Resolved unanimously, That the thanks of this society be given to John Horne Tooke, Esq., for his meritorious support of our lawful privileges, as a firm advocate of our natural and just rights, the establishment of an equal representation of the people.

Resolved unanimously, That this society disdaining to be considered either of a ministerial or opposition party (names of which we are tired, having been so often deceived by both) do ardently recommend it to all their fellow-citizens, into whose hands these resolutions may come, to confer seriously and calmly with each other on the subject alluded to; and to manifest to the world, that the spirit of true liberty is a spirit of order; and that to obtain justice it is consistent that we be just to ourselves.

Resolved unanimously, That these resolutions be printed, and that a copy thereof be transmitted to the Society for Constitutional Information, London, requesting their approbation for twelve of our friends to be entered into their society for the purpose of establishing a connexion and a regular communication with that and all other similar societies in the kingdom.

By order of the committee.
March 14, 1792.'   DAVID MARTIN, *Chairman.*

The above were selected from a number of others of a similar description. They show that Mr. Paine had the approbation of the most independent portion of the people, though his writings were not sanctioned by the aristocracy, the landed interest, or any other class interested in the protection of a corrupt system of government

pose of the moment in decrying the character of a work, and defaming the reputation of a man whose arguments were unanswerable, and whose character was irreproachable. A great number of pamphlets, intended as answers to the 'Rights of Man,' had issued from the press, but such was the irresistible nature of truth, that these puny and feeble efforts on the part of wounded corruption no sooner appeared than they vanished, and a few short weeks consigned them and their authors to eternal oblivion. They therefore determined that an appeal to popular clamor would serve their cause better than an appeal to reason, and the verdict of a packed jury would answer their purpose better than any attempt to argue the merits of the work on the principles of truth and justice.

While the ministers of despotism were thus revelling in the anticipation of their plots and schemes for crushing the rising spirit of the country, the author of the 'Rights of Man' was resolved not to shrink from the discussion which his writings had occasioned. He was urged by several gentlemen of the law to prefer a bill of indictment against the publisher of the proclamation as a publication tending to influence the decision of the jury; but conscious of the rectitude of his intentions, and of the strength of his arguments, he preferred meeting the proclamation on its own ground, and defending the principles of the work which had been falsely stigmatized as wicked and seditious. Accordingly, about the month of August, 1792, he prepared another publication in defence of the 'Rights of Man' and of his own conduct, entitled, 'An Address to the Addresers on the late Proclamation.' This is one of the severest pieces of satire that ever issued from the press. The parliamentary orators on both sides the house, anxious to raise a popular outcry against the 'Rights of Man,' had commenced the session, by describing to the country and to each other blessings which were enjoyed under the British constitution. The praises which were bestowed upon the 'radical beauties' of this constitution, and the motives which produced them, are ridiculed by Mr. Paine in a fine strain of irony. Having informed the *addressers* of these symptoms of alarm, on the part of their mild and merciful governors, he proceeds to a defence of the principles of the 'Rights of Man.' He repeats his former arguments, and offers additional reasons for the positions he had advanced. He concludes this part of the pamphlet with these words, in reference to the impending prosecution: 'If to expose the fraud and imposition of every species of hereditary government; to lessen the oppression of taxes; to propose plans for the education of helpless infancy, and the comfortable support of the aged and distressed; to endeavor to conciliate nations to each other; to extirpate the horrid practice of war; to promote universal peace, civilization, and commerce; and to break the chains of political superstition, and raise degraded man to his proper rank; if these things be libellous, let me live the life of a libeller, and let the name of *libeller* be engraven on my tomb.'

But though Mr. Paine was determined to take every opportunity of defending his principles, he maintained that the case was deserving of a much more extensive consideration than could be bestowed upon it by any jury, whether special or common. He contends in the work before us, that the question was not so much whether he had or had not written what crown lawyers and packed juries are in the habit of condemning as wicked and seditious libels, but whether individuals had the right to investigate systems and principles of government, and to publish the conclusions resulting from such investigation. It was *this* right which the ministry were invading under the pretence of prosecuting the author of the 'Rights of Man,' and while in appearance they were merely attempting to suppress what they called the seditious writings of Mr. Paine, they were, in fact, aiming a deadly blow at the rights of every man in the country.

It was at first Mr. Paine's intention to have defended himself personally, but an event happened about two months previous to the trial which disconcerted his purpose. While he was preparing his 'Letter to the Addressers,' his friends and admirers in France were preparing a wreath of civic honors, as a reward for his intrepid exertions in defence of universal liberty. About the middle of September, 1792, a French deputation announced to him in London, that the department of Calais had elected him as their representative in the national convention. This was a matter of greater interest to him than the attorney-general's prosecution, and he proceeded to Dover with the intention of embarking immediately to Calais. The treatment which he met with at Dover was disgraceful in the extreme,[*] his trunks were all opened, and the contents examined. Some of his papers were seized, and it is probable that the whole would have shared the same fate, but for the cool and steady conduct of Mr. Paine and his attendants. When the custom-house officers had indulged themselves in this manner as long as they thought proper, Mr. Paine and his friends were suffered to embark, and they arrived at Calais, after a pleasant passage of three hours. He very narrowly escaped the vigilance of the despots he had provoked, for it appears that an order to detain him was received at Dover, in about twenty minutes after his embarkation. The reception which he met with at Calais, furnished a striking contrast to the conduct of the government agents at Dover. On the name of Paine being announced, the soldiers at the gates were drawn up, and the officers on guard having embraced him, presented him with

---

[*] For a full account of this scandalous transaction, see his Second Letter to Mr. Secretary Dundas, dated Calais, September 15, 1792.

the national cockade. A very pretty woman, who was standing by, desired she might have the honor of putting it in his hat, expressing her hopes that he would continue his exertions in favor of liberty, equality, and France. A salute was then fired from the battery, to announce the arrival of their new representative. This ceremony being over, he walked to Deissein's, in the *Rue de l'Egalité* (formerly *Rue de Roi*), the men, women, and children, crowding around him, and calling out '*Vive* Thomas Paine!' He was then conducted to the town-hall, and there presented to the municipality, who with the greatest affection embraced their representative. The mayor addressed him in a short speech, which was interpreted to him by his friend and conductor, M. Audibert, to which Mr. Paine, laying his hand on his heart, replied, that his life should be devoted to their service.

At the inn he was waited upon by the different persons in authority, and by the president of the Constitutional society, who desired he would attend their meeting of that night: he cheerfully complied with the request, and the whole town would have been there, had there been room: the hall of the '*Minimes*' was so crowded that it was with the greatest difficulty they made way for Mr. Paine to the side of the president. Over the chair he sat in, was placed the bust of Mirabeau, and the colors of France, England, and America united. A speaker acquainted him from the tribune with his election, amid the plaudits of the people. For some minutes after this ceremony, nothing was heard but '*Vive la Nation! Vive* THOMAS PAINE,' in voices male and female.

On the following day an extra meeting was appointed to be held in the church in honor of their new deputy to the convention, the *Minimes* being found quite suffocating from the vast concourse of people which had assembled on the previous occasion. A play was performed at the theatre on the evening after his arrival, and a box was specifically reserved 'for the author of the "Rights of Man," the object of the English proclamation.'

Mr Paine was likewise elected as deputy for Abbeville, Beauvais, and Versailles, as well as for the department of Calais, but the latter having been the first in their choice, he preferred being their representative.

After remaining with his constituents a short time, he proceeded to Paris in order to take his seat as a member of the National Assembly. On the road he met with similar honors to those which he had received at Calais. As soon as he had arrived at Paris, he addressed a letter to the people of France thanking his fellow-citizens for adopting him as their deputy to the convention.

Mr. Paine was, shortly after his arrival in Paris, appointed a member of the committee for framing the new constitution.

While he was peaceably and patriotically performing the duties of his station, the ministry of England were using every effort to counteract the (to them) dangerous principles which he had disseminated. For this purpose they filed a number of informations against the different individuals who had retailed the work. The trial of Mr. Paine came on at Guildhall, on the 18th of December, before Lord Kenyon,* and a special jury. The former being pensioned, and the latter being packed, a verdict of guilty followed as a matter of course. The proceedings on this trial are not of much interest, except as they tend to develop the inquisitorial character of an English court of law in matters of libel. The attorney-general had selected a few passages from the second part of the 'Rights of Man,' which he thought were most likely to answer his purpose, and these, in the verbose vulgarity of the law, he stigmatized as false, wicked, scandalous, and seditious. He was prudent enough to refrain from any attempt to *prove* the truth of his charge, well knowing that, with such a judge and such a jury, abuse would be received as a substitute for argument, and the coarsest and most improbable calumnies would be admitted as evidence of the writer's evil intention. The greater part of his speech to the jury was taken up with a comment on a letter relative to the prosecution, which Mr. Paine had written to him from Paris. In this letter he says: 'Had not my duty as a member of the national convention of France called me from England, I should have stayed to have contested the injus-

---

* This man was one of the most cruel, vindictive, and merciless characters that ever disgraced the bench of a British court of justice. As an illustration of his conduct, the following anecdote will be sufficient: in the year 1799, a gentleman with whom I have the pleasure of being acquainted, of the name of Waddington. speculated very largely in *hops*. It is the custom, and has been so time out of mind, to purchase many of the hops of the growers before they are gathered, and to give so much a pound for them when gathered and put into bags. Mr. Waddington (who was an opulent banker, and whose character, as a commercial man, stood very high), about the time he was making large purchases of this sort, took the lead in calling a meeting in the city of London to petition against the war. The myrmidons of Pitt were set to work to discover how he might be annoyed. They trumped up a charge of forestalling against him for having purchased hops before they were brought to market. Nothing could be more unfounded than this charge, seeing that it had been the practice of thousands of persons for perhaps more than a century. In the reigns of Edward VI., Mary, Elizabeth, Charles II., and Anne, divers acts of parliament had been passed against forestalling, regrating, engrossing, &c. But in time it was discovered that these acts were not only foolish, but mischievous, and in the 12th year of the reign of the present king, the whole of them were repealed; upon the ground that they tended to produce *dearth* and *misery*. But the common law had not been repealed, or at least Kenyon *said so*. Upon this was Mr. Waddington indicted, and a jury, packed for the purpose, found him guilty of dealings as honest and common as any in the country: in consequence of this verdict, the wicked and malignant judge sentenced this worthy and respectable man to be imprisoned as well as fined, which, considering that it dissolved all his contracts, produced a forfeiture of his deposites, and caused a run upon his house and his bank, was, in fact, sentencing him to ruin, and almost to actual beggary. The result of these proceedings brought forth a number of informations against forestallers—fortunately for Kenyon he died soon after, and his successor declared that *not* to be an offence, which Kenyon had declared *to be* an offence for the sole purpose of ruining a man whom Pitt and his colleagues had marked out for destruction.

tice of that prosecution; not upon my own account, for I cared not about the prosecution, but to have defended the principles' I had advanced in the work.' He likewise delivers his opinion very freely, upon the capacity of the reigning king, and the profligacy of his sons, and very pointedly asks the attorney-general, whether he conceives such persons are necessary to the government of a nation? Mr. Erskine contended against the legal right of the prosecutor to avail himself of the contents of this letter, but the judge overruled the objection. Indeed the whole of the proceedings seem to have been marked out beforehand, and the trial seems to have been nothing but a convenient farce. Mr. Erskine addressed the jury for some hours, but his speech was rather an *evasion* of the charge, than a justification of the principles he professed to defend. It was, as Mr. Paine observed, on seeing the report of the trial, 'a good speech for himself, but a very poor defence of the " Rights of Man." ' The jury found a verdict for the crown, without the trouble of deliberation.

With respect to the different retailers of the work against whom informations were filed, their fate now became pretty evident. The ministry were not satisfied with punishing the venders of 'Rights of Man;' they likewise instituted prosecutions against the publishers of the '*Letter to the Addressers*,' and obtained several convictions. The following statement contains, I believe, a correct account of the number of prosecutions against these works:—

A LIST OF THE PERSONS WHO HAVE BEEN PROSECUTED FOR THE PUBLICATION OF PAINE'S WORKS.

December 18, 1792. Thomas Paine, 'Rights of Man, Part II.' convicted; went to France previous to the trial.

February 26, 1793. Thomas Spence, 'Rights of Man, Part II.' flaw in the indictment; acquitted.

William Holland. 'Address to the Addressers,' one year's imprisonment, and £100 fine.

H. D. Symonds. 'Rights of Man,' two years imprisonment, and £20 fine. 'Letter to the Addressers,' one year's imprisonment, £100, and two sureties of £250 each, and self for £500, for three years, and imprisonment till the fine be paid and sureties given.

April 15. Thompson, printer, Birmingham, 'Rights of Man' and 'Address to the Addressers;' acquitted.

April 17. Richard Phillips, printer, Leicester, 'Rights of Man;' eighteen months' imprisonment.

May 8. J. Ridgway, bookseller, London; 'Rights of Man,' one year's imprisonment, and £100. 'Letter to the Addressers,' one year's imprisonment, and £100 fine; in each case, two sureties of £250 each, and self for £500 for three years, and imprisonment till the fine be paid, and sureties given.

June 3. D. I. Eaton, 'Rights of Man:' verdict which amounted to an acquittal. *July* 11. Do. 'Address to the Addressers:' do.

Richard Peart and William Belcher, 'Address to the Addressers,' and 'Rights of Man;' imprisonment three months.

August 10. Messrs. Robinsons, 'Rights of Man;' fine.

Daniel Holt, bookseller, Newark, 'Address to the Addressers;' four years' imprisonment, and £50 fine.

These prosecutions, though they were far from tranquillizing or satisfying the public mind, were certainly followed by one of their intended effects, that of suppressing the circulation of the work. Such was the acrimony with which the admirers of Mr. Paine were persecuted in all parts of the country, that it was regarded as highly dangerous for any person to be found with the book in his possession; for though the law took no cognizance of such an act, the individual became a marked object of destruction, and so vigilant were the agents of tyranny, that their malice was sure to be gratified by one means or other. On the trials of Hardy, Tooke, and Thelwall, the circumstance of their having patronised the 'Rights of Man' was made a very material ground for the charge of high treason, and though the accusation failed, the obloquy, which by this and other means was cast upon the work, tended very greatly to prevent its farther dissemination."

We have hitherto only noticed the public character of Mr. Paine in England. Before we follow him into France, we shall extract from Clio Rickman's life of Paine, an article on his civil, social, or domestic habits, observing that Mr. Rickman was his friend and companion, a man of amiable disposition, extensively known, and esteemed wherever known. We knew the family, and are at this time intimate with those who were familiar with and companions of Mr. Rickman. This gentleman remarks:—

"Mr. Paine's life in London was a quiet round of philosophical leisure and enjoyment. It was occupied in writing, in a small epistolary correspondence, in walking about with me to visit different friends, occasionally lounging at coffee-houses and public places, or being visited by a select few. Lord Edward Fitzgerald, the French and American ambassadors, Mr. Sharp, the engraver, Romney, the painter, Mrs. Wolstonecroft, Joel Barlow, Mr. Hull, Mr. Christie, Dr. Priestly, Dr. Towers, Colonel Oswald, the walking Stewart,

Captain Sampson Perry, Mr. Tuffin, Mr. William Choppin, Captain de Stark, Mr. Horne Tooke, &c., &c., were among the number of his friends and acquaintance; and, of course, as he, was my inmate, the most of my associates were frequently his. At this time he read but little, took his nap after dinner, and played with my family at some game in the evening, as chess, dominoes, or draughts, but never at cards; in recitations, singing, music, &c.; or passed it in conversation: the part he took in the latter was always enlightened, full of information, entertainment, and anecdote. Occasionally we visited enlightened friends, indulged in domestic jaunts and recreations from home, frequently lounging at the White Bear, Piccadilly, with his old friend, the walking Stewart, and other clever travellers from France, and different parts of Europe and America.

When by ourselves we sat very late, and often broke in on the morning hours, indulging the reciprocal interchange of affectionate and confidential intercourse. 'Warm from the heart and faithful to its fires,' was that intercourse, and gave to us the 'feast of reason and the flow of soul.'"

"To return to Mr. Paine and the French convention. On the 25th of July, 1792, the Duke of Brunswick issued his sanguinary manifesto: in this he stated that the allies were resolved to inflict the most dreadful punishments on the national assembly, and on the city of Paris, for their treatment of the royal family; he even went so far as to threaten to give up the place to military execution. The publication of this document threw the people of Paris into a state of complete confusion. They became frantic and furious, and the manifesto, instead of lulling them into repose, drove them to deeds of desperation. A party was soon formed in the convention for putting the king to death, and the agitated condition of the people facilitated the design. Mr. Paine labored hard to prevent this object from being carried into execution; but though his efforts produced a few converts to his doctrine, the majority of his colleagues were too enraged with the duplicity of the king, and the detestable conduct of the foreign monarchs, with whom he was leagued, to listen to anything short of the most unlimited vengeance. The conduct of Louis was too reprehensible to be passed over in silence; Mr. Paine therefore voted that he should be tried, but when the question whether he should be condemned to death, was brought forward, he opposed it by every argument in his power. His exertions were, however, ineffectual, and sentence of death was passed, though by a very small majority. Mr. Paine was determined to let slip no opportunity of protesting against this measure, and when the question, whether the sentence should be carried into execution, was discussed, he combated the proposition with great energy. As he was not in the habit of pronouncing

French, one of the secretaries read his discourse translated from the original English.

It is evident that his reasoning was thought very persuasive, since those who had heard the discourses of Buzot, Condorcet, and Brissot, to the same purpose without interruption, broke out in murmurs while Paine's opinion was reading; and Marat, at length, losing all patience, exclaimed that Paine was a quaker, and insinuated that his mind being contracted by the narrow principles of his religion, was incapable of the liberality that was requisite for condemning men to death. This shrewd argument not being thought convincing, the secretary continued to read, that 'the execution of the sentence, instead of an act of justice, would appear to all the world, and particularly to their allies, the American States, as an act of vengeance, and that if he were sufficiently master of the French language, he would, in the name of his brethren of America, present a petition at their bar against the execution of the sentence.' Marat and his associates said that these could not possibly be the sentiments of Thomas Paine, and that the assembly was imposed upon by a false translation. On comparing it with the original, however, it was found correct.

Though these exertions were frustrated, they were attended with one effect, that of rendering Mr. Paine an object of hatred among the most violent actors in the revolution. They found that he could not be induced to participate in their acts of cruelty; they dreaded the opposition which he might make to these sanguinary deeds, and they therefore marked him out as a victim to be sacrificed the first opportunity.

The humanity of Mr. Paine was, indeed, one of the most prominent features in his character, and it was equally a matter of indifference to him whether the exercise of this high attribute of the human heart was required on a trivial or important, a public or private occasion. Of his strict attention to his public duty in this respect, even at the hazard of his own safety, we have a convincing proof in his opposition to the execution of the king, and of his humane and charitable disposition in a private point of view, the following circumstances are sufficient to warrant the most unqualified conclusion.

Mr. Paine happened to be dining one day with about twenty friends at a coffee-house in the *Palais Egalite*, now the *Palais Royal*, when, unfortunately for the harmony of the company, a captain in the English service contrived to introduce himself as one of the party. The military gentleman was a strenuous supporter of the constitution in church and state, and a decided enemy of the French revolution. After the cloth was drawn, the conversation chiefly turned on the state of affairs in England, and the means which had been adopted by the government to check the increase of political knowledge. Mr. Paine delivered his opinion very freely, and much to the satisfaction of every one present, with the exception of Captain Grimstone, who returned his arguments by calling him a traitor to his country, with a variety of terms equally opprobious. Mr. Paine treated his abuse with much good humor, which rendered the captain so furious, that he walked up to the part of the room where Mr. Paine was sitting, and struck him a violent blow, which nearly knocked him off his seat. The cowardice of this behavior from a stout young man toward a person of Mr. Paine's age (he being then upward of sixty) is not the least disgraceful part of the transaction. There was, however, no time for reflections of this sort; an alarm was instantly given, that the captain had struck a citizen deputy of the convention, which was considered an insult to the nation at large; the offender was hurried into custody, and it was with the greatest difficulty that Mr. Paine prevented him from being executed on the spot.

It ought to be observed, that an act of the convention had awarded the punishment of death to any one who should be convicted of striking a deputy: Mr. Paine was therefore placed in a very unpleasant situation. He immediately applied to Barrere, at that time president of the committee of public safety, for a passport for his imprudent adversary, who after much hesitation complied with his request. It likewise occasioned Mr. Paine considerable personal inconvenience to procure his liberation; but even this was not sufficient; the captain was without friends, and penniless, and Mr. Paine generously supplied him with money to defray his travelling expenses.

The gentleman who favored me with the account of the foregoing circumstance, has likewise informed me of another anecdote equally honorable to Mr. Paine's feelings. A Major Munroe, who at the beginning of the revolution was employed by Mr. Pitt to send an account to the ministry of what was going on in Paris, remained there till after the declaration of war, when he, with many others, was sent to prison. He had previously occupied the same hotel with Mr. Paine, and though the latter was aware of his errand, he found him an intelligent companion. When the major was imprisoned, he applied to Mr. Paine, who after considerable trouble obtained his release. The major was recently living, and it is but fair to say, that he has often observed to his friends, he should ever feel indebted to the kindness of Mr. Paine, for the interest he employed in procuring his discharge.

I have already noticed the feeling of hostility with which our author's exertions in the cause of humanity were received by some of the members of the convention. Those who had deserted the principles of liberty, and who, from the most treacherous and tyrannical motives, were anxious to plunge the nation into a state of anarchy, were naturally the enemies of the great defender of the 'Rights of Man,' and they were determined to gratify their vengeance, whenever a possibility of so doing should offer itself. Before entering into a description of the steps that were taken for this purpose I will give the reader an account of the mode in which he passed his time at the period we are speaking of.

'In Paris, in 1793,' he observes, ' I had lodgings in the *Rue Fauxbourg St. Denis*, No. 63. They were the most agreeable for situation of any I ever had in Paris, except that they were too remote from the convention, of which I was then a member. But this was recompensed by their being also remote from the alarms and confusion into which the interior of Paris was then often thrown. The news of those things used to arrive to us, as if we were in a state of quietude in the country. The house, which was enclosed by a wall and gateway from the street, was a good deal like an old mansion farm-house, and the court-yard was like a farm-yard stocked with fowls, ducks, turkeys, and geese; which, for amusement, we used to feed out of the windows of the parlor on the ground-floor. There were some huts for rabbits, and a stye with two pigs. Beyond, was a garden of more than an acre of ground, well laid out, and stocked with excellent fruit-trees. The orange, apricot, and the green-gage plum, were the best I ever tasted; and it is the only place where I saw the wild cucumber, which they told me is poisonous. The place had formerly been occupied by some curious person.'

In allusion to the dreadful proceedings which were making such havoc among the best patriots of France, he continues:—

'As for myself, I used to find some relief by walking alone in the garden after it was dark, and cursing with hearty good will the authors of that terrible system that had turned the character of the revolution I had been proud to defend.

I went but little to the convention, and then only to make my appearance; because I found it impossible for me to join in their tremendous decrees, and useless and dangerous to oppose them. My having voted and spoken extensively, more so than any other member, against the execution of the king, had already fixed a mark upon me: neither dared any of my associates in the convention to translate, and speak in French for me anything I might have dared to write. Pen and ink were then of no use to me. No good could be done by writing, and no printer dared to print; and whatever I might have written for my private amusement, as anecdotes of the times, would have been continually exposed to be examined, and tortured into any meaning that the rage of party might fix upon it; and as to softer subjects, my heart was in distress at the fate of my friends, and my harp was hung upon the weeping willows.'

At this period the national convention was divided into factions, each intent on their own aggrandizement, and each possessing a powerful host of partisans among the people. Terror, hatred, suspicion, revenge, and every other dark and deadly passion, had supplanted the just, liberal, and humane principles which marked the commencement of the revolution, and the wide empire of France became one vast slaughter-house, where the supporters of freedom and the advocates of despotism were alternately sacrificed at the shrine of factious violence. The exertions of the friends of liberty sooner increased than lessened the effects of the storm, and to defend the interests of truth and the rights of the people, was to invite destruction. The voice of humanity was mute, for the ear of humanity was closed. It is painful to recur to these heart-rending scenes, but justice requires it, and more particularly so, as Mr. Paine was very near falling a victim to the violence of the contending factions.

The gentle, conciliating, and open method in which he had conducted himself, had prevented the possibility of impeaching his political conduct, and to this we must attribute the circumstance of his remaining so long at liberty. The first attempt that was made against him, was by means of an act of the convention, which decreed that all persons residing in France who were born in England should be imprisoned; but as Mr. Paine was a member of the convention, and had been complimented with the title of 'citizen of France,' the decree did not extend to him. A motion was afterward made by Bourdon de l'Oise, for expelling foreigners from the convention. It was evident from the speech of the mover, that Mr. Paine was the principal object aimed at, and as soon as the expulsion was effected, an application was made to the two committees of public safety and general surety, of which Robespierre was the dictator, and they immediately put him in arrestation under the former decree for imprisoning persons born in England. On his way to the Luxembourg he contrived to call upon his intimate friend and associate, Joel Barlow, with whom he left the manuscript of the first part of the 'Age of Reason.'* This work he intended to be the last of his life, but the proceedings in France, during the year 1793, induced him to delay it no longer. 'The circumstance,' says he, 'that has now taken place in France, of the total abolition of the whole national order of priesthood, and of everything appertaining to compulsive systems of religion, and compulsive articles of faith, has not only precipitated my intention, but rendered a work of this kind exceedingly necessary, lest in

* See Mr Barlow's letter, page 135.

the general wreck of superstition, of false systems of government, and false theology, we lose sight of morality, of humanity, and of the theology that is true.' At the time this performance was written, Mr. Paine was in almost daily expectation of being sent to the guillotine, where many of his friends had already perished; the doctrines, therefore, which it inculcates, must be regarded as the sentiments of a dying man. This is at least a conclusive proof that the work was not the result of a wish to deceive, that, whether true or false, it was the effusion of a disinterested mind; and, in ordinary cases, the fact of a man writing a book under such circumstances, would be admitted as a logical evidence of the rectitude of the doctrines it contained. I do not, however, intend to enter into any discussion relative to our author's religious opinions, until we arrive at the second part of the work. It is, therefore, only necessary at present, to observe, that Mr. Paine had measured his time with such a degree of precision, that he had not finished the book more than six hours before he was arrested and conveyed to the Luxembourg.*

Mr. Paine had remained in prison about three weeks, when it was ascertained to the satisfaction of every one in Paris, except the tyrants who had sent him there, that he had committed no offence; and in consequence of this, the Americans residing in that city, went in a body to the convention to demand the liberation of their fellow-citizen and friend. The following is a copy of the address presented by them to the president of the convention; an address which sufficiently shows the high estimation in which Mr. Paine was at this time held by the citizens of the United States:—

'Citizens! The French nation had invited the most illustrious of all foreign nations to the honor of representing her.

Thomas Paine, the apostle of liberty in America, a profound and valuable philosopher, a virtuous and esteemed citizen, came to France and took a seat among you. Particular circumstances rendered necessary the decree to put under arrest all the English residing in France.

Citizens! representatives! We come to demand of you Thomas Paine, in the name of the friends of liberty, and in the name of the Americans, your brothers and allies; was there anything more wanted to obtain your demand we would tell you. Do not give to the leagued despots the pleasure of seeing Paine in irons. We shall inform you that the seals put upon the papers of Thomas Paine have been taken off, that the committee of general safety examined them, and far from

---

* Had such a singularly favorable coincidence as this happened in the transactions of a Christian theological writer, it would undoubtedly have been ascribed to the interposition of Divine Providence, but in the present instance (whatever rational men may think on the subject) the faithful will perhaps find it convenient to attribute the circumstance to the influence of a power of quite an opposite character.

finding among them any dangerous propositions, they only found the love of liberty which characterized him all his lifetime, that eloquence of nature and philosophy which made him the friend of mankind, and those principles of public morality which merited the hatred of kings, and the affection of his fellow-citizens.

In short, citizens! if you permit us to restore Thomas Paine to the embraces of his fellow-citizens, we offer to pledge ourselves as securities for his conduct during the short time he shall remain in France.'

The Americans who presented the foregoing address, received for answer, that 'Mr. Paine was born in England,' and it was likewise hinted to them that their attempt to reclaim him as a citizen of the United States, could not be listened to, in consequence of its not being *authorized* by the American government.

A few days after this, all communication between persons imprisoned, and any person without the prison, was cut off, by an order of the police. In this forlorn and solitary situation Mr. Paine continued for six months, and the only hope that remained for him was, that a new minister would arrive from America to supersede Morris, and that he would be authorized to inquire into the causes of his imprisonment; 'but even this hope,' Mr. Paine observes, 'in the state in which matters were daily arriving, was too remote to have any consolatory effect; and I contented myself with the thought that I might be remembered when it would be too late.'

During this long imprisonment he amused himself as well as such a gloomy situation would allow, by writing various pieces of fancy, both in poetry and prose, some of which have since been published. He likewise wrote a considerable proportion of the second part of the 'Age of Reason' during his incarceration. When he had been in prison about eight months, he was seized with a violent fever, which nearly deprived him of life, and from the effects of which he never afterward perfectly recovered. This fever, which rendered him completely insensible for more than a month, was evidently the means of preserving his life. Had he remained in health he would probably, according to the routine of the times, have been dragged before the tribunal, and sent to the guillotine, without the trouble of proving either his guilt or his innocence. But the fever fortunately averted the impending danger, and the first thing he heard of after his recovery was the fall of Robespierre. But the fate of this sanguinary man did not restore him to liberty. The desolator was overthrown, but his faction still remained, and, though considerably humbled, their hostility toward Mr. Paine was unabated. The latter seeing that several of his fellow-prisoners were released, addressed a memorial to Mr. Monroe (who it appears had received no instructions from the American government respecting Mr. Paine), on the subject of his confinement, who behaved toward him with great kindness and attention. The following is a copy of Mr. Monroe's letter to Mr. Paine on this occasion :—

PARIS, September 18, 1794.

'DEAR SIR : I was favored, soon after my arrival here, with several letters from you, and more latterly with one in the character of a memorial upon the subject of your confinement : and should have answered them at the times they were respectively written, had I not concluded, you would have calculated with certainty upon the deep interest I take in your welfare, and the pleasure with which I shall embrace every opportunity in my power to serve you. I should still pursue the same course, and for reasons which must obviously occur, if I did not find that you are disquieted with apprehensions upon interesting points, and which justice to you and our country equally forbid you should entertain. You mention that you have been informed you are not considered as an American citizen by the Americans, and that you have likewise heard that I had no instructions respecting you by the government. I doubt not the persons who gave you the information meant well, but I suspect he did not even convey accurately his own ideas on the first point : for I presume the most he could say is, that you had likewise become a French citizen, and which by no means deprives you of being an American one. Even this, however, may be doubted, I mean the acquisition of citizenship in France, and I confess you have said much to show that it has not been made. I really suspect that this was all that the gentleman who wrote to you, and those Americans he heard speak upon the subject, meant. It becomes my duty, however, to declare to you, that I consider you as an American citizen, and that you are considered universally in that character by the people of America. As such you are entitled to my attention ; and so far as it can be given, consistently with those obligations which are mutual between every government and even transient passenger, you shall receive it.

The congress have never decided upon the subject of citizenship, in a manner to regard the present case. By being with us through the revolution, you are of our country as absolutely as if you had been born there, and you are no more of England than every native American is. This is the true doctrine in the present case, so far as it becomes complicated with any other consideration. I have mentioned it to make you easy upon the only point which could give you any disquietude.

It is necessary for me to tell you, how much all your countrymen—I speak of the great mass of the people—are interested in your welfare. They have not forgotten the history of their own revolution, and the difficult scenes through which they passed; nor do they review its several stages without reviving in their bosoms a due sensibility of the merits of those who served them in that great and arduous conflict. The crime of ingratitude has not yet stained, and I trust never will stain, our national character. You are considered by them, as not only having rendered important services in our own revolution, but as being, on a more extensive scale, the friend of human rights, and a distinguished and able advocate in favor of public liberty. To the welfare of Thomas Paine, the Americans are not, nor can they be, indifferent.

Of the sense which the president has always entertained of your merits, and of his friendly disposition toward you, you are too well assured, to require any declaration of it from me. That I forward his wishes in seeking your safety is what I well know: and this will form an additional obligation on me to perform what I should otherwise consider as a duty.

You are in my opinion, at present, menaced by no kind of danger. To liberate you will be an object of my endeavors, and as soon as possible. But you must, until that event shall be accomplished, bear your situation with patience and fortitude; you will likewise have the justice to recollect, that I am placed here upon a difficult theatre, many important objects to attend to, and with few to consult. It becomes me in pursuit of those, to regulate my conduct with respect to each, as to the manner and the time, as will, in my judgment, be best calculated to accomplish the whole.

With great esteem and respect consider me personally your friend.

JAMES MONROE.'

Mr. Paine was released from prison on the 4th of November, 1794, having been in confinement for eleven months.

After his liberation he was kindly *invited* to the house of Mr. Monroe, with whom he remained for about eighteen months. I intend to be as brief in my extracts as the subject will admit; but the following, which is taken from one of his letters, written after his return to America, is so descriptive of his situation while in prison, and of another narrow escape which he had in addition to the one already noticed, that I consider it necessary for the information of the reader.

'I was one of the nine members that composed the first committee of constitution. Six of them have been destroyed. Syeyes and myself have survived. He by bending with the times, and I by not bending. The other survivor joined Robespierre, and signed with him the warrant of my arrestation. After the fall of Robespierre, he was seized and imprisoned in his turn, and sentenced to transportation. He has since apologized to me for having signed the warrant, by saying, he felt himself in danger and was obliged to do it.

Herault Sechelles, an acquaintance of Mr. Jefferson, and a good patriot, was my *suppliant* as member of the committee of constitution; that is, he was to supply my place, if I had not accepted or had resigned, being next in number of votes to me. He was imprisoned in the Luxembourg with me, was taken to the tribunal and the guillotine, and I, his principal, was left.

There were but two foreigners in the convention, Anacharsis Cloots and myself. We were both put out of the convention by the same vote, arrested by the same order, and carried to prison together the same night. He was taken to the guillotine, and I was again left. Joel Barlow was with us when we went to prison.

Joseph Lebon, one of the vilest characters that ever existed, and who made the streets of Arras run with blood, was my suppliant as member of the convention for the department of the Pais de Calais. When I was put out of the convention he came and took my place. When I was liberated from prison, and voted again into the convention, he was sent to the same prison and took my place there, and he went to the guillotine instead of me. He supplied my place all the way through.

One hundred and sixty-eight persons were taken out of the Luxembourg in one night, and a hundred and sixty of them guillotined the next day, of which I know I was to have been one; and the manner I escaped that fate is curious, and has all the appearance of accident.

The room in which I was lodged was on the ground floor, and one of a long range of rooms under a gallery, and the door of it opened outward and flat against the wall; so that when it was open the inside of the door appeared outward, and the contrary when it was shut. I had three comrades, fellow-prisoners with me, Joseph Vanhuile of Bruges, since president of the municipality of that town, Michael Robins, and Bastini of Louvain.

When persons by scores and hundreds were to be taken out of prison for the guillotine, it was always done in the night, and those who performed that office had a private mark or signal by which they knew what rooms to go to, and what number to take. We, as I have said, were four, and the door of our room was marked unobserved by us, with that number in chalk; but it happened, if happening is a proper word, that the mark was put on when the door was open and flat against the wall, and thereby came on the inside when we shut it at night, and the destroying angel passed by it. A few days after this Robespierre fell, and the American ambassador arrived and reclaimed me and invited me to his house.

During the whole of my imprisonment, prior to the fall of Robespierre, there was no time when I could think my life worth twenty-four hours, and my mind was made up to meet its fate. The Americans in Paris went in a body to the convention to reclaim me, but without success. There was no party among them with respect to me. My only hope then rested on the government of America that it would remember me. But the icy heart of ingratitude, in whatever man it may be placed, has neither feeling nor sense of honor. The letter of Mr. Jefferson has served to wipe away the reproach, and done justice to the mass of the people of America.'

Soon after Mr. Paine's release from prison the convention passed a unanimous vote to invite him to return to the seat he had formerly occupied. The times were still dangerous, as well from without as within, for the coalition of foreign despots was unbroken, and the constitution not settled. Mr. Paine however, thought proper to accept the invitation, being resolved to show that he was not to be alarmed either by prospects or retrospects of danger, and that his principles were neither to be perverted by disgust nor weakened by misfortune.

He was liberated, as before stated, in November, 1794; his bodily health was at this time very much impaired by long confinement, and in September following he was taken dangerously ill. He states that he had felt the approach of his disorder for some time, which occasioned him to hasten to a conclusion of the second part of the 'Age of Reason.' This work was published at Paris, early in 1795, and was very shortly afterward reprinted in England, and the United States. At the time he wrote the first part of the work he was without a bible, nor could he procure one. The investigation which it contained was therefore rather a general, than a detailed inquiry into the Jewish and Christian systems of belief. The first point which he attacks is the doctrine of revelation. He admits the possibility, though he denies the probability of the Supreme Being having ever held personal communication with man. But even allowing this to be the case, he observes, that 'revelation is necessarily limited to the first communication. After this it is only on account of something which that person says was revelation made to him; and though he may find himself obliged to believe it, it cannot be incumbent on me to believe it in the same manner, for it was not revelation made to *me*, and I have only his word for it that it was made to him.'*

In this manner he proceeds to controvert the principal arguments in favor of Christianity. He asserts that it is a system founded entirely upon hearsay evidence, and that we are not obliged to believe it. He next endeavors to show the similarity of the heathen mythology, and that of the Christians, from

* Age of Reason, Part I.

which he infers that the latter is a copy of the former. Among the novel positions which he advanced, was an argument to prove that the word *prophet* had changed its original meaning, that in former times it was synonymous with that of *poet* or *musician*; to prove this he cites the part of the Bible, where we are told the prophets of old performed the functions of their vocation by means of pipes, tabrets, horns, harps, and other musical instruments. Having declared his disbelief of what is called revealed religion, and his reasons for such disbelief, he next gives his opinion as to what he conceives to be the only true word of God—the only true revelation; and as his ideas on this subject are of no ordinary stamp, I insert them in his own words, as the best mode of doing justice to the author :—

'It is only in the CREATION that all our ideas and conceptions of a *word of God* can unite. The creation speaketh a universal language, independently of human speech or human language, miltiplied and various as they be. It is an ever-existing original, which every man can read. It cannot be forged; it cannot be counterfeited; it cannot be lost; it cannot be altered; it cannot be suppressed. It does not depend upon the will of man whether it shall be published or not: it publishes itself from one end of the earth to the other. It preaches to all nations and to all worlds; and this *word of God* reveals to man all that is necessary for man to know of God.

Do we want to contemplate his power? We see it in the immensity of the creation. Do we want to contemplate his wisdom? We see it in the unchangeable order by which the incomprehensible Whole is governed. Do we want to contemplate his munificence? We see it in the abundance with which he fills the earth. Do we want to contemplate his mercy? We see it in his not withholding that abundance even from the unthankful. In fine, do we want to know what God is? Search not the book called the Scripture, which any human hand might make, but the scripture called the Creation.'

It is not hazarding too much to say that the above breathes as pure a spirit of morality and philosophy, as anything that was ever written on the subject, in either ancient or modern times. It is superior to the bible description of the Deity, for it ascribes to him none of those weaknesses and passions which are so frequently attributed to him by the authors of that book. It is not at all wonderful that the ministers of a corrupt system of religion should calumniate the character of a work, which inculcates the practice of morality as the only religious duty that men are bound to perform, which teaches the most sublime and reverential ideas of the Creator of the universe, and which represents the intercessions of ignorant and bigoted priests, as unnecessary either to the present or future happiness of mankind—it is not at all wonderful that such men should look upon such a work with horror, and load its author with every epithet of calumny and reproach. They are in religion, what courtiers are under a limited monarchy. Both parties are, in nine cases out of ten, aware of the farce, and they tremble at the approach of reason and investigation.

From a great portion of the work before us, it is evident that Mr. Paine possessed an extensive knowledge of astronomy and mathematics, and the mode in which he applies these branches of science, to prove the ignorance of the bible writers, and the falsehood of their statements, is worth the reader's attention. For this, however, I must refer him to the work itself. The extract which I have already given will enable any person to form an idea of the general character of the book, its principles and tendency; I therefore proceed to offer a few observations on the second part.

This work is divided into an examination, first, of the Old, and, secondly, of the New Testament. In the former our author examines the different books of the Bible in rotation, and proves, very clearly, as far as the evidence of circumstances can go, that they were not written by the persons to whom they are ascribed, and, therefore, that they are anonymous and without authority. He likewise reasons very forcibly against the various acts of horrid cruelty, and gross immorality, which are attributed to the Almighty by Moses, and the other reputed authors of the Bible. In this examination the ancient Jews are stripped of the disguise in which commentators generally clothe them, and exposed in their true character—that of the most ignorant and ferocious race of beings which ever disgraced the character of human nature. Their ignorance is inferred from the circumstance of there not being in the whole Bible more than one book in which any branch of useful or scientific knowledge is mentioned (the book of Job) and this it appears is a book of the Gentiles and not of the Jews. The ferocity of their character is established by the almost innumerable and unprovoked murders with which the Scriptures are filled, and which are blasphemously ascribed to the God of mercy and eternal beneficence.

These are the principal grounds on which our author argues against the divinity of the Bible. In the examination of the New Testament, he exposes the contradictions of the different writers, he cites authorities to prove that the gospels were not written till a long time after the evangelists are reported to have lived; and that they were not formed into a book for more than three hundred years after the death of Christ. They were then collected together by the church, and it was decided by vote which were and which were not the word of God.

The work likewise contains some fine ideas on the doctrine of immortality: these form a striking contrast to the gloomy and unnatural doctrines of the resurrection.

On a superficial view of the subject it appears wonderful that a system of belief which is liable to so many objections, not only on the score of probability, but on that of the common principles of morality, should have obtained so general an influence among mankind. But when we look at the means which have been used to propagate its principles, we may cease to be surprised at the general credence it has acquired. Its professors preached peace and humility, until, by the increase of their numbers, they were enabled to assume a more formidable tone, but so slow was their progress, and with such general contempt were their doctrines viewed, that even this accession of strength did not take place until three or four centuries after the death of their founder. As the number of their converts increased, their temporal power became more extensive, and all attempts to investigate the truth of their pretensions were put down as impious heresies. Thus, in the first instance, their faith was protected by its obscurity and the professed humility of its disciples; in latter times it has been promoted by means of the sword, and the assiduity of the priesthood; while all inquiry into the probability or improbability of its precepts, has been suppressed by the powerful reasoning of the fagot and the inquisition.

It is not to be denied that the New Testament contains some good moral maxims, but these are no proofs of its divinity, for they existed thousands of years before the appearance of Christ, and they will exist when all the desolating wars and shocking persecutions which have been occasioned by the Christian system of faith, shall be sunk in the Lethean stream of oblivion. They are inherent in human nature, and they consequently do not depend upon the belief of any particular system of opinions. It may suit the convenience of the pious teachers of our established religion, to tell us that the practice of virtue, the foundation of our happiness here and of our hopes hereafter, are dependant on the practice of their absurd ceremonies, and the belief of their improbable doctrines; but it is impossible for the reflecting mind to discover in these dogmas anything more than the motives of an interested priesthood, or the effusions of a distempered imagination. The principles of moral virtue are essentially distinct from the belief of any existing system of faith, they result from the relations of a being with his fellow-beings; justice toward ourselves is wisdom; justice toward others is virtue. In society all is relative, there is no happiness independent; we are compelled to sacrifice a part of what we might enjoy, not to be deprived of the whole, and to secure a portion against all assaults. Even here the balance is in favor of reason.

However laborious may be the life of the honest man, however encompassed with dangers, however beset with difficulties it may be, that of the vicious character must be more so. He can seldom be tranquil who stands in opposition to the interests of his fellow-men; it is impossible for him to conceal from himself that he is surrounded by enemies, or by those who are ready to become so, and this situation is always painful, however splendid may be appearances. Let us add to these considerations, the sublime rectitude of instinct, which corruption may lead astray, but which no false philosophy can ever annihilate, which impels us to admire and love wisdom and generosity of conduct, as we do grandeur and beauty in nature and the arts; and we shall have the source of human virtue, independent of every religious system of the intricacies of metaphysics, and of the impostures of priests.

The publication of the 'Age of Reason' called forth a great variety of replies, but the only one which is now remembered is the Bishop of Llandaff's 'Apology for the Bible.' It is much to be doubted whether this work, which is written in open defiance of the plainest rules of reason and logic, would have survived the fate of its companions in the same cause, if it had been written by any other person. His character in the world of letters, and in several of the departments in science, coupled with his conduct in parliament, which induced many to regard him as an independent promoter of the gospel, gave the work an importance which its contents by no means deserved, and the friends of the church lost no time in publishing it throughout the country. Their zeal in this respect, perhaps, in some measure, answered the purpose they had in view, but it certainly conferred no honor on the bishop's literary reputation.

Whether the advocates of the Christian faith were or were not conscious of the imperfections of their system, it is evident they were afraid of an inquiry into its merits, and a prosecution was commenced against Mr. Williams, the publisher of the 'Age of Reason.' By way of giving a color to this proceeding, they retained Mr. Erskine on the part of the crown, who strained every effort to procure a verdict. Mr Kyd made an ingenious and argumentative reply, in behalf of the defendant, but the jury, being special, readily found him guilty, June 4, 1797. Mr. Paine addressed a letter to Mr. Erskine on the proceedings of this trial, in which he ridicules the absurd practice of discussing theological subjects before such men as special juries are generally composed of, and cites fresh evidence in support of his former arguments respecting the Bible.

Mr. Paine now attended his duty as a member of the convention, in which capacity he delivered his opinions whenever occasion required. In April, 1795, a committee was appointed to form another new constitution (the former one having been abolished) and the report of this committee was brought forward on the 23d of June following, by Boissy d'Anglas. This was the constitution of elders and youngsters, a council of five hundred, a council of ancients, and an executive directory of five. Mr. Paine wrote a speech in opposition to several of the articles of this constitution, which was translated and read to the convention by Citizen Lanthera, on the seventh of July. One of the subjects against which Mr. Paine contended, was the unjust distinction that was attempted to be made between direct and indirect taxes. Whatever weight these objections ought to have carried, they were not listened to by the convention, and the constitution of Boissy d'Anglas was adopted. By this decree the convention was formally destroyed, and as Mr. Paine was not afterward re-elected, it likewise terminated his public functions in France.

The reign of terror having in some degree subsided, our author's political pen returned to its former employment. About the time that he brought out the second part of the 'Age of Reason,' he published several pamphlets on subjects less likely to inflame the passions of the bigoted and the ignorant, than investigations into the nature of theology. The principal of these are his 'Dissertation on first Principles of Government,' 'Agrarian Justice opposed to Agrarian Law,' and the 'Decline and Fall of the English System of Finance.' The first of these is a continuation of the arguments advanced in the 'Rights of Man;' the second is a plan for creating in every country a national fund 'to pay to every person when arrived at the age of twenty-one years the sum of fifteen pounds sterling, to enable him or her to begin the world, and also ten pounds sterling, per annum, during life, to every person, now living, of the age of fifty years, and to all others, when they shall arrive at that age, to enable them to live in old age without wretchedness, and to go decently out of the world.'

This little essay contains a good deal of original thinking, and close reasoning, though in the present state of society it is not very probable that its recommendations will be ever adopted. The pamphlet on finance is a proof of Mr. Paine's extensive knowledge on this complicated subject. The events of every day serve to confirm the truth of his opinions respecting the English system, and the agitations which have prevailed throughout the country rendered the fulfilment of his predictions exceedingly probable.

In 1796, he published at Paris a 'Letter to General Washington.' The principal subject of this letter is the treaty which had recently been concluded between the United States and Great Britain. From the articles of the treaty, Mr. Paine contends, that those who concluded it had compromised the honor of America, and the safety of her commerce, from a disposition to crouch to the British minister. The cold neglect of Mr. Washington toward Mr. Paine during his imprisonment, forms likewise a prominent subject of the letter and but for this circumstance it is probable it would never have appeared. Notwithstanding the high opinion which Mr. Washington professed to entertain of his services in behalf of American independence, he abandoned him in a few years afterward to the mercy of Robespierre, and during his imprisonment of eleven months he never made a single effort to reclaim him. This was not the treatment which the author of 'Common Sense' deserved at the hands of Mr. Washington, either as a private individual, or as president of America. Exclusive of Mr. Paine's being a citizen of the United States, and of his being consequently entitled to the protection of the government, he had rendered America services which none but the ungrateful could forget; he had therefore no reason to expect that her chief magistrate would abandon him in the hour of difficulty. However deserving of our admiration some parts of General Washington's conduct may be, his behavior in this instance certainly reflects no honor upon his character.

From a variety of circumstances it appears that Mr. Paine regarded the United States as the land of his home. His spirit of universal philanthropy, his republican principles, and his resolution in attacking fraud and superstition, whether in politics or religion, rendered him in a great measure an inhabitant of the world, more than of any particular country; but notwithstanding these peculiarities of disposition, he had domestic feelings and local attachments which neither time nor distance could obliterate. During his residence in Europe, he always declared his intention of returning to America: the following extract from a letter of his to a female literary correspondent at New York, will show the affectionate regard which he constantly cherished for the safety and freedom of the country whose affairs were the means of first launching him into public life:—

'You touch me on a very tender point, when you say, *that my friends on your side of the water cannot be reconciled to the idea of my abandoning America even for my native England.* They are right. I had rather see my horse, Button, eating the grass of Bordentown, or Morrissania, than see all the pomp and show of Europe.

A thousand years hence, for I must indulge a few thoughts, perhaps in less, America may be what England now is. The innocence of her character, that won the hearts of all nations in her favor, may sound like a romance, and her inimitable virtue as if it had never been. The ruins of that liberty, which thousands bled to obtain, may just furnish materials for a village tale, or extort a sigh from rustic sensibility; while the fashionable of that day, enveloped in dissipation, shall deride the principle and deny the fact.

When we contemplate the fall of empires, and the extinction

of the nations of the ancient world, we see but little more to excite our regret than the mouldering ruins of pompous palaces, magnificent monuments, lofty pyramids, and walls and towers of the most costly workmanship: but when the empire of America shall fall, the subject for contemplative sorrow will be infinitely greater than crumbling brass or marble can inspire. It will not then be said, Here stood a temple of vast antiquity, here rose a Babel of invisible height, or there a palace of sumptuous extravagance; but here, ah! painful thought! the noblest work of human wisdom, the greatest scene of human glory, the fair cause of freedom, rose and fell! Read this, then ask if I forgot America.'

The name of the lady to whom the above was addressed, was Nicholson. She was afterward married to Colonel Few. Whether or not it was owing to Mr. Paine's opinions on religion I do not know, but on his return to America he was totally forsaken by her and her husband. When, however, Mr. Paine's dissolution was at hand, they sought his company, and Mrs. Few expressed a wish to renew their former friendship. But Mr. Paine, weak and debilitated as he was, refused to shake hands with her, and indignantly observed, 'You have neglected me, and I beg you will leave the room.'

In 1797, a society was formed of a number of persons in Paris, under the title of 'Theophilanthropists.' Of this society Paine was one of the principal promoters. Their objects were the propagation of morality and extinction of religious prejudices, and their faith the belief of one God. At one of their meetings Mr. Paine delivered a public discourse, in which he stated his reasons for rejecting the doctrines of atheism, which at that time prevailed in many parts of France.

This year he likewise published a 'Letter to the People of France, on the Events of the eighteenth Fructidor.' Of the merits or demerits of this pamphlet, I am unable to say anything as I have not been able to procure a copy. I believe it was never reprinted.

About the middle of the same year he also addressed a letter to Camille Jordan, one of the council of five hundred, respecting his report on the priests, public worship, and bells. I have only seen a mutilated copy of this production, but as far as I can judge from that, it deserves to be classed with the best works of the author. 'It is want of feeling,' says he, 'to talk of priests and bells, while so many infants are perishing in the hospitals, and aged and infirm poor in the streets from the want of necessaries. The abundance that France produces is sufficient for every want, if rightly applied; but priests and bells, like articles of luxury, ought to be the least articles of consideration.'

The publication of his deistical opinions certainly lost our author a great number of friends, and, it is possible, that this might be one of the causes of General Washington's indifference. The clear, open, and undisguised method in which he had contested established opinions, called forth the united indignation of the whole order of priesthood in England and America, and there was scarcely a house of devotion, in the old world or the new, which did not resound with their pious execrations. They witnessed with amazement and terror the immense circulation of the work, and they trembled at the possibility that men might assume sufficient courage to think for themselves. Thousands of persons who had never seen the book, and who knew nothing of its contents, except through the perverted medium of their spiritual teachers, rent the air with exclamations against the blasphemies of Thomas Paine, and to conclude these truly charitable proceedings, the English government called upon the public to condemn the work which they had suppressed by a legal prosecution.

Such are the means adopted by the professors of Christianity to suffocate inquiry, and to dispel the doubts of skepticism.

To the credit of mankind it ought to be observed, that the powers of the hierarchy are upon the decline. There was a time when Mr. Paine would have been roasted alive for daring to dispute the dogmas of the church, but the progress of science, and its handmaid, civilization, has softened the ferocity of human nature, and a somewhat milder punishment is now reserved for those who may question the divinity of the Christian religion. For this, however, we are not indebted either to the morality of the religion, or the piety of its professors—we owe it to the progress which mankind have made in freeing themselves from the profane and barbarous notions which such a system of belief is calculated to diffuse wherever it is tolerated."

Mr. Paine, it appears, lived long enough in France to become unpopular, at least for a time. His opposition to the dominant party of Robespiere, and to the death of the king of France, were the political offences which rendered him so. While his "Age of Reason," written in defence of deism, and for the express purpose of arresting the progress of atheism, as he himself informs us, still farther contributed to his unpopularity, for atheism and violence, although not necessarily connected, at one time prevailed; and during the reign of terror, and even after the death of Robespiere, men who were not of his party, nor intolerant democrats, assumed to be so, to avoid suspicion and death by the guillotine: these therefore dared not associate with Mr. Paine, who steadfastly adhered to his republican principles without cringing to an intolerant party. When Mr. Paine became unpopular he lived chiefly in retirement; and, though a member of the national assembly, he did not make himself prominent, as he could not sanction their proceedings, and opposition was useless, especially, as he did not speak the language fluently, and never in public. While Mr. Paine was unpopular in France, and when he had but few friends, he resided chiefly with Mr. Bonneville and family. Mr. Bonneville at that time edited a paper, was in good circumstances, and when Mr. Paine's remittances from this country were not regular, he cheerfully lent him money. This kindness, on the part of Bonneville, shown at a time when Mr. Paine most needed it, was not lost on him, for he was as grateful as generous, moral qualities always in the same ratio; and Mr. Paine had afterward an opportunity of returning this kindness; for, on the elevation of Bonaparte to supreme power, the press of Mr. Bonneville was stopped, and himself injured in his property. At this time Mr. Paine resolved to quit France, where liberty appeared hopelessly absorbed by the splendid military talents and achievements of Napoleon. Mr. Paine then offered an asylum to Mr. Bonneville and family in the United States, and this offer Mr. Bonneville accepted, and soon after Mr. Paine returned to this country. In 1802 Mr. Bonneville forwarded his wife and three sons, intending to follow them as soon as he could settle his affairs. Accident or change of purpose delayed his arrival till after Mr. Paine's death, and hence he became charged with the maintenance of Mrs. Bonneville and family (except the elder son, who returned to his father) till his death. To this subject we shall again refer in the fourth part of this life, especially as it afforded Cheetham the subject of a libel, of which he was convicted, after the death of Mr. Paine.

The social and moral character of Mr. Paine while in France appears to have been the same as in England, and as in this country during the revolution; yet Sherwin, in his life, seems to admit that at one period, when unpopular, he became intemperate. Joel Barlow, who certainly knew him well, partially admits the charge while he vindicates the general character of Mr. Paine, in a letter to Cheetham, which we shall extract. In spite of these admissions, and others, with various allusions from persons who knew something of him, we are sceptical of the fact, because we were nearly betrayed into an error on this subject, in relation to his course of life after his return to this country. The statement that Mr. Paine was intemperate was so commonly asserted, that we never contemplated looking for proof to the contrary, till this fact was forced upon us by the uniform testimony of his most intimate acquaintances; but as this subject relates to the fourth part of his history, we shall reserve it for its proper place. We introduced it merely to justify our scepticism in relation to his habits in France, when partially in seclusion. This doubt in us does not arise from any desire to screen Mr. Paine from any supposed blemish; for, if this were the fact, we feel more disposed to justify than to screen him. We know that he was not only temperate in after life, but even abstemious; and he would therefore stand as a monument of reform in old age, on a subject where reform is most uncommon at that period. Mr. Paine lived in an age when hospitality and excess were so identified that the one could not be shown without the other. In our boyish days bumpers were drank in good society, on public occasions; the toasts must go round, and the glasses *drained* in honor to the toast, and occasional excess, even when no public cause induced it, was only a proof of good fellowship. Nor would the host be satisfied that the guests had done him honor, if noisy mirth, excited by wine, did not finish the repast; while the guest did not scruple, on his next-day visit, to complain of present headache, and of double sight, and a staggering gait on the previous evening, as proofs of his good entertainment, and of the liberality of his friend and host. At that time Pitt was a *four-bottle* man, Fox, when in exertion, would drink wine from a great bowl, and the heir-apparent to the British crown might even go to greater excesses, surrounded by the brilliants of the nation; among whom Sheridan and Fox were not the least distinguished. If Mr. Paine, then, the companion of some of these men, had done as they did, he would only have been on a level with them, and to the *custom* of the times must the folly be ascribed. Since that age the custom has changed, bumpers are not insisted on in good society, except in song. A drained glass is not a *sine que non*. The host indeed spreads the table abundantly, but excess is not the fashion; each helps himself, and 'the flow of reason and wit, and innocent games, supply the place of boisterous mirth. The change is rational, but the present age must not condemn the past, for all *follow custom*. We feel then no disposition to screen Mr. Paine, but so many falsehoods have been told on this subject, that we honestly doubt various assertions unsupported by facts. Mr. Clio Rickman followed Mr. Paine to France, became again his companion, and parted with him on the shore when he finally left that country for this. We shall give that gentleman's account of Mr. Paine's habits in France, as far as he knew.

"Mr. Paine was acknowledged deputy for Calais, the 21st of September, 1792. In France, during the early part of the revolution, his time was almost wholly occupied as a deputy of the convention and as a member of the committee of constitution. His company was now coveted and sought after universally among every description of people, and by many who for some reasons never chose to avow it. With the Earl of Lauderdale, and Dr. Moore, whose company he was fond of, he dined every Friday, till Lord Gower's departure made it necessary for them to quit France, which was early in 1793.

About this period he removed from White's hotel to one near the Rue de Richelieu, where he was so plagued and interrupted by numerous visiters, and sometimes by adventurers, that in order to have some time to himself he appropriated two mornings in a week for his levee days.* To this indeed he was extremely averse, from the fuss and formality attending it, but he was nevertheless obliged to adopt it.

Annoyed and disconcerted with a life so contrary to his wishes and habits, and so inimical to his views, he retired to the Fauxbourg St. Dennis, where he occupied part of the hotel that Madame de Pompadour once resided in.

Among these adventurers was a person calling himself Major Lisle : Mr. Paine was at breakfast when he was announced ; he stated himself to be lately arrived from Ireland ; he was dressed in the Irish uniform, and wore a green cockade ; he appeared to be a well-informed man, and was gentlemanly in his manners, but extremely voluble. He ran over the number of sieges and battles he had been at, and ended with professing a zealous desire to serve the republic, wishing Mr. Paine to give him a letter of recommendation to the minister at war. Mr. Paine was extremely observing, shrewd, and cautious; he treated him with hospitality and politeness, and inquired after some of the leading characters in Ireland, with whom he found the major not at all acquainted ; he then recommended him to take the credentials of his services to the military committee, but declined every importunity to interfere himself. The adventurer turned out afterward to be the notorious Major Semple.

Here was a good garden well laid out, and here too our mutual friend Mr. Choppin occupied apartments; at this residence, which for a town one was very quiet, he lived a life of retirement and philosophical ease, while it was believed he was gone into the country for his health, which by this time indeed was much impaired by intense application to business, and by the anxious solicitude he felt for the welfare of public affairs.

Here with a chosen few he unbent himself; among whom were Brissot, the Marquis de Chatelet le Roi of the gallerie de honore, and an old friend of Dr. Franklin, Bançal, and sometimes General Miranda. His English associates were Christie and family, Mary Wolstonecraft, Mr. and Mrs. Stone, &c. Among his American friends were Capt. Imlay, Joel Barlow, &c., &c. To these parties the French inmates were generally invited.

It was about this time a gentleman at Paris thus writes of him to his friend: 'An English lady of our acquaintance, not less remarkable for her talents than for her elegance of manners, entreated me to contrive that she might have an interview with Mr. Paine. In consequence of this I invited him to dinner on a day when we were to be favored with her company. For above four hours he kept every one in astonishment and admiration of his memory, his keen observation of men and manners, his numberless anecdotes of the American Indians, of the American war, of Franklin, Washington, and even of his majesty, of whom he told several curious facts of humor and benevolence. His remarks on genius and taste can never be forgotten by those present.'"

The above extract is a part of Mr. Yorke's letter, published we believe in this country, but as that letter contains some falsehoods we have no confidence in it; for Mr. Yorke says Paine could repeat by heart anything he had written: and Sherwin repeats the statement. This is a mistake, as we are informed by Mr. John Fellows and others, his intimates. Mr. Paine would necessarily express himself nearly in the same style, on the same subject, because it was the most clear, the fewest words, and combined the greatest strength. Men who say the best thing first, can but repeat them on a future occasion. Mr. Clio Rickman goes on to remark:—

"He usually rose about seven, breakfasted with his friend Choppin, Johnson, and two or three other Englishmen, and a Monsieur La Borde, who had been an officer in the ci-devant garde du corps, an intolerable aristocrat, but whose skill in mechanics and geometry brought on a friendship between him and Paine; for the undaunted and distinguished ability and firmness with which he ever defended his own opinions when controverted, do not reflect higher honor upon him than that unbounded liberality toward the opinions of others which constituted such a prominent feature in his character, and which never suffered mere difference of sentiment, whether political or religious, to interrupt the harmonious intercourse of friendship, or impede the interchanges of knowledge and information.

After breakfast he usually strayed an hour or two in the garden, where he one morning pointed out the kind of spider whose web furnished him with the first idea of constructing his iron bridge; a fine model of which, in mahogany, is preserved at Paris.

The little happy circle who lived with him here will ever remember these days with delight: with these select friends he would talk of his boyish days, play at chess, whist, piquet, or cribbage, and enliven the moments by many interesting anecdotes: with these he would sport on the broad and fine gravel walk at the upper end of the garden, and then retire to his boudoir, where he was up to his knees in letters and papers of various descriptions. Here he remained till dinner-time; and unless he visited Brissot's family, or some particular friend in the evening, which was his frequent custom, he joined again the society of his favorites and fellow-boarders, with whom his conversation was often witty and cheerful, always acute and improving, but never frivolous.

Incorrupt, straightforward, and sincere, he pursued his political course in France, as everywhere else, let the government or clamor or faction of the day be what it might, with firmness, with clearness, and without a 'shadow of turning.'

In all Mr. Paine's inquiries and conversations he evinced the strongest attachment to the investigation of truth, and was always for going to the fountain-head for information. He often lamented we had no good history of America, and that the letters written by Columbus, the early navigators, and others, to the Spanish court, were inaccessible, and that many valuable documents, collected by Philip II, and deposited with the national archives at Simania, had not yet been promulgated. He used to speak highly of the sentimental parts of Raynal's History."

As farther illustration of the character of Mr. Paine while in France we shall now introduce the letter of Joel Barlow to Cheetham, when Cheetham was getting up the life of Paine, just after the death of the latter. He wrote for in information to various persons, suggesting what answers they should give by leading questions. These answers, if they suited his purpose, he published, if not, he suppressed them, or he took the liberty of publishing detached parts of what he had been told, or related direct falsehoods, as in the case of Mr. Jarvis, who has explicitly denied to us the words which Cheetham puts into his mouth in relation to Mr. Paine. Cheetham, among others, wrote to Mr. Barlow, and to him put such sort of questions as we have noticed. Mr. Barlow, in reply, states as follows:—

TO JAMES CHEETHAM.

"Sir : I have received your letter calling for information relative to the life of Thomas Paine. It appears to me that this is not the moment to publish the life of that man in this country. His own writings are his best life, and these are not read at present.

The greatest part of the readers in the United States will not be persuaded as long as their present feelings last, to consider him in any other light than as a drunkard and a deist. The writer of his life who should dwell on these topics, to the exclusion of the great and estimable traits of his real character, might, indeed, please the rabble of the age who do not know him ; the book might sell ; but it would only tend to render the truth more obscure, for the future biographer than it was before.

But if the present writer should give us Thomas Paine *complete* in all his character as one of the most benevolent and disinterested of mankind, endowed with the clearest perception, an uncommon share of original genius, and the greatest breadth of thought; if this piece of biography should analyze his literary labors, and rank him as he ought to be ranked among the brightest and most undeviating luminaries of the age in which he has lived—yet with a mind assailable by flattery, and receiving through that weak side a tincture of vanity which he was too proud to conceal; with a mind, though strong enough to bear him up, and to rise elastic under the heaviest load of oppression, yet unable to endure the contempt of his former friends and fellow-laborers, the rulers of the country that had received his first and greatest services— a mind incapable of looking down with serene compassion, as it ought, on the rude scoffs of their imitators, a new generation that knows him not; a mind that shrinks from their society, and unhappily seeks refuge in low company, or looks for consolation in the sordid, solitary bottle, till it sinks at last so far below its native elevation as to lose all respect for itself, and to forfeit that of his best friends, disposing these friends almost to join with his enemies, and wish, though from different motives, that he would haste to hide himself in the grave—if you are disposed and prepared to write his life, *thus entire*, to fill up the picture to which these hasty strokes of outline give but a rude sketch with great vacuities, your book may be a useful one for another age, but it will not be relished, nor scarcely tolerated in this.

The biographer of Thomas Paine should not forget his mathematical acquirements, and his mechanical genius. His invention of the *iron bridge*, which led him to Europe in the year 1787, has procured him a great reputation in that branch of science, in France and England, in both which countries his bridge has been adopted in many instances, and is now much in use.

You ask whether he took an oath of allegiance to France. Doubtless, the qualification to be a member of the convention required an oath of fidelity to that country, but involved in it no abjuration of his fidelity to this. He was made a French citizen by the same decree with Washington, Hamilton, Priestley, and Sir James Mackintosh.

What Mr. M——— has told you relative to the circumstances of his arrestation by order of Robespierre, is erroneous, at least in one point. Paine did not lodge at the house where he was arrested, but had been dining there with some Americans, of whom Mr. M——— may have been one. I never heard before, that Paine was intoxicated that night. Indeed the officers brought him directly to my house, which was two miles from his lodgings, and about as much from the place where he had been dining. He was not intoxicated when they came to me. Their object was to get me to go and assist them to examine Paine's papers. It employed us the rest of that night, and the whole of the next day at Paine's lodgings; and he was not committed to prison till the next evening.

You ask what company he kept—he always frequented the best, both in England and France, till he became the object of calumny in certain American papers (echoes of the English court papers), for his adherence to what he thought the cause of liberty in France, till he conceived himself neglected and despised by his former friends in the United States. From that moment he gave himself very much to drink, and, consequently, to companions less worthy of his better days.

It is said he was always a peevish inmate—this is possible. So was Lawrence Sterne, so was Torquato Tasso, so was J. J. Rousseau; but Thomas Paine, as a visiting acquaintance and as a literary friend, the only points of view in which I knew him, was one of the most instructive men I ever have known. He had a surprising memory and brilliant fancy; his mind was a storehouse of facts and useful observations; he was full of lively anecdote, and ingenious original, pertinent remark upon almost every subject.

He was always charitable to the poor beyond his means, a sure protector and friend to all Americans in distress that he found in foreign countries. And he had frequent occasions to exert his influence in protecting them during the revolution in France. His writings will answer for his patriotism, and his entire devotion to what he conceived to be the best interest and happiness of mankind.*

This, sir, is all I have to remark on the subject you mention. Now I have only one request to make, and that would doubtless seem impertinent, were you not the editor of a newspaper ; it is, that you will not publish my letter, nor permit a copy of it to be taken.

I am, sir, &c.,
Joel Barlow.

Kalorama, *August* 11, 1809."

Mr. Barlow was not always so candid. He has published a poem on the revolution, in which he does not mention Mr. Paine, whose " Common Sense " produced the declaration of independence, and who, throughout the contest, did more toward producing unanimity and funds (the two essentials in war) than any other man. We have now in our house a compact history of the revolution, by S. F. Wilson, published in Baltimore, in which the same injustice is done to Mr. Paine, for he scarcely occupies *one line* in the history, although " *political writings*," without giving a name, are referred to, as being very efficacious. Paul Allen in a larger work does him the same injustice. In a biography of distinguished American characters, by Colonel Knapp, published by Conner, a short notice was inserted of Mr. Paine, being a *republication of an English biography*. This Mr. Conner was obliged to alter, after stereotyping, at the instigation of Collins and Hanna, and other booksellers, not because the facts and sentiments were incorrect, but because the *praise* of Mr. Paine would spoil the sale of the book. These facts we learn from Mr. John Fellows and Mr. Conner. In the case of Joel Barlow, there was no personal objection, but he knew that prejudices existed against Mr. Paine, and he succumbed to public feeling; and such we believe the case with other writers.

---

* Mr. Barlow might have added, in regard to Mr. Paine's religion, that as it was the religion of most of the men of science of the present age, and probably of three fourths of those of the last, there could be no just reason for making it an exception in his character.

While Mr. Paine was in France, and partly detached from politics, in consequence of imprisonment and the violence of party, he was not idle. Mr. Yorke remarks, in his letter published in Sherwin's Life:—

"In showing me one day the beautiful models of two bridges he had devised, he observed that Dr. Franklin once told him, that 'books are written to please, houses built for great men, churches for priests, but no bridge for the people.' These models exhibit an extraordinary degree, not only of skill, but of taste, in mechanics; and are wrought with extreme delicacy, entirely by his own hands. The largest is nearly four feet in length; the iron works, the chains, and every other article belonging to it, were forged and manufactured by himself. It is intended as the model of a bridge, which is to be constructed across the Delaware, extending 480 feet with only *one arch*. The other is to be erected over a lesser river, whose name I forget, and is likewise a single arch, and of his own workmanship, excepting the chains, which instead of iron, are cut out of pasteboard, by the fair hand of his correspondent, the 'Little Corner of the World,' whose indefatigable perseverance is extraordinary. He was offered three thousand pounds for these models, and refused it. The iron bars, which I before mentioned that I noticed in a corner of his room, were also forged by himself, as the model of a crane, of a new description. He put them together, and exhibited the power of the lever, to a most surprising degree."

"Mr. Yorke in the above extract states the correspondence between Lady Smith and Mr. Paine to have been extremely beautiful and interesting; as a proof of this, the following specimen is subjoined:—

'FROM "THE CASTLE IN AIR," TO THE ' LITTLE CORNER OF THE WORLD."

In the region of clouds where the whirlwinds arise,
  My castle of fancy was built;
The turrets reflected the blue of the skies,
  And the windows with sun-beams were gilt.

The rainbow sometimes, in its beautiful state,
  Enamelled the mansion around,
And the figures that fancy in clouds can create,
  Supplied me with gardens and ground.

I had grottoes and fountains and orange tree groves,
  I had all that enchantment has told;
I had sweet shady walks for the gods and their loves,
  I had mountains of coral and gold.

But a storm that I felt not, had risen and rolled,
  While wrapt in a slumber I lay:
And when I looked out in the morning, behold!
  My castle was carried away.

> It passed over rivers, and valleys, and groves—
>   The world, it was all in my view—
> I thought of my friends, of their fates, of their loves,
>   And often, full often, of you.
>
> At length it came over a beautiful scene,
>   That nature in silence had made :
> The place was but small—but 't was sweetly serene,
>   And chequered with sunshine and shade.
>
> I gazed and I envied with painful good will,
>   And grew tired of my seat in the air :
> When all of a sudden my castle stood still,
>   As if some attraction was there.
>
> Like a lark from the sky it came fluttering down,
>   And placed me exactly in view—
> When who should I meet, in this charming retreat,
>   This corner of calmness—but you.
>
> Delighted to find you in honor and ease,
>   I felt no more sorrow nor pain ;
> And the wind coming fair, I ascended the breeze,
>   And went back with my castle again.'

The above was written during his residence in Paris. Mr. Paine had very early in life corresponded with the lady to whom it was addressed, his letters, like the foregoing, being dated from the 'Castle in the Air,' and hers from the 'Little Corner of the World.' For reasons which he knew not, their intercourse was suddenly suspended, and for some time he believed his friend in obscurity and distress. Many years afterward, he met her unexpectedly at Paris, in the most affluent circumstances, and married to Sir Robert Smith.

In Mr. Yorke's Letters there is another piece, on *forgetfulness*. This is replete with the most beautiful imagery, but Mr. Yorke, from some motive which I cannot discover, has cancelled so great a part of it, that much of the interest is lost which it would otherwise possess.

As the letter of Mr. Jefferson which Mr. Yorke alludes to, shows the high opinion which that gentleman entertained of our author's services, and his wish to accommodate him by every possible kindness, I here subjoin a copy of it :—

'You express a wish in your letter to return to America by a national ship ; Mr. Dawson, who brings over the treaty, and who will present you with this letter, is charged with orders to the captain of the Maryland to receive and accommodate you back, if you can be ready to depart at such a short warning. You will in general find us returned to sentiments worthy of former times ; in these it will be your glory to have steadily labored, and with as much effect as any man living. That you may live long to continue your useful labors, and reap the reward in the thankfulness of nations, is my sincere prayer. Accept the assurances of my high esteem, and affectionate attachment.
                                    THOMAS JEFFERSON.'

Soon after Mr. Paine's release from the Luxembourg, it appears he made an effort to return to America, but he found the obstacles more numerous than he expected. The misconduct of Mr. Monroe's predecessor had rendered his reception in France a very unpleasant one, and as soon as he had effected a good understanding with the government of that country, he wished to transmit some despatches to America, by a person with whom he could likewise confide a verbal communication, and he fixed upon Mr. Paine. For this purpose he applied to the committee of public safety for a passport, but as Mr. Paine had been voted again into the convention, it was only the convention who could grant the passport, and as an application to them would have made his departure publicly known, he was obliged to sustain the disappointment, and Mr. Monroe to lose the opportunity.

When Mr. Monroe left France, our author was to have accompanied him, but owing to some unforeseen circumstances he was unable to complete his arrangements for that purpose. It was fortunate he could not, for the vessel in which the minister returned was boarded by a British frigate in her passage, and every part of her searched, down even to the hold, for Thomas Paine. He then went to Havre, thinking that he should be able to embark there without its being known, but he found that several British frigates were cruising in sight of the port, and he thereupon returned to Paris. Seeing himself cut off from every opportunity that was within his power to command, he wrote to Mr. Jefferson requesting that if the fate of the election should put him in the chair of the presidency, and he should have occasion to send a frigate to France, he would give him the opportunity of returning by it. This application produced an answer from Mr. Jefferson of which the letter before cited is a copy. He did not, however, go by this vessel, the notice being too short. He next agreed to embark with Commodore Barney, in a vessel he had engaged, but in this, as in some of the former cases, the protecting hand of Providence was very visible, he was accidently detained beyond the time, and the vessel sunk at sea. Such a multitude of difficulties and narrow escapes were perhaps never concentrated together in the execution of so simple a project. He finally embarked from Havre on the 1st of September, and arrived at Baltimore on the 30th of October, 1802."

PART IV.

FROM THE ARRIVAL OF MR. PAINE IN BALTIMORE, OCTOBER 30, 1802, TO HIS DEATH IN 1809.

The most interesting period of Mr. Paine's life has necessarily already been given. He was now an old man, between sixty and seventy, yet vigorous, with his mental faculties unimpaired. His strong desire to end his days in the United States was beautifully and pathetically expressed to a lady, in a letter from France, a few days before his arrival. This we have already given, page 127. The reception of Mr. Paine in the United States was such as might have been expected from his fame and independent course. In a letter to his friend Clio Rickman he thus expresses himself:—

"My dear friend: Mr. Monroe, who is appointed minister extraordinary to France, takes charge of this, to be delivered to Mr. Este, banker in Paris, to be forwarded to you.

I arrived at Baltimore 30th October, and you can have no idea of the agitation which my arrival occasioned. From New Hampshire to Georgia (an extent of 1500 miles), every newspaper was filled with applause or abuse.

My property in this country has been taken care of by my friends, and is now worth six thousand pounds sterling; which put in the funds will bring me £400 sterling a year.

Remember me in friendship and affection to your wife and family, and in the circle of our friends.
Yours in friendship,
Thomas Paine."

What course he meant to pursue in America his own words will best tell, and best characterize his sentiments and principles; they are these:—

"As this letter is intended to announce my arrival to my friends, and my enemies if I have any, for I ought to have none in America, and as introductory to others that will occasionally follow, I shall close it by detailing the line of conduct I shall pursue.

I have no occasion to ask, nor do I intend to accept, any place or office in the government.

There is none it could give me that would in any way be equal to the profits I could make as an author (for I have an established fame in the literary world) could I reconcile it to my principles to make money by my politics or religion; I must be in everything as I have ever been, a disinterested volunteer : my proper sphere of action is on the common floor of citizenship, and to honest men I give my hand and my heart freely.

I have some manuscript works to publish, of which I shall give proper notice, and some mechanical affairs to bring forward, that will employ all my leisure time.

I shall continue these letters as I see occasion, and as to the low party prints that choose to abuse me, they are welcome; I shall not descend to answer them. I have been too much used to such common stuff to take any notice of it.

THOMAS PAINE.

CITY OF WASHINGTON."

Mr. Paine did not remain long at Baltimore, but while there the following characteristic circumstance occurred :—

"Passing through Baltimore, he was accosted by the Rev. Mr. Hargrove, minister of a new sect, called the New Jerusalemites. 'You are Mr. Paine,' said Mr. Hargrove. 'Yes.' 'My name is Hargrove, sir; I am minister of the New Jerusalem church here. We, sir, explain the Scripture in its true meaning. The key has been lost above four thousand years, and we have found it.' 'Then,' said Paine, drily, 'it must have been very rusty.'

Mr. Paine visited Washington, and was kindly received by Jefferson, then president; indeed this gentleman kept up a constant correspondence with him to the day of his death. He had invited him to return to the United States, had sent out a ship for him, and on being asked if he had done so, he replied, "I have, and when he arrives, if there be an office in my gift, suitable for him to fill, I will give it to him; I will never abandon old friends to make room for new ones." Mr. Paine, it appears, had resolved not to take office, his wants were moderate and his means sufficient. Mr. Paine visited the heads of the departments, and the various leading political characters, by whom he was received with pleasure, and remembered with gratitude, not, however, to be depended on when such remembrances came in contact with their popularity.

Soon after Mr. Paine came to New York, and put up at the City hotel, then Lovett's hotel, where Grant Thorburn, well known in New York, says, in a pamphlet before noticed, that he visited him, introduced himself, shook hands with him, declared that his only object in thus visiting Mr. Paine was to *see* the man who had written " Common Sense," and was so much talked about; and having gratified his curiosity, as he says, he abruptly retired, to the no small amusement of the party. Thorburn had formerly adopted Mr. Paine's principles, but at this time he was a professor of religion, and held some office in a baptist church, the members of which, hearing that Mr. Grant Thorburn had shaken hands with Thomas Paine, thought proper to suspend him from the church on that account; for this reason we have introduced the anecdote, as it explains the situation of all the friends of Mr. Paine, who were connected with churches, either from principle or policy.

While Mr. Paine was at Lovett's hotel, in spite of the influence of the church, he was honored with a public dinner by a respectable and numerous party, and his after-enemy, Cheetham, then editor of a daily paper, the organ of the democratic party, was particularly active in making the arrangements. Notwithstanding this public declaration in favor of Mr. Paine, he was not popular; the church feared him and had set their curse upon him; children had been taught to lisp his name in connexion with blasphemy; and those political leaders who sought after place, without regarding the means to be employed, and who needed the suffrages of the pious, and above all feared their united opposition, shunned the company of Mr. Paine as something contaminating. The people were deceived by the church, and those who knew better wanted the honesty to stem the torrent. Jefferson, Clinton, the mayor of New York, and a number of others, high in politics, literature, and situation in life, were honorable exceptions; while the independence of Mr. Paine would not allow him to conceal his principles or conform in practices which involved even a portion of hypocrisy. On a morning visit to Dr. Mitchill, in company with Mr. John Fellows, the latter reminded Mr. Paine, while in a gig, before they reached the doctor, that Mr. Paine had a morning gown on; Mr. Paine replied, "Let those dress who need it." Cheetham has said much about the slovenly habits and appearance of Mr. Paine. Mr. Fellows, who knew him well from his first return to this country till his death, denies the whole of it. He remarks that he was careless of his appearance (as the above little anecdote shows), but always cleanly and decent; and, as we before remarked, that he never saw him disguised in liquor but once, when he had been to a dinner-party, and that he was then only excited. This opinion we find uniformly supported by every credible person who knew him.

The partial desertion of Mr. Paine, as a matter of policy, by many of the prominent leading political characters, opened a way to others of less influence in society, but more fearless of public opinion; and some of these, with an indiscreet zeal, thrust themselves upon Mr. Paine, and claimed a sort of championship in his support. At this time Mr. Carver introduced himself to Mr. Paine, as a fellow-townsman, who, when a boy, remembered the fame of the latter, at Lewes, in Sussex. Mr. Paine, too, probably, remembered him, for Carver had sometimes saddled his horse, and could remind him of these services and former times. Mr. Carver was at this period a respectable tradesman, a blacksmith and veterinary surgeon. He had a comfortable home, was liberal, and kept a horse and chaise; but, above all, he was honest, independent, and openly avowed the opinions, political and theological, of Mr. Paine. With him Mr. Paine consented to live till he went to his farm at New Rochelle; and thus he became a guest, and afterward a boarder and lodger of a man who, without meaning it, did his memory a great injustice, by becoming the tool of Cheetham in a fit of anger.

Mrs. Bonneville and her three sons soon after arrived from France, on invitation from Mr. Paine to Mr. Bonneville and the whole family, as mentioned in the introduction to this life. Mr. Paine, who was simple in his habits, indeed economical, offered Mrs. Bonneville his small farm at Bordentown, where he wished to establish her in a school; but this employment did not suit the habits or taste of this lady, and thus the expense of herself and family fell entirely on Mr. Paine. He retired to New Rochelle, and boarded with Purdy, who lived on Paine's farm. Madam Bonneville, however, preferred New York, where she occasionally taught French, while the two boys were sent to school at New Rochelle by Mr. Paine; the eldest, a youth of fourteen, returned to France. Mr. Paine was godfather to one of the others, who had been named after him. He now divided his time between New York and New Rochelle, boarding in various places, and sometimes living on his farm.

Cheetham has represented Mr. Paine at this period, as disgustingly dirty, drunken, ill-tempered, and quarrelsome, and with much impudence he has referred to living characters as proofs, and thus he gives to his falsehoods the appearance of truth; while a portion of the clergy, eager to believe what they wished to be true, have propagated these falsehoods with the utmost zeal. We are, however, fortunate in being acquainted with those who were about him at this time, and with some of those to whom Cheetham refers; and these latter do not hesitate to blast the memory of this writer of Paine's life as a deliberate falsifier, and as an unprincipled man. Both Carver and Mr. Jarvis, the celebrated painter, thus speak of Cheetham, and yet he has had the impudence to refer to them for events as facts which he knew to be fabricated. At this time, 1803 and 1804, when Mr. Paine was backward and forward, from New York to New Rochelle, he resided for several weeks at the private house of Captain Pelton, who also kept the store at New Rochelle. He resided also for two months in the winter with Mr. Staple, at New Rochelle. Mr. D. Burger, the brother-in-law of Mr. Staple, was the clerk to Captain Pelton, and when Mr. Paine was rather poorly, he drove him in a gig daily about the neighborhood. He, too, supplied Mr. Paine with all the liquor he took, which was one quart of rum in a week, to serve himself and visiters. Mr. Burger[*] is well known to us, he has since lived for many years in New York, as a watch and clock-maker, and for

[*] This gentleman is since dead, but his eldest son lives and remembers the statement of his father.

some time he had the care of the public clocks; his veracity is not disputed.' He describes Mr. Paine as really abstemious, and when pressed to drink by those on whom he called during his rides, he usually refused with great firmness, but politely. In one of these rides he was met by De Witt Clinton, and their mutual greetings were extremely hearty. Mr. Paine at this time was the reverse of morose, and though careless in his dress and prodigal of his snuff, he was always clean and well clothed. Mr. Burger describes him as familiar even with children, and humane to animals, occasionally sitting by the store, playing with the neighboring children, and communicating a friendly pat, even to a passing dog, assuring him he would not see him hurt. Such were the simple habits of the man, described to be wallowing in filth, drunkenness, and brutality. At the time of Mr. Paine's residence at his farm, Mr. Ward, now a coffee-roaster in Gold street, New York, and an assistant alderman, was then a little boy and residing about Rochelle. He remembers the impressions his mother and some religious people made on him by speaking of *Tom* Paine, so that he concluded *Tom* Paine must be a very bad and brutal man. Some of his elder companions proposed going into Mr. Paine's orchard to obtain some fruit, and he, out of fear, kept at a distance behind, till he beheld, to his surprise, Mr. Paine come out and assist the boys in getting apples, patting one on the head and caressing another, and directing them where to get the best. He then advanced and received his share of encouragement, and the impression this kindness made on him determined him at a very early period to examine his writings. His mother at first took the books from him, but at a later period restored them to him, observing that he was then of an age to judge for himself; perhaps she had herself been gradually undeceived, both as to his character and writings.

In 1804, Mr. Purdy having left his farm, Mr. Paine hired one Derick to cultivate it, when he and the family of the Bonnevilles boarded for some time at Mr. James Wilburn's, in Gold street. At this period Mr. John Fellows, still living in New York, and respected as a good citizen, boarded at the same house, and testifies to the propriety both of Mr. Paine's and Madame Bonneville's conduct. Mr. Paine's notions of economy did not however accord with those of Madame Bonneville. She was constantly incurring expenses which he deemed unnecessary, while she, relying upon the protection which he had promised both her and her husband, did not scruple to send bills in to him which he had not sanctioned. One of these was presented by Mr. Wilburn, for board to the amount of thirty-five dollars, which she had incurred beyond what he had sanctioned. This demand Mr. Paine resisted, perhaps to check Mrs. Bonneville, and make her either content with a simple competence at his farm in Bordentown, or with him at Rochelle, or that she should by industry acquire the means of a more ample expenditure. The action was brought, and Mr. Fellows was a witness; but the plaintiff was nonsuited, for the debt had been incurred without Mr. Paine's consent. No sooner, however, was the trial ended in the favor of Mr. Paine than he paid Mr. Wilburn the money; thus justifying the view we have taken of this subject. Honorable and liberal as this transaction is to Mr. Paine, Cheetham, and after him Mr. Paine's enemies, have retailed this story as if it were to his discredit. There is no reconciling tastes or standards of expenditure. Madame Bonneville's was probably too high to be prudent. Taste is a gift of nature, but partly depending on education. A difference of tastes, where two persons are interested, will always lead to divisions, and Madame Bonneville does not seem to have readily yielded, or to have been very scrupulous as to the means she employed. On one occasion, as we learn from Mr. Carver, and as Cheetham has expressed in a note (if such authority can be relied on),

"Before his return to the city, Madame Bonneville paid him a visit, and arrived just at candle-light. She told him she had an order which she wished him to sign, for clothing for herself and the children, who were all in fact nearly naked. She presented the order. Paine said, 'I'll put it in my pocket and read it in the morning.'—'No,' said she, 'you must sign it to-night: I want to return and get the things to-morrow.'—'I cannot read in the night, I'll keep it till morning.'—'Then,' said Madame Bonneville, with some temper, 'if you won't read it to-night, give it me back.' Paine resisted all her importunities: he kept the paper until the morning, when he found, that instead of an order for clothing, it was a bond, duly drawn, for seven hundred pounds. Quite enraged, he went to Mrs. Dean's and told her the story, by whom, and by Mr. Carver, it is mentioned to me."

In these circumstances Madame Bonneville was sometimes left to want what she thought comforts, yet it does not appear that they had any serious quarrels, although these differences interrupted that cordial intimacy which both perhaps expected. Yet, at his death, we shall find he left her, her husband, and family, the bulk of his property, which was then very considerable.

During this time Mr. Paine was not idle, he had generally some work on politics, science, or literature, on hand. He mixed a little too with party politics, communicated with some papers and periodicals, and, when Cheetham deserted the democratic cause, he lashed him with the severity of party spirit, but not unjustly; and hence the revenge which Cheetham afterward took. Mr. Paine now, too, published many little things which had been written long before for amusement when in France or in England. One of these was a piece of poetry in the style of "Chevy Chase," entitled, "The Strange Story of Korah, Dathan, and Abiram," perhaps the severest thing ever written upon tythes. In 1804 he published an essay on the invasion of England, and a treatise on gun-boats, full of valuable maritime information; and, in 1805, a treatise on the yellow fever, and suggests modes of prevention, especially in the improvement of the docks, so as to favor cleanliness. He had now been residing for some time at New Rochelle, when Mr. Carver rode out to see him, and in his zeal urged him to come into the city to oblige his friends, and offered him a room in his house. Mr. Paine consented, and thus again became an inmate with Mr. Carver, without any engagement as to terms, an error extremely injurious in its consequence. Mr. Paine lived with the family, and occasionally made purchases for them, thus complicating the accounts. While he thus resided in Cedar street, with Mr. Carver, his friend, Elihu Palmer, with his wife, boarded in the same street, and within sight of Mrs. Burtsell's; him Mr. Paine visited daily, and when Mr. Paine was seized with an epileptic fit, and fell down stairs, Mrs. Palmer attended on him. The attendance which he thus required, when ill, still farther served to complicate the accounts between him and Mr. Carver. Mrs. Burtsell, still living in Cedar street, speaks with enthusiasm of the agreeable manners of Mr. Paine. She declares she never saw him intoxicated, though he was daily in her house. By the advice of a medical man Mr. Paine now left Mr. Carver's, and lived in Church street with Mr. Jarvis, the celebrated painter, still living.* Here he soon recovered, and he and Mr. Jarvis became good companions; the one the greatest wit of the age, and the other, though now an old man, not deficient in sprightly thoughts or conversation, and abounding in information. Mr. Jarvis still speaks of their agreeable companionship with much gust, and relates a number of anecdotes highly characteristic; and he positively denies to us the language ascribed to him by Cheetham. As Mr. Jarvis was at this time in good circumstances, and received Mr. Paine as a companion, the Cheetham stories of Mr. Paine's dirtiness kill themselves, for it is absurd to suppose Mr. Jarvis would have had such a companion. The following are among the anecdotes related by Mr. Jarvis in relation to Mr. Paine:—

"He usually took a nap after dinner, and would not be disturbed let who would call to see him. One afternoon, a very old lady, dressed in a large scarlet cloak, knocked at the door, and inquired for Thomas Paine. Mr. Jarvis told her he was asleep. 'I am very sorry,' she said, 'for that, for I want to see him very particularly.' Thinking it a pity to make an old woman call twice, Mr. Jarvis took her into Paine's bed-room and waked him. He rose upon one elbow, and then, with an expression of eye that staggered the old woman back a step or two, he asked—'What do you want?'—'Is your name Paine?'—'Yes,' Well then, I come from Almighty God, to tell you, that if you do not repent of your sins and believe in our blessed Savior Jesus Christ, you will be damned, and'——— 'Poh, poh, it is not true. You were not sent with such an impertinent message. Jarvis, make her go away. Pshaw, he would not send such a foolish ugly old woman, as you about with his messages. Go away. Go back. Shut the door.' The old lady raised both her hands, kept them so, and without saying another word, walked away in mute astonishment."

Died since the manuscript was written.

Mr. Paine still visited New Rochelle, while ostensibly with Mr. Jarvis. He had left Mr. Carver without any direct settlement of accounts. Mr. Carver's circumstances had now altered from some family affairs which he could not control, and altered circumstances produced altered feelings. When Mr. Carver was in good circumstances, he thought only of the honor and pleasure of having Mr. Paine under the same roof with him, the terms of his board were a secondary consideration. We have already remarked that no agreement was made. Now in altered circumstances, of which Mr. Paine does not appear to be aware, his charge was an object. In the first note from Carver to Mr. Paine on this subject, published by Cheetham, Mr. Carver uses this expression, " *I have made a calculation of my expenditures on your account, the last time you were at my house, and find they amount to one hundred and fifty or sixty dollars.*" He charges for twenty-two weeks for Mr. Paine and twelve for Mrs. Palmer, who assisted him in his illness; and he takes no notice of the few things Mr. Paine had purchased. He reminds Mr. Paine of his riches, and concludes by saying that he should not ask *one cent* if he could afford it. Mr. Paine at this time did not expect a long life. The fit and subsequent sickness had shaken his constitution. He had put Mr. Carver down in his will for a handsome sum; and from the manner of the invitation and supposed circumstances of Mr. Carver, perhaps he never expected a formal charge. At any rate, Mr. Paine was indignant at this charge, which he considered unjust, and proposed paying the money down at once, and having nothing more to do with him. This he was prevented from doing by Mr. John Fellows, who was present when the demand was made by Mr. Carver's boy. Mr. Fellows and Mr. Morton, the friends of Mr. Paine, considered the charge too high; and these finally settled the account upon what they considered just principles. The charge might have been perfectly just, as, in Mr. Carver's altered circumstances, he might have remembered former hospitalities, for he refers to them in one of his letters. There might have been but a trifling difference had Mr. Paine made up the account. The fault was, not having a definite agreement; and this foolish affair produced a quarrel. Mr. Paine replied to this note in an angry manner to Mr. Carver, and Carver, remarkable for his boldness, replied in the severest terms possible, giving the very worst construction to every event concerning Mr. Paine he could think of. His epileptic fit he insinuates was drunkenness; and he *infers* an improper connexion with Madame Bonneville, merely however in an inuendo, with a sarcastic remark about young Thomas, the godson, being like Mr. Paine. He refers to his trouble when Mr. Paine was sick, and reminds him of the quantity of water he procured for his personal cleanliness. This personal quarrel was soon forgotten, and the angry letters should have been destroyed; but both letters had been read in public by some zealous friends, and copies were taken. They ought to have been obliterated; but after Mr. Paine's death, in 1809, Cheetham sought out Mr. Carver, obtained a copy, deceived him as to his intention and the nature of his publication, and published these letters against Carver's will. The mere publication of these letters would avail nothing among a candid people; they were avowedly written in anger, but there were persons who *wished* to believe. Even among such these angry letters could avail but little; but Mr. Cheetham, with fiendish ingenuity, not only inserted these letters, but in other parts of his life, presuming on their publication, boldly asserts as facts what Carver had only insinuated, leaving the impression that these letters are *additional* confirmations of the facts, instead of the *only* foundation for such reports. Thus he directly charges Mr. Paine with adultery with Madame Bonneville. He charges him with drunkenness, coarseness, and dirtiness directly, which are only insinuated or implied in Carver's angry letters. In the first charge Mrs. Bonneville was implicated, and she very properly prosecuted Cheetham. On the trial, which we have read, he could only bring Mr. Carver as witness, and Mr. Carver could only say what he had before written, and his counsel was obliged to withdraw the justification and acknowledge that the accusation was a FALSE and MALICIOUS libel. The other charges applied to Mr. Paine *only*, and he was dead and could not prosecute. We, after diligent inquiry, believe them also *false* and malicious, and that they have no other foundation than the angry letter of Mr. Carver, and the malicious revengeful spirit of Cheetham; for this reason we have detailed this foolish quarrel.

We have now approached the year 1807, the seventieth of Mr. Paine's life, and two years only before his death. In the spring of this year he removed to Broome street, at one Mr. Hitt's, a baker; here he lived some time; and while in Broome street he published an examination of the passages in the New Testament, quoted from the Old, and called "Prophesies of Jesus Christ," &c. This work shows all the acumen of his former works; it marks the most laborious examination of the Scriptures. The Bible of Mr. Paine had been most carefully read, it was marked all over; indeed, no book had been read by him more than that.

Mr. Paine lived successively in Partition street and afterward in Greenwich street, near the state-prison; but his sickness increased on him, and boarding-house attention was scarcely sufficient. Madame Bonneville took a small house for him, May, 1809, in Columbia*street, and here she attended on him till his death. Mr. Paine was perfectly conscious of his approaching dissolution, and some time before he wished to arrange for his burial in the quakers' burying-ground, as the least obnoxious to his feelings; and for this purpose he applied to Mr. Willit Hicks, a preacher and influential member of that body, as his father had been of that persuasion. Mr. Hicks saw no objection, he had no prejudice on his own account, and brought this subject before the church; and to their discredit they denied the request.

While Mr. Paine was at Mr. Jarvis's he seemed to foresee what would be the scene of his death-bed, and what some fanatical persons would attempt after his death. With that shrewdness of judgment which he always possessed, and which displayed itself during the revolution, by his instantly anticipating what the British government would do, he was enabled to prepare the people for the various proclamations and deceptive propositions before they arrived; nay, some of these appeared but a repetition of Paine's statements. The consequence was, they lost their effect, as far as his influence went. So, on this occasion, he foretold that when on a sick bed attempts would be made to convert him to Christianity,

* Now Grove street.

or to make it appear that he was converted; and that after his death reports would be spread of his death-bed repentance, of his unbelief; then, appealing to Mr. Jarvis, he observed, "Now I am in health, and in perfect soundness of mind; now is the time to express my opinion." And thus having called Mr. Jarvis to witness, he solemnly repeated his belief in his already written opinions.

What Mr. Paine had foreseen came to pass. As his illness assumed a fatal appearance he was visited by men and women who obtruded upon his last moments their religious principles, either from christian simplicity and ignorant sincerity, and, most likely, in some of them, from hypocrisy; in the hopes of being able to contort some of his answers into a manifestation of fear or conversion, or to give them an opportunity of inventing a recantation for him. This is by no means an uncharitable supposition from the facts which followed his death, when the second part of Mr. Paine's prophesy was fulfilled by an invention of the kind, and by pious falsehoods promulgated to willing ears. The position is not uncharitable, for the dying moments of Voltaire have been misrepresented by similar pious frauds. Nor are these the only instances where base falsehoods have been perpetrated in the name of God for a supposed pious purpose. Even the judge, who afterward sentenced Cheetham for a false and malicious libel on the memory of Mr. Paine and Madame Bonneville, declared Cheetham's life a *useful* book, because it tended to suppress the influence of Mr. Paine's writings. After these and other proofs of lying, for the sake of God, in remembrance too of the counterpart, we think we are justified in assuming that some of the visiters were hypocrites, and came there to distort his answers, or as an excuse for invention, than for any reasonable hope of converting and saving his soul. Among the most prominent and zealous visiters of Mr. Paine in his last days were the Rev. Mr. Milledollar, a presbyterian clergyman, and the Rev. Mr. Cunningham, about a fortnight before Mr. Paine's death. This latter gentleman told Paine that they visited him as friends and neighbors, and added, "You have now a full view of death, you cannot live long, and whosoever does not believe in Jesus Christ will assuredly be damned." Mr. Paine replied, "Let me have none of your popish stuff. Get away with you. Good morning, good morning." Mr. Milledollar attempted to address him, but was interrupted by Mr. Paine; and when they were gone, he said to Mrs. Hedden, his housekeeper, "Don't let'em come here again, they trouble me." In spite of Mr. Paine's declaration these gentlemen again attempted to obtrude themselves upon him, but they were refused admittance, as directed, by Mrs. Hedden, who piously added, "If God does not change his mind, she was sure no human power could."

Mr. Willit Hicks, himself a preacher, a most respectable member of the friends, and a man of high standing in the community, yet alive, was then a neighbor of Mr. Paine, and in his last illness visited him daily, and on the day of his death. This gentleman, whom we especially visited, assured us that Mr. Paine was beset by clergymen; that on one occasion a methodist minister obtruded on Mr. Paine when he, Mr. Hicks, was present. The minister, we suppose sincerely, declared to Mr. Paine, with uplifted hands, that "unless he repented of his unbelief he would be damned." Mr. Hicks describes Mr. Paine as rising in his bed with indignation at the intrusion and ignorant presumption, and, sick as he was, declaring that if he was able he would immediately put him out of the room. We recently met one of these visiting parties who sought to convert Mr. Paine on his death-bed, a Mr. Pigott, formerly a legislator, and now a man of high moral standing. He has a brother a minister, a learned studious man, but unfortunately blind. He was so at the time of Mr. Paine's death, and he felt desirous of converting Mr. Paine, and engaged his brother, Mr. Pigott, our informant, to go with him. With some difficulty they obtained access, for Mr. Paine was then annoyed, as we have seen, by obtruders; but as this gentleman had once adopted the opinions of Mr. Paine, and was then blind, these qualities obtained the brothers an audience. Mr. Pigott remarked that Mr. Paine was in bed and sick, but that he received them with politeness, and cheerfully conversed with his brother, who was a learned thoughtful man; but when his brother proceeded to state that he had changed his opinions, and about to urge on Mr. Paine, sincerely in this case no doubt, the necessity of re-examination and conversion, Mr. Paine abruptly closed the conversation, and intimated his displeasure, and a wish for their immediate departure; and they thus left the room. Mr. Pigott describes Mr. Paine as a large-faced man, with a most penetrating eye, and immense expression of countenance, marking lively sensibilities, which the peculiar character of the visit brought out; for he had seen him pleased with his brother, intelligent and communicative, and then *indignant* at supposing the brother could change his opinions.

The friends of Mr. Paine visited him till his death. Mr. Jarvis saw him one or two days before his dissolution, and on that day he had expected to die during the night, to Mr. Jarvis he expressed a continued belief in his written opinions; of this we are informed by Mr. Jarvis. Mr. Thomas Nixon, and his old friend Mr. Pelton, visited him expressly on the subject of his opinions, so did Mr. B. F. Hasken, a respectable attorney, now residing in Chambers street, New York; and, as they say, aware that falsehoods might be resorted to, because such means had before been used with others, they put down Mr. Paine's answers in writing. But when they first proposed their questions, as Mr. Paine did not know their motive, he seemed hurt that they should suppose he had any doubts on the subject. We have this account personally from Mr. Hasken, and we shall give a letter from Mr. T. Nixon and Mr. D. Pelton in another place. Mr. Paine suffered considerably in his illness, but he retained his mental faculties to the last. Death made slow approaches, and dropsy, attended by a cough and vomiting, were the last symptoms of approaching dissolution. On the eighth of June, about nine in the morning, he died, placid and almost without a struggle, notwithstanding his previous sufferings. And his last words, as recorded by Dr. Manley were—" I have no wish to believe on the subject," in answer to the question, " Do you wish to believe that Jesus is the Son of God ?" put by the pious doctor himself, who was curious on the subject.

Fortunately we have the living testimony of the person who sat up with Mr. Paine on the night previous to his death. This testimony cost us a journey to Boston, but we are amply repaid for our labor. On our return we published the testimony in the Beacon of June 5, 1839, Vol. III., page 240. A precaution we have taken for these eight years, during which time we have had the command of a press; for aware that many of the witnesses to this history, being then advanced in years, might die, we published their testimony in detail while yet alive, and capable of verifying our statements if correct, or of contradicting them if erroneous. As a specimen of this method of chronicling events, which we meant to imbody in this work, we extract the following from the Beacon (see reference above):—

THOMAS PAINE'S DEATH-BED.

"We have just returned from Boston. One object of our visit to that city, was to see a Mr. Amasa Woodsworth, an engineer, now retired in a handsome cottage and garden at East Cambridge, Boston. This gentleman owned the house rented by Mrs. Bonneville for Mr. Paine at his death; while he lived next door. As an act of kindness Mr. Woodsworth visited Mr. Paine every day for six weeks before his death; he frequently sat up with him, and did so on the last two nights of his life. He was always there with Dr. Manley the physician, and assisted in removing Mr. Paine, while his bed was prepared: he was present when Dr. Manley asked Mr. Paine 'if he wished to believe that Jesus Christ was the Son of God,' and he describes Mr. Paine's answer as animated. He says, that lying on his back, he used some action, and with much *emphasis* replied, 'I have no wish to believe on that subject.' He lived a short time after this, but was not known to speak, for he died tranquilly. He accounts for the insinuating style of Dr. Manley's letter, by stating that that gentleman just after its publication joined a church. He informs us that he has openly reproved the doctor for the falsity contained in the *spirit of that letter*, boldly declaring before Dr. Manley, who is yet living, that nothing which he saw justified his (the doctor's) insinuations. Mr. Woodsworth assures us that he neither heard nor saw anything to justify the belief of any mental change in the opinions of Mr. Paine previous to his death; but that being very ill and in pain, chiefly arising from the skin being removed in some parts by long laying, he was generally too uneasy to enjoy conversation on abstract subjects. This, then, is the best evidence that can be procured on this subject, and we publish it while the contravening parties are yet alive, and with the authority of Mr. Woodsworth.—G. V."

Mr. Woodsworth is yet alive, and his testimony has derived additional importance from the evidence of Mr. Willet Hicks, which we shall shortly give. We refer especially to his remarks on the conduct of Dr. Manley; and when we produce Mr. Hicks' evidence, we shall have to request that our readers will return to the previous page, and again read this testimony, and compare it with that evidence.

The day after the death of Mr. Paine he was taken from his house in Greenwich village to New Rochelle, attended by a few friends, and was there buried on his farm, and a plain stone was erected to his memory, with the following inscription:—

THOMAS PAINE,

AUTHOR OF "COMMON SENSE."

Died June 8, 1809, aged seventy-two years and five months.

Mr. Paine left behind him a manuscript in answer to Bishop Watson. A copy of this is now in the hands of Madame Bonneville. A catholic priest in this country borrowed another copy of her, which has never been returned.

In reviewing the life of Mr. Thomas Paine, we can see no defect in his public character. He was a citizen of the world, and served its interests to the best of his abilities, which were great. "Where liberty is, that is my country," said Dr. Franklin. Mr. Paine replied, "Where liberty is *not*, that is my country," in reference to his exertions for liberty in the United States, England, and France. Paine wrote for mankind, and he may be emphatically styled " the friend of man." *Here* he was a good citizen, and a firm supporter of thé government; because that government is based upon the rights of man, with the exception of the recognition of slavery in the southern states, unfortunately engrafted on the community before the war of independence. Whatever may be the opinion of Mr. Paine's theological works, his honesty in publishing them cannot be doubted by any impartial reader. He believed those opinions true, and he believed the *truth* useful to mankind; while his especial object was to establish a religious principle in France, then becoming atheistical. The best argument in support of deism is to be found in the first part of the "Age of Reason." In this view of the subject Mr. Paine ought to have been taken by the hand by every believer in the existence, wisdom, power, and goodness of one supreme God, the maker and sustainer of the universe. Mr. Paine gave up the copyright of his theological works, just as he had done that of his political, and for the same reason, *public good.* His *prudence* in publishing his "Age of Reason," has been doubted; and if he had been ambitious, and had consulted his own interest, he would have abstained from such a publication; but he was neither ambitious nor covetous, except of honest fame, from honest and intelligent men, and that he has obtained. His political career was run, and the doors apparently closed against an extension of liberty at that time, and therefore his political usefulness was not injured. The United States had accomplished her independence; the revolution in France was completed, and liberty disgraced by excesses which the "Age of Reason" was intended to restrain, as it taught toleration; while in England the cause of liberty was checked by war, and his political works suppressed; but church aggressions were oppressive; *there* the "Age of Reason" had *nearly* effected a revolution, and the odious system of tythes was almost prostrated. We cannot then admit that Mr. Paine was imprudent in the publication. The *age of reason* has now arrived, at least in New York, and every man chooses to read and think for himself, whatever may be his conclusions; and Mr. Paine was *scarcely* in advance of the age.

Of Mr. Paine's private character, we cannot say it was perfect. We should be sorry if we could; for then we could not hope to be believed. Mr. Paine was a part of human nature, and partook of its imperfections. He wrote a foolish angry letter to Carver. He was, no doubt, penurious, to a limited extent, in his old age; and in sickness we can easily conceive of his being sometimes peevish and angry; he would not be man if he were not; but these are all the personal blemishes we can discover, and these are counterbalanced by the most noble and social qualities. He had a heart to feel for the distresses of mankind, and a head to conceive the

clear, by fixing on so small a vice as inebriety for the subject of slander, that there was no *pretence* even for other vices. Had he been *unjust*, not addicted to truth, a man wanting principle, or possessed of any *public* vice, these would necessarily have been laid hold of; and this is a negative evidence that no *pretence* for public vice existed. But how are we to regard his slanderers, the great body of whom are *sincere*, religious, and feminine. What an amalgamation do the slanderers of Paine present. The young girl of pious education vociferating *Tom* Paine, the filthy, drunken, *Tom* Paine; the pious teacher, perhaps also deceived, but without examination, preaching from the pulpit, that the opponent of the gospel scheme lived and died a degraded, a drunken being. To these are added the arch hypocrite, who knows the slander, but, from interested motives, joins the bitter cry of *Tom* Paine and inebriety. To these again are added the *thousands* of decent people of all religions, who, finding it fashionable to pronounce the name of Paine with a sneer, generously believe what everybody says; and these add their mite of slander, making in the aggregate a mountain. But to these must yet be added the politician, the sneaking artful man who could not afford to lose a vote, and who, conscious of the contrary, chimes in with the pious, and pronounces *Tom* Paine and excess with supreme disgust, as an assurance that the speaker, the politician, is neither sot, drunkard, nor infidel; but even the political drunkard will join the throng, and in his beer become extremely pious, and denounce *Tom* Paine as drunken and dirty, being *willing* to believe what he wishes to be true, as an excuse for himself, and degrading to the principles which Paine manifested, and which our drunken politician eschews. This mass have sought to overwhelm the name of Paine by associating it with intoxication, for which there is not a particle of proof. We cannot say a *shadow*, for a shadow there was, and this, perhaps, rendered the extension of the slander easy. Mr. Paine *used*, but did not abuse, liquor. He had a large florid face, and this, we believe, favored the report among those who only knew him by sight. If now we push back the slander, on whom does it rest. Are the *sincere* justified, because of their sincerity, in propagating slander? Is it in accordance with their religion? It is evident it exists, with religion most sincere. It exists with the ministers of religion, some of whom were sincere but ignorant, others, not sincere, but interested; but the whole body was contaminated, minister and people, by circulating slander. This then was the visible religion Mr. Paine would have uprooted, while the political tyrants and sycophants, who joined the crusade, from the basest motives, and they have now their representatives, but ill contrast in sentiment and feelings with the noble principles of the man whose fame they would suppress. "The world my country, to do good my religion," were the sublime sentiments of this sincere and able advocate of human rights, whose fair fame has been thus abused.

Immediately on the death of Mr. Paine, Cheetham, his political enemy, began to collect materials for his life; which was published the same year. We have already noticed the manner in which he collected those materials, and the recklessness with which he repeated the grossest and most malicious falsehoods, while in the most impudent manner he inserted the names of living witnesses. His conviction in the case of Madame Bonneville did something to undeceive the public; still Mr. Paine's memory suffers from this malignity. We had by us Mr. Carver's copy of Cheetham's first edition of the "Life of Paine," including the matter for which he (Cheetham) was prosecuted. This copy Mr. Carver sold to Mr. Parkins, ex-sheriff of London, and he, Mr. Parkins, loaned it to us. The book is margined by notes in Carver's handwriting; a few of which we shall notice or extract, although they are extremely coarse.

The first note on the blank leaf after the preface, charges Cheetham with villifying Mr. Paine, and also Mr. Palmer, and plainly calls Mr. Cheetham a hypocrite. To this Carver puts his name and address, 36 Cedar street. Page 47, Cheetham says, "'Common Sense' has *no merit*." Carver adds, "One more of Cheetham's lies." Page 209, Cheetham pretends a great reverence for received religious opinions. Carver adds, "I believe Cheetham was an athiest, as he told me that Mirabeau's 'System of Nature' could never be answered. He was a hypocrite." Page 210, Carver says, "Cheetham fol-

means of relief. The charge of Madame Bonneville and family was at once an act of generosity and gratitude, however unpleasant their different tastes, or sense of propriety rendered their mutual duties. Mr. Paine possessed every prominent virtue (if not in perfection, which human nature forbids) in large proportions; and to these he added the most social qualities. in public, without being a great talker, he was cheerful, communicative, abounding in information and anecdote, and in private he was not less agreeable, on the testimony of Mr. John Fellows, Mr. Jarvis, and a host of others, his companions. Few people are aware of the morals and decorum of Mr. Paine. We have already observed that he never used vulgar oaths, and that he even goodhumoredly reproved his friends who did. Mr. Jarvis, who gave us the above information, observed that he once, by way of a joke, advised Mr. Paine to recant, and publish his recantation as a hoax, assuring him that he would then make a large fortune and get a good living. Mr. Paine, shaking his head, replied, "Tom Paine never told a lie." We do not discover in Mr. Paine, on any account, even a prevarication; such was his love of truth, while he had too much sense to be the dupe of the falsehood of others. The charge of drunkenness we can find no ground for, unless it occurred in France for a short period; and yet the company he there kept seems to forbid it. But as this charge is so generally believed we shall take the liberty of naming a few persons who knew him personally during his last residence in New York, some of whom were in the habit of meeting him in public, and others in public and private societies, his companions for years; and of these, none ever saw him drunk, and most of them are well known and respected for their veracity. Among others, are Mr. John Fellows,[*] Mr. D. Burger,[†] Mr. Ming, senr., Judge Herttell, Mr. Jarvis, Mr. Bassinet, Nassau street, Mr. B. F. Haskin, attorney, Chambers street, Mr. H. Magary, Willet Hicks, &c., &c., to which we could add a number now dispersed about the states, as Amasa Woodsworth, near Boston, and all the old inhabitants of New Rochelle.

There exists, too, a note on this subject to Mr. Caleb

[*] Saw him once elevated, after attending a dinner-party.
[†] Since dead.

Bingham, bookseller, Boston, from Mr. Lovett, now deceased, but formerly of the City hotel, New York, where Mr. Paine put up after his last return to this country. In that note Mr. Lovett declares that Mr. Paine drank less than any of his other boarders, while at his hotel: and this accords with what Mr. Jarvis and others have informed us, that " he did not, and could not, drink much." Our author, for the existence of this note, is Mr. John Fellows, a gentleman well known, and whose veracity was never doubted. The note was written to answer an inquiry, and shown to Mr. John Fellows, our informant. This subject is puerile in itself, were there not a *host* who sincerely believe Mr. Paine to have been disgustingly a drunkard or a sot. Others of liberal minds, would at once perceive that he who possessed all his faculties to an advanced age unimpaired, could not commonly indulge in such gross excesses; and if he had indulged in excesses sometimes only, it was merely a fault in the age which has passed. But we have a much more important inference, beside a desire to undeceive those who have been duped. We think we have given abundant evidence that Mr. Paine was neither a sot nor drunkard; and we know of *no contrary* evidence, nothing but hearsay, which, when approached, vanishes. How then are we to regard this slander, its circulation, its reiteration, the boldness of the assailants, and the variety of forms it assumed, from the pulpit, the press, and in prints; and in private, from mouth to mouth, till his very friends were deceived, as we were, till we commenced this investigation. What now is the secret cause of slander, but the desire to check the influence of an individual or his writings. Could the "Age of Reason" and "Rights of Man" have been replied to, as he replied to Burke, we should never have heard these slanders; and kings and priests, lordlings, an aristocracy and their sycophants, and the sincerely pious, but duped disciples of Jesus, never would have formed one mighty mass to circulate a petty slander but from *fear*. Some feared the truth—it would disturb their old prejudices; but others feared *reform*, because where equal rights are maintained, privileges must be yielded, and the leeches on society must give up their hold. But why did the slanderers fix on the minor vice of inebriety? It is

lowed Palmer in principles, but was not half as good and moral a man." He adds, "Cheetham was an abominable liar." This last expression is repeated in various parts of the book, with some variations, such as, "Cheetham was a liar, and, if reports are true, he should have treated his wife better." On the last page Carver adds, "I once told Cheetham in his own house, as that he had had his hands crossed with British gold." This is one of the witnesses to whom Cheetham constantly refers; and this witness thus denounces the man who refers to him, in the plain language we have shown, as not to be relied on. Mr. Jarvis is another, and he too uses the same expressions, in relation to Cheetham, which Carver does. Could we then get access to the *other* living witness to whom Cheetham refers for proofs of Mr. Paine's failings, we might find in them the same indignation and conviction of Cheetham's impudence and falsehoods.*

The cunning of Cheetham, in getting up materials for the life of Paine, will clearly be seen by again referring to Joel Barlow's letter to Cheetham (page 135). It is clear that Barlow was deceived, and we were deceived when we first read this letter in Cheetham's life of Paine, and continued deceived till we had examined the question of Mr. Paine's habits of temperance during the last years in New York. We then *re*-read Barlow's letter, and discovered the cunning. Mr. Barlow was in France at the time of Mr. Paine's death and knew not his habits. Cheetham wrote to him, informed him of his object, mentioned that Paine was *drunken* and *low* in his company toward the latter years of his life, and says he was *informed* that he was *drunk* when taken to prison in France. Now Mr. Barlow does not contradict Cheetham; he could not, as Cheetham had the better opportunity of knowing facts, and Mr. Barlow does not suspect him of falsehood; as who would? He therefore

---

* Cheetham sported with truth. He published in his paper an account of Burr's duel with Hamilton, in which he declared that Burr had undergarments of silk, to turn off the ball if hit, and that a garment of silk would do this; for that a Mr. Lawrence, then well known, had by accident fired off a pistol, that the ball struck his leg, and turned off from the effect of the silk-stocking. On the Sunday following Judge Herttell dined where Cheetham was, when he related the story of this publication as a hoax, and laughed at the people's credulity; as we are informed by Mr. Herttell.

presumes Mr. Cheetham correct in the statement, and goes on, not to excuse Paine, but to present his acknowledged good qualities as a set-off. Then Cheetham publishes this letter, and presents, to a cursory reader, Mr. Joel Barlow as acknowledging Mr. Paine's intemperance, and other infirmities, which had no other foundation than Cheetham's declaration, given to deceive Barlow; who afterward, as we have seen, gives Barlow's letter to deceive the public. In the next place *Cheetham informs* Mr. Barlow that he *had heard* Mr. Paine was drunk when sent to prison, and *boldly* gives his authority; as he did in the libel case. Here Mr. Barlow happened to be qualified to judge, for Paine was brought to his house when he was arrested, and Mr. Barlow distinctly disavows the statements; but he is too polite, or too unsuspicious, to suppose himself cheated; yet it is evident on this assertion and alleged evidence, had Mr. Barlow not known by accident the contrary, he too would have presumed the fact on Cheetham's statement, and, perhaps, would have endeavored to *excuse* Mr. Paine for being intoxicated at such a time; when the fact was, he was not intoxicated, nor is there any evidence that he was in the habit of being intoxicated. Of the referee, Mr. Murray, our friend Mr. John Fellows thus speaks:—

"I happen to know something of the Mr. Murray alluded to above, whose testimony Mr. Barlow proves to be false. It is thus, that Cheetham collected stories injurious to the character of Paine. Mr. Murray was an English speculator in France, in the time of the revolution, and was once imprisoned as a spy. His enmity to Paine and the principles for which France was contending, I am confident (from my knowledge of the man), would induce him to fabricate any story calculated to throw obloquy upon either."

Now who can doubt but that Cheetham knew the qualities of this man, whom he used as a referee, especially after we have seen the unscrupulous character of Cheetham as to truth. But perhaps it will be asked, what could induce Cheetham thus to lie? We have before remarked, that Cheetham had edited the leading republican paper; but that he had become a renegade, and was then in support of the English tory party, and was preparing to go to England, when he died. His life

of Paine he knew was a passport to the English court, and he
intended to defend the Bible and crown against Cobbet, who
had shortly before broken his connexion with the English
government, and was then in successful opposition. Such is
the evidence we obtained from a gentleman who was then
head-clerk to Cheetham, and this we find sustained by others.
Besides, Paine had been very severe on Cheetham for his
political change; and this would stimulate his revenge. The
following, published by Mr. Paine a short time before his
death, will show the relation Mr. Cheetham bore to Mr. Paine
at that time, and how badly qualified such a man must be for
an impartial biographer. Mr. Paine had published an article
in the Public Advertiser, on the defence of the harbor of New
York. Cheetham had attacked Paine on that article, and Mr.
Paine in his reply remarks:—

"Mr. Cheetham speaks much about Locke, and says, that
'all political elementary writers on government since the days
of Locke, including Mr. Paine, are but the mere retailers of
his ideas and doctrines.' This is John Bullism all over.

He also says, that ' on hereditary and elective government,
Mr. Paine, in his "Common Sense" and "Rights of Man,"
has followed Locke idea for idea.' It may be so for what I
know, for I never read Locke, nor ever had the work in my
hand, and by what I have heard of it from Horne Tooke, I had
no inducement to read it. It is a speculative, not a practical
work, and the style of it is heavy and tedious, as all Locke's
writings are.

I suppose Locke has spoken of hereditary and *elective monarchy*, but the representative, as laid down in 'Common
Sense' and 'Rights of Man,' is an entirely different thing to
elective monarchy. So far from taking any ideas from Locke
or from anybody else, it was the absurd expression of a mere
John Bull in England, about the year 1773, that first caused
me to turn my mind to systems of government. In speaking
of the then king of Prussia, called the Great Frederick, he
said, 'He is the right sort of man for a king, for he has a deal
of the devil in him.' This set me to think if a system of government could not exist that did not require the devil, and I
succeeded without any help from anybody. It is a great
deal that may be learned from absurdity, and I expect to learn
something from James Cheetham. When I do, I will let him
know in the Public Advertiser.

In the conclusion of the piece of mine, which Mr. Cheetham
has vomited his spleen upon, I threw out some reproach

against those who, instead of practising themselves in arms and artillery, that they might be prepared to defend New York, should it be attacked, were continually employing themselves on imaginary fortifications, and skulking behind projects of obstruction. As Mr. Cheetham supposed himself included in this description (and he thought right), he made, as he imagined, an effectual retort, but in doing this, as in everything else he does, he betrayed his want of knowledge, both as to the spirit and circumstances of the times he speaks of.

'I would not,' says Mr. Cheetham, ' charge with cowardice that gentleman [meaning me], who, in the " times that tried men's souls," stuck very correctly to his pen in a *safe retreat*, and never handled a musket offensively.'

By this paragraph, Mr. Cheetham must have supposed, that when congress retreated from Philadelphia to Baltimore, in the ' times that tried men's souls,' that I retreated with them as secretary to the committee for foreign affairs.

In the first place, the committee for foreign affairs did not exist at that time.

In the next place, I served in the army the whole of the ' time that tried men's souls,' from the beginning to the end.

Soon after the declaration of independence, July 4, 1776, congress recommended that a body of ten thousand men, to be called the flying camp, because it was to act wherever necessary, should be formed from the militia and volunteers of Jersey, Pennsylvania, and Maryland. I went with one division from Pennsylvania, under General Roberdeau. We were stationed at Perth Amboy, and afterward at Bergen; and when the time of the flying camp expired, and they went home, I went to Fort Lee, and served as aid-de-camp to Greene, who commanded at Fort Lee, and was with him through the whole of the black times of that trying campaign.

I began the first number of the ' Crisis,' beginning with the well-known expression, ' These are the times that try men's souls', at Newark, upon the retreat from Fort Lee, and continued writing it at every place we stopped at, and had it printed at Philadelphia the 19th of December, six days before the taking the Hessians at Trenton, which, with the affair at Princeton, the week after, put an end to the black times.

It therefore is not true, that I stuck to my pen in a safe retreat with congress from Philadelphia to Baltimore in the ' times that tried men's souls.' But if I had done so, I should not have published the cowardice James Cheetham has done. In speaking of the affair of the Driver sloop-of-war, at Charleston, South Carolina, he said in his paper, if the Driver and her comrades should take into their heads to come here (New York), we must submit. What abominable cowardice, for a man to have such a thought in his mind, that a city containing twenty thousand able-bodied men, numbers of them as stout in person as himself, should submit to a sloop-of-war containing about a hundred and fifty men.

After this, Mr. Cheetham will take care how he attacks old revolutionary characters, whose undiscouraged intrepidity, in the 'times that tried men's souls,' made a home for him to come to.

THOMAS PAINE

NEW YORK, *Aug.* 21, 1807."

"REPRIMAND TO JAMES CHEETHAM.

If James Cheetham, editor of the 'New York American Citizen,' thinks to draw me into a controversy with him, he is greatly mistaken. In the first place, I hold him too cheap; and his well-known character for abuse and blackguarding, renders any altercation with him dishonorable; and beside this, it would take up too much of my time to put his blunders to-rights. He cannot write without blundering, neither can he write truth, of which I will give another instance.

He quotes the following paragraph from the first part of 'Rights of Man,' and then grounds a false assertion upon it :—

'Every age and generation must be as free to act for itself, in all cases, as the ages and generations that preceded it. The vanity and presumption of governing beyond the grave, is the most ridiculous and insolent of all tyrannies. Man has no property in man, neither has one generation a property in the generation that is to follow.'

Mr. Cheetham having made this short quotation says: 'Mr. Paine here and there glances at the absurdity of hereditary government, but the passage just quoted is the *only* attempt at *argument* against it contained in the " Rights of Man."'

Is James Cheetham an idiot, or has the envy and malignity of his mind possessed him with a spirit of wilful lying?

The short passage he has quoted (which is taken from the middle of a paragraph) is on the third, and in some editions on the fourth page of the first part of 'Rights of Man.' It contains a general principle, on which the arguments and statements against hereditary succession are founded in the progress of that work.

If Mr. Cheetham had looked farther into the work, 'Rights of Man,' he would have come to a paragraph ending with the expression, ' *hereditary succession cannot be established as a legal thing.*' The work then goes on to say :—

' In order to arrive at a more perfect decision on this head (that is, that hereditary succession cannot be established as a legal thing), it is proper to consider the generation which undertakes to establish a family with hereditary powers, apart and separate from the generations which are to follow, and also to consider the character in which the generation acts with respect to succeeding generations.

'The generation which selects a person and puts him at the head of its government with the title of king, or any other distinction, acts its own choice, be it wise or foolish, as a free agent for itself. The person so set up is not hereditary, but selected and appointed, and the generation which sets him up do not live under an hereditary government, but under a government of its own choice and establishment. Were the generation which set him up, and the person so set up, to live for ever, it never could become hereditary succession; and, of consequence, hereditary succession can only take place on the death of the first parties.

As, therefore, hereditary succession is out of the question with respect to the first generation, we have now to consider the character in which that generation acts with respect to the commencing generation, and to all succeeding ones.

It assumes a character to which it has neither right nor title. It changes itself from a legislator to a testator, and affects to make its will, which is to have operation after the demise of the makers, to bequeath the government; and it not only attempts to bequeath, but to establish over the succeeding generation a new and different form of government from that under which itself lived. Itself, as already observed, lived not under an hereditary government, but under a government of its own choice and establishment, and it now attempts, by virtue of a will and testament, which it has no authority to make, to take from the commencing generation, and all succeeding ones, the right and free agency by which itself acted.'

Now, without giving any farther extracts from the work, 'Rights of Man,' on the subject of hereditary succession, what is here given ought to cover James Cheetham with shame for the falsehood he has advanced. But as a man who has no sense of honor has no sense of shame, Mr. Cheetham will be able to read this with an unblushing front.

Several writers before Locke had remarked on the absurdity of hereditary succession, but there they stopped. Buchanan, a Scots historian, who lived more than a hundred years before Locke, reproaches Malcolm II., king of Scotland, and his father, Kenethus, for making the crown of Scotland hereditary in his family, 'by which means,' says Buchanan, 'the kingdom must frequently be possessed by a child or a fool; whereas before, the Scots used to make choice of that prince of the royal family that was best qualified to govern and protect his people.'

But I know of no author, nor of any work, before 'Common Sense' and 'Rights of Man' appeared, that has attacked and exposed hereditary succession on the ground of illegality, which is the strongest of all grounds to attack it upon; for if the right to set it up do not exist—and that it does not is certain, because it is establishing a form of government, *not for themselves*, but for a future race of people—all discussion upon the subject ends at once. But James Cheetham has not sense enough to see this.

He has got something into his head about Locke, and he keeps it there, for he does not give a single quotation from him to support the random assertion he makes concerning Locke.

'It is to Locke in particular,' says Cheetham, ' who wrote his incomparable essay on government in 1689, that we are almost wholly indebted for those political lights which conducted *us* to *our* revolution.'

This is both libellous and false. The revolutionary contest began in opposition to the assumed rights of the British parliament '*to bind America in all cases whatsoever*,' and there can be nothing in Locke, who wrote in 1689, that can have reference to such a case. The tax upon tea, which brought on hostilities, was an experiment on the part of the British government to enforce the practice of that assumed right, which was called *the declaratory act.* James Cheetham talks of times and circumstances he knows nothing of, for he did not come here till several years after the war; yet in speaking of the revolution, he uses the words *we*, and *us*, and *our* revolution. It is common in England, in ridiculing self-conceited importance, to say, ' What a long tail *our* cat has got!'

The people of America, in conducting their revolution, learned nothing from Locke; nor was his name, or his work, ever mentioned during the revolution, that I know of. The case America was in was a new one, without any former example, and the people had to find their way as well as they could by the lights that arose among themselves, of which I can honestly and proudly say, I did my part. Locke was employed by the first settlers of South Carolina to draw up a form of government for that province, but it was such an inconsistent aristocratical thing, that it was rejected. Perhaps Mr. Cheetham does not know of this, but he may know it if he will inquire.

Mr. Cheetham hypocritically says, ' I advise Mr. Paine, as a friend, to write no more.'

In return for this civility in *words*, I will inform him of something for his good, which is, that he has been going down hill in the opinion of the republicans for a long time past. Good principles will defend themselves; but the abuse and scurrility in Cheetham's paper have given very general offence to his subscribers. Another complaint is, that his paper is not a newspaper. It does not give the news from Europe till it becomes old in every other paper. There are, perhaps, two causes for this: as a John Bull, he does not like the news from Europe; and as a dabbler in scribbling, he prefers filling his paper with his own stuff.

It is probable he will be called upon to explain on what ground of compromise (for it has the appearance of a compromise) the intimacy between him and the Anglo-Irish emissary Cullen, alias Carpenter, began and continued. He is now giving symptoms of becoming a successor of Cullen, as Cullen was the successor of Cobbett. As there is now a well-conducted republican paper established in New York (the Public Advertiser), Mr. Cheetham cannot have the same range for his scurrility he had before.

THOMAS PAINE

September 5, 1807."

" CHEETHAM AND HIS TORY PAPER.*

Cheetham is frequently giving symptoms of being the successor of *Cullen*, alias *Carpenter*, as Cullen was the successor of *Cobbett*, alias *Porcupine*. Like him, he is seeking to involve the United States in a quarrel with France for the benefit of England.

In his paper of Tuesday, September 22, he has a long abusive piece against France, under the title of " *Remarks*" on the speech of the arch-chancellor of France to the French senate. This is a matter that Cheetham, as an adopted American citizen, has no business with; and as a John Bull it is impertinence in him to come here to spit out his venom against France. But Cheetham cannot live without quarreling, nor write without abuse. He is a disgrace to the republicans, whose principle is to live in peace and friendship with all nations, and not to interfere in the domestic concerns of any.

Cheetham seems to regret that peace is made on the continent of Europe, and he shows his spleen against it by the following roundabout scurrilous paragraph.

'The people of France,' says he, 'now breathe the air of peace, under slavery, closer, more systematic, military, and universal [Cheetham knows nothing about it], than that with which they were overwhelmed previous to the beginning of the long continued calamity.' This is spoken exactly in the character of a stupid prejudiced John Bull, who, shut up in his island, and ignorant of the world, suppose all nations slaves but themselves; whereas, those at a distance can see, that of all people enslaved by their own governments, none are so much so as the people of England. Had Cheetham stayed in England till this time, he would have had to shoulder a musket, and this would have been dreadful to him, for, as all

---

* This piece was the cause of a duel between Cheetham and Frank.

bullies are cowards, the smell of gunpowder would be as horrid to Cheetham, as the scent of a skunk to other animals.

The danger to which the city of New York was exposed, by the continual abuse of France in such papers as Cullen's, was, that the French government might be induced to consider the city of New York as a British colony, such as it was during the revolutionary war, and exclude her from the commerce of the continent of Europe, as she has excluded Britain. Cheetham is following the footsteps of Cullen.

The French nation, under all its changes of government, has always behaved in a civil and friendly manner to the United States. We have no cause of dispute with France. It was by the aid of France in men, money, and ships,* that the revolution and independence of the United States were so completely established, and it is scarcely sufferable that a prejudiced and surly-tempered John Bull should fix himself among us to abuse a friendly power.

September 25, 1807."

"NOTE TO CHEETHAM.

MR. CHEETHAM: Unless you make a public apology for the abuse and falsehood in your paper of Tuesday, October 27, respecting me, I will prosecute you for lying.

It is by your talent for abuse and falsehood, that you have brought so many prosecutions on your back. You cannot even state truth without running it to falsehood. There was matter enough against Morgan Lewis without going a syllable beyond the truth.

THOMAS PAINE

October 27, 1807."

"TO THE CITIZENS OF NEW YORK.

In a letter from the president of the United States, of October 9, after his mentioning that he did not expect the Revenge back under a month from that date, adds, '*In the meantime, all the little circumstances coming to our knowledge are unfavorable to our wishes for peace.*'

As this might be useful information to men in mercantile pursuits and speculations, and who had no guide to go by, whether to send out their vessels, or not, I mentioned it to such of my republican friends as called to see me; and that the information, if so useful, might not be confined to one distinction of men only, I mentioned it also to Mr. Coleman, of the Evening Post, who came to me on account of a piece I

---

* Six thousand French troops under General Rochambeau, and thirty-one sail-of-the-line under Admiral de Grasse, assisted at the capture of Cornwallis at Yorktown, Virginia, which put an end to the war.

sent to him concerning Cheetham's insulting message to Mr. Frank, of the Public Advertiser. How it got into the newspapers I know not; Mr. Coleman, I suppose, can give the best account of that.

Cheetham then published a most abusive piece in his paper, and in his vulgar style of language said, "*Paine has told a lie,*" and then insinuated as if I had forged the letter. It is by his propensity to blackguarding and lying, that he has brought so many prosecutions on his back. He says he has nine. He will now have one more. If an unprincipled bully cannot be reformed, he can be punished.

THOMAS PAINE.

November 20, 1807."

"THE EMISSARY CHEETHAM.

Cheetham can now be considered in no other light than a British emissary, or successor to the impostor Cullen, alias Carpenter, whom Cheetham handed out in his newspaper, as a gentlemanly sort of a man. Cheetham finding the republicans are casting him off, is holding out signs to be employed as a British partisan.

Cheetham, in his papers of December 29 and 30, has two long pieces about the embargo, which he labors to prove is not laid on in consequence of any dispute with England, but in consequence of some imperious demands on the part of France. This John Bull is an idiot in diplomatic affairs.

Cheetham says, 'Mr. Monroe's despatches, which were laid before congress, and which congress *concluded did not authorize an embargo*, are dated London, October 10th. In the opinion of congress,' continues Cheetham, 'and I venture to say of Mr. Monroe, an immediate war with England was therefore by no means probable.'

Cheetham has been so long in the habit of giving false information, that truth is to him like a foreign language.

The president laid the despatches of Mr. Monroe, of October 10th, before congress; but as they were in daily expectation of later information by the arrival of the Revenge schooner, and also of the personal arrival of Mr. Monroe, congress received it as preparatory information, but came to no conclusion on their contents.

Cheetham says, that the Leopard, which brought Mr. Monroe's despatches, of October 10th, sailed from London on the 16th of October, and that the Revenge sailed from London for Cherbourg, on the same day, at which time, says Cheetham, there was no probability of an immediate war with England.

In a letter I received from London, dated October 15th, and which I published in the Philadelphia Aurora, and in the New York Public Advertiser, the writer, in speaking of the British ministry, says, 'Their cup of iniquity is nearly full, they only want to go to war with America to fill it up; and it is the opinion here [London] that that measure is resolved on. They will make no concessions unless it be to deceive.' The letter is dated one day before the Revenge sailed from London, and I suppose came by the Revenge; yet Cheetham tells his readers there was then no probability of a war with America. Cheetham's information is never entitled to credit.

When the Revenge sailed with the president's proclamation, and the instructions to Mr. Monroe, the writer of this knows she was ordered to come from London to France. It was expected she would be detained in the two countries about a month, and be back here about the 16th of November.

Her coming from London to France, would give Mr. Monroe the opportunity (for foreign ministers do not correspond by post, but by express) of communicating to Mr. Armstrong, at Paris, the plans and projects of the British ministry.

Soon after the arrival of the Revenge at Cherbourg, a French port on the channel, General Armstrong sent circular letters to the American consuls in France, to hasten the departure of the American vessels as fast as possible. Several paragraphs in the English newspapers, and which have been copied into the American papers, stated, that the British ministry intended to seize American vessels coming to, or going from, any port in France. As Mr. Monroe would get knowledge of this, as well as the writer of the letter to Thomas Paine, of October 15th, he would communicate it to General Armstrong at Paris; and this accounts for General Armstrong's circular letter, after the arrival of the Revenge schooner from London.

If Britain put her threat in force, that of taking American vessels going to or coming from France, it is probable the French government will retaliate, and take American vessels going to or coming from England; and this resolution on the part of France, had a natural tendency to prevent American vessels being taken, because Britain, by setting the example, will suffer more by it than France.

The British blockading decree, that of seizing neutral vessels going to or from France, was to have been published on the 14th of November, but the news from London of the 14th by the Jane, is silent on the subject. The apprehension of retaliation has, most probably, stopped the British ministry in their career.

Jan. 7, 1808."

In another letter, dated August 25, 1808 (and Mr. Paine died, as we have seen, in 1809), he thus expresses himself of Cheetham, that " in religion he was a hypocrite, and in politics a John Bull," said in reference to Cheetham's abuse of Bonaparte and the French. Mr. Paine adds in the same letter: "The ward meetings have done exceedingly right in posting Cheetham. The people in the country and abroad will now know that he does not belong to the popular republican party, and that he is an English impostor."

Whether these letters derive some asperity from party politics or not, is a matter of no consequence to our subject. The statement of facts is no doubt correct, and the feelings of Cheetham toward Paine must be anything but friendly. When, therefore, a party hack, as Cheetham doubtless was, disappointed and a renegade, with talents, as he certainly possessed, but embittered in feelings and regardless of truth, as all circumstances contribute to show, what could be expected from such a man, but just what he produced—a life of Paine abounding in bold falsehoods, cunningly contrived, and addressed to a people who *wished* to be deceived? The compliment paid Cheetham by Judge Hoffman, in extenuation of heavy damages, when convicted by the clearest evidence of gross slander in the case of Madame Bonneville, viz, that "he had produced a work useful to religion," explains the position of Cheetham, his life of Paine, and the public. The politicians *succumbed* to the religious part of the community, and both sacrificed the fame of Paine to their supposed interest. The religious because they thought they did God service, and hypocrites and politicians because they imagined an injury from the association of the name of Paine with theirs. Individuals did lift up their voices in defence of the memory of Paine, but as these had neither the press nor public sympathy, nor public opinion, nor fashion, on their side, their voices were not heard, and falsehood triumphed for a time; not, however, without witnesses, whose testimony was recorded from time to time, which might be accumulated and presented at a proper season, a time to which Joel Barlow looked forward. That time we believe has now arrived, and Judge Hoffman, were he now alive, dare not repeat his infamous sentiment, that "Cheetham had written a book *useful* to religion." The very sentiment is now scoffed by the religious people of the age, who are so far advanced in civilization as to scorn a religion that needs falsehood for its support. In the history of nations there are periods of fanaticism, but a steady progress in liberality. Cromwell's time was a period of fanaticism, succeeded indeed by licentiousness; and after the French revolution a *re*-action took place, and fanaticism prevailed, first in England, and then on this side the Atlantic; and in the darkness of which Cheetham slipped in his life of Paine. But we yet believe that justice will be done to the memory of the man who caused the declaration of independence, showed how it could be maintained, and was the *light* of the republic in the "times which tried men's souls," (*Paine*). And we farther believe that *this age* is sufficiently intelligent to investigate the merits of *one* of the *men* of the revolution, and sufficiently honest to do his memory justice.

The second part of Mr. Paine's prophecy was not suffered to want fulfilment. In vain did his friends witness the sincerity of his belief, his firmness and calmness at the last moment; in vain did Dr. Manley *try* to extort from him a recantation, and in vain did clerical gentlemen assail him when infirm in body. In vain did Mr. Jarvis, Colonel Daniel Pelton, and our living friend Mr. Haskins, and the respected Willet Hicks, receive his last declaration in presence of death; in vain was all this. A few zealous pious hypocrites had determined on a conversion, or on a conviction and remorse, and therefore a woman was made a tool of to propagate such charges; and one Charles Collins, now alive, was found base enough to publish her foolish tales, not avowed till some years after the death of Mr. Paine; such a circumstance however is easily jumped over, when that is revealed which is wanted. This subject has however been treated on in the preface to the Boston edition of Mr. Paine's theological works, written by our friend Mr. John Fellows, now alive, and frequently alluded to in this work, from which we shall therefore extract, as we have examined into it, and, with one exception, are satisfied with the correctness of the statement.

"I cannot relinquish this subject without taking notice of one of the most vile and wicked stories that was ever engendered in the fruitful imagination of depraved mortals. It was fabricated by a woman, named Mary Hinsdale, and published by one Charles Collins, at New York, or rather, it is probable that this work was the joint production of Collins, and some other fanatics, and that they induced this stupid, ignorant woman to stand sponsor for it.

It states, in substance, that Thomas Paine, in his last illness, was in the most pitiable condition for want of the mere necessaries of life; and that the neighbors, out of sheer compassion, contributed their aid to supply him with sustenance: that he had become converted to Christianity, and lamented that all his religious works had not been burnt: that Mrs. Bonneville was in the utmost distress for having abandoned her religion, as she (M. H.) said, for that of Mr. Paine, which he now told her would not answer the purpose, &c. In all this rodomontade there is not a single, solitary ray of truth to give it a colorable pretext. It is humiliating to be under the necessity of exposing such contemptible nonsense. Collins, if he was not the author, was assured of its falsity. But being *full of the spirit* of fanaticism and intolerance, and believing, no doubt, that the end sanctified the means, he continued to circulate the *pious fraud*, and the clergy exultingly retailed it from the pulpit. Nothing but religious phrensy could have induced Collins, after being warned of the crime he was committing, to persist in publishing this abominable trash.* He had the hardihood even to apply to William Cobbett for the purpose of inducing him to insert it in the life of Thomas Paine, which Mr. Cobbett then contemplated to write. For which he received due chastisement from the pen of that distinguished writer, in a number of his Register. Mr. Cobbett subsequently having taken great pains to investigate the falsity of this story, exposed and refuted it in the most ample manner This I have not seen, nor is the Register, containing the article alluded to, before me. Mrs. Bonneville was absent in France at the time of its first appearance in New York, and when shown to her on her return to America, although her feelings were highly agitated at the baseness of the fabrication, she would not permit her name to appear in print in competition with that of Mary Hinsdale. No notice, therefore, has been taken of it, excepting by Mr. Cobbett. Indeed, it was considered by the friends of Mr. Paine generally to be too contemptible to controvert. But as many *pious* people continue to believe, or pretend to believe in this stupid story, it was thought proper to say a few words upon it in this publication.

The facts are as follow: Mary Hinsdale was hired at service in the family of Mr. Willet Hicks, residing at Greenwich

---

* Since writing the above, it has been suggested to me, by a gentleman who knows him, that this base act of Collins is attributable more to his actual stupidity than to either his fanaticism or malice. That he is too weak to be aware of the sin of slander; and has no doubt, in this case, been made use of, as a mere puppet, by others behind the scene, more knowing and more wicked than himself. If this be the fact, it is charity to state it to the public, as his case will tend to excite pity, and depreciate, in some measure, the enormity of his guilt in this transaction.

village, in the neighborhood of Mr. Paine, who occasionally sent some little delicacies to him in the time of his sickness, as every good neighbor would do; and this woman was the bearer. Here is the whole foundation upon which the distorted imagination of Mary Hinsdale, or some one for her, has raised this diabolical fiction. Mr. Hicks was in the habit of seeing Mr. Paine frequently, and must have known if such a wonderful revolution had taken place in his mind, as is stated, and he does not hesitate to say, that the whole account is a *pious fraud.* Mr. Hicks is a respectable merchant at New York, and any one there, who has any doubts on the subject, by calling on him will be satisfied. Even James Cheetham, the libeller of Mr. Paine, acknowledges that he died in the religious faith which he had inculcated in his writings. Which is also attested by his physician, Dr. Manley, and all those who visited him in his last illness. But to put this matter beyond all cavil, I shall add the certificate of two old and highly respectable citizens, Thomas Nixon of New York, and Captain Daniel Pelton of New Rochelle. It was addressed to William Cobbett, under an expectation that he was about to write the life of Thomas Paine, and left with a friend to be handed to him; but as the undertaking was relinquished, it was never delivered, and is now in my possession, in the hand writing of the signers; and is as follows:—

TO MR. WILLIAM COBBETT.

Sir: Having been informed that you have a design to write a history of the life and writings of Thomas Paine, if you have been furnished with materials in respect to his religious opinions, or rather of his recantation of his former opinions before his death, all you have heard of his recanting is false. Being aware that such reports would be raised after his death by fanatics which infested his house at the time it was expected he would die, we, the subscribers, intimate acquaintances of Thomas Paine, since the year 1776, went to his house—he was sitting up in a chair, and apparently in the full vigor and use of all his mental faculties. We interrogated him on his religious opinions, and if he had changed his mind or repented of anything he had said or wrote on that subject. He answered, 'not at all,' and appeared rather offended at our supposition that any change should take place in his mind. We took down in writing the questions put to him, and his answers thereto, before a number of persons then in his room, among whom were his doctor, Mrs. Bonneville, &c. This paper is mislaid and cannot be found at present, but the above is the substance, which can be attested by many living witnesses. Thomas Nixon.
Daniel Felton

New York *April* 24, 1818."

We had resolved on so much of the manuscript before we saw Mr. Willet Hicks, before mentioned ; and if it were not a rule in evidence to obtain the best, in the most direct manner, we should not have sought an interview, for we had supposed that those who had gone before us had obtained all that was desirable from that gentleman ; but, to our surprise, on seeing Mr. Hicks, as a duty which we owed the public, we learned that Mary Hinsdale never saw Paine to Mr. Hicks's knowledge ; that the fact of his sending some delicacy from his table as a compliment occurred but a very few times, and that he *always* commissioned his *daughters* on this errand of kindness, and he designated Mrs. Cheeseman, then a little girl, but now the wife of one of our celebrated physicians, as the daughter especially engaged, and that she states that Mary Hinsdale *once* wished to go with her, but was *refused*. So that on the testimony of Mr. Willet Hicks, the whole story of confession of Paine to such a woman, remorse, wretchedness, despair, and conversion, rests on Mary Hinsdale *once wishing* to go with Mr. Hicks's daughter to Mr. Paine's. The secret of such a fabrication on such a foundation is easily explained. On farther conversation with Mr. Hicks, he informed us, that when it was known that he visited Mr. Paine daily, many, of the FRIENDS (to which sect he belonged, and of which he was a preacher), thought he would make some religious impression on Mr. Paine, and that after his death he was extremely annoyed at numbers of them pressing him to say something detrimental of Paine, or that he was converted. The old gentleman remarked to us : " You can have no idea of the anxiety of our people on this subject ; I was *beset* by them, both here and in England, where I soon after went on a journey." He remarked, they wished to convict Mr. Paine of calling on Jesus ; they would say, he observed, " Didst thee never hear hear him call on Christ ?" On reference to our notes, which we took for accuracy, we find, Mr. Hicks even declared : " You cannot conceive what a deal of trouble I had, and as for money, I could have had any sums if I would have said anything against Thomas Paine, or if I would even have consented to remain silent. They informed me that the doctor was willing to say something that would satisfy them if I would engage to be silent only; but," remarked Mr. Hicks to us, "they observed, he (the doctor) knows the standing of Willet Hicks, and that he knew all about Paine, and if he (Mr. Hicks) should contradict what I say, he would destroy my testimony." Such is the simple testimony recently obtained of this gentleman, who is yet alive, and was, when we saw him, at the residence of his son-in-law, Dr. Cheeseman. Mr. Hicks, in conclusion, remarked of Mr. Paine, that " he was a *good* man, an honest man," and with great indignation he remarked, " he was not a man to talk with Mary Hinsdale." Here then is the KEY to Mary Hinsdale's fabrication ; the *intense feeling of a portion of the friends on the subject of Mr. Paine's works.* We say a *portion* ; for, though Mr. Hicks uses the expression, " he was *beset* with them, both here and in England," a *portion* could *beset* him. Mr. Hicks was himself a *friend*, a pious friend, and a preacher, and an honorable man of high standing, and such as he was and is, such we have no doubt were and are many. Besides, we can readily conceive that this intense feeling was chiefly among the more orthodox, as some of these in every sect have always *felt* the most. From the multitude who raised the cry of *Tom* Paine, we need not minutely examine the question as to *numbers* in this portion of the FRIENDS; we can readily believe there would be enough to effect the object. If, too, Mr. Hicks, who was rich, could have had *any sum*, as he expresses himself, then Mary Hinsdale could have had any sum for her invention. We do not know that she did ; but we can readily believe that she would not want a Charles Collins, or any one else, to assist her in getting out such a work; and that those who wished to believe would not be at much trouble to inquire after the credibility of the evidence. Will our readers now turn to page 156, where we have inserted Mr. Amasa Woodsworth's testimony, and observe in what language he speaks of Dr. Manley, yet alive, and enjoying a post of honor. Now we do not know that Mr. Hicks referred to Dr. Manley, when he says that the *friends* informed him the doctor was willing to say *something*, he might have meant some other doctor ; we merely give his words as he gave them to us. But there is a curious coincidence in these two witnesses, both respectable, but who have moved in very different spheres, and who, perhaps, have never seen each other since the death of Paine. Their evidence was taken, the one near Boston, two years ago, the other two months ago, in New York, and they both infer a disposition to cheat the public by those who were professionally about Mr. Paine on his death-bed. Dr. Manley has published a letter, and has thus thrown himself on the public, and we have a right to examine that letter. He there, indeed, gives you the last words of Paine, "I have no wish to believe on that subject." But what would he have said had Willet Hicks consented to silence, and if Amasa Woodsworth had not been present. We again remark that we do not know that Mr. Hicks referred to Dr. Manley, but we do know that Dr. Manley published a pamphlet, in which he endeavors to *insinuate*, that in spite of Mr. Paine's declaration, that he did *conceal* his real sentiments; and this he infers from *looks* and *exclamations* which he *alone* saw and heard. And now let us remind our readers that Amasa Woodsworth says, he was *always* there *with* Dr. Manley; yet Amasa Woodsworth saw none of these expression, and heard no exclamations indicating mental agony, but such expressions as resulted from bodily pain, and that from a cause explicitly given, viz, " the skin in some parts being removed from long lying." The judge, Hoffman, who tried Cheetham on the libel against Madame Bonneville, complimented Mr. Cheetham for writing a very useful book in *favor of religion*, although it did contain falsehoods and libel; and in the same way the doctor may think his published letter may be useful to hundreds of thousands, and he no doubt did, and perhaps does think so; and no doubt some persons will regret that Mr. Willet Hicks stood in the way of some more dignified person than Mary Hinsdale, belying Mr. Paine on his death-bed. The whole, however, is explained by the "intense feelings of a portion of the FRIENDS, who could *beset* Mr. Hicks in the manner they did, 'Didst thee never hear him call on Christ?'" or who could intimate a wish that he would say that Paine recanted, or, at least, that he would *promise silence*, while others should testify falsely; and who could intimate reward for such perfidy. "As for money I could have had *any* sum," is the language of Mr. Hicks toward the portion of "FRIENDS" that *beset* him Now if this feeling could exist among the FRIENDS, carried out as we have seen it in the case of Mary Hinsdale, to what extent must it have existed in other classes, more superstitious, less educated, less accustomed to truth and more to passion, as the devoutly pious among every class, who believe their feelings the effects of divine influence, and who are consequently easily misled by these feelings. And when we consider that all this pious feeling was backed by an interested class of clergy, and by corrupt politicians, who wished the votes of the pious, can we be surprised at the calumny under which he has lain, and that even his friends should have been deceived on some points, from the incessant clamor and apparent universality of the accusations.

We shall now furnish Mr. W. Cobbett's account of this transaction of Mr. Collins and Mary Hinsdale, on which, perhaps, we have thrown some light:—

" CURIOUS HISTORY OF A CALUMNY ON PAINE.

It is a part of the business of a press, sold to the *cause of corruption*, to calumniate those, dead or alive, who have most effectually labored against that cause; and, as Paine was the most powerful and effectual of those laborers, so to calumniate him has been an object of their peculiar attention and care. Among other things said against this famous man, is, that he *recanted* before he died; and that in his last illness, he discovered horrible fears of death. This is, to be sure, a very good *answer* to what these same persons say about his *hardened infidelity*. But, it is a pure, unadulterated falsehood. This falsehood, which I shall presently trace to its origin (the heart of a *profound hypocrite*), was cried about the streets of *Liverpool*, when I landed there in November last. Thence it found its way to the grand receptacle and distributor of falsehood and calumny, the *London press*, which has sent it all over this kingdom. One *country paper*, however, pre-eminent in all that is *foul* and *mean*, affects to possess *original* matter and *authentic* information on the subject; and, indeed, it *pledges* itself for the *character* of the *gentleman* from whom it says it has *received* the pretended authentic account. The country paper I allude to, is the Norwich Mercury, printed and published by one Burks.

The Norwich Mercury did not imagine that any one would take the pains to expose this tissue of falsehoods. In the first place, why does he not *name* his ' *gentleman*' of such excellent character? How these informers *skulk!* Mr. Burks can *pledge* himself for the *character* of the " gentleman" informer; but, where are we to get a pledge for the character of Mr. Burks, who, if we are to judge from this act of his, stands in need of very good sponsors.

Let us look, a little, at the *internal evidence* of the falsehood of this story. Mr. Paine possessed, at his death, an unencumbered estate of *two hundred and fifty acres* of land, *not more than twenty miles from New York.* He possessed a considerable sum beside. These he left by will. Will any one believe, that he was, on his dying-bed, in the want of *proper nourishment*, and that he was in a *deplorable* state as to apartments and necessaries? Then, was it likely, that when a *neighbor's maid-servant* went to carry him a little present of sweetmeats, or the like, that he would *begin a conversation on theology with her?* And is it not monstrous to suppose, that he would call himself the *devil's agent* to HER, and not *leave behind him* any recantation at all, though he had such ample time for doing it, and though this *confidant* was so ready to *receive it and to take care of it?* The story is false upon the face of it: and nothing but a simpleton, or something a great deal worse, would have given it circulation and affected to believe it to be true.

I happen to know the *origin* of this story: and I possess the real, *original document*, whence have proceeded the divers *editions* of the falsehood, of the very *invention* of which I was, perhaps, *myself*, the innocent *cause!*

About two years ago, I, being then on Long Island, published my intention of writing an account of the life, labors, and death of Paine. Soon after this, a quaker at New York, named *Charles Collins*, made many applications for an *interview* with me, which at last he obtained. I found that his object was to persuade me that Paine had *recanted*. I laughed at him, and sent him away. But he *returned again and again to the charge.* He wanted me to promise that I would say that '*it was said*,' that Paine had recanted. ' No,' said I; 'but I will say that *you say it*, and that you *tell a lie*, unless you *prove the truth* of what you say; and if you do that, I shall gladly insert the fact.' This *posed* ' friend Charley,' whom I suspected to be a most consummate hypocrite. He had a *sodden* face, a *simper*, and manœuvred his features, precisely like the *most perfidious wretch that I have known, or ever read or heard of.* He was precisely the reverse of my honest, open, and sincere quaker friends, the Pauls of Pennsylvania. Friend Charley plied me with remonstrances and reasonings, but I always answered him. ' Give me *proof;* name *persons;* state *times;* state *precise words*, or I denounce you as a '*liar*.' Thus put to his trumps, friend Charley resorted to the aid of a person of his own stamp; and, at last, he brought me a paper, containing matter, of which the above statement of Mr. Burks is a *garbled edition!* This paper, very cautiously and craftily drawn up, contained only the *initials* of names. This would not do. I made him, at last, put down the full name and the address of the *informer,* 'Mary Hinsdale, No.10 Anthony street, New York.' I got this from friend Charley some time about June last; and had no opportunity of visiting the party till late in October, just before I sailed.

The informer was a quaker woman, who, at the time of Mr. Paine's last illness, was a servant in the family of Mr. Willet Hicks, an eminent merchant, a man of excellent character, a quaker, and even, I believe, a quaker preacher. Mr. Hicks, a kind and liberal and rich man, visited Mr. Paine in his illness, and, from his house, which was near that of Mr. Paine, little nice things (as is the practice in America) were sometimes sent to him; of which this servant, friend Mary, was the bearer; and *this* was the way in which the lying cant got into the room of Mr. Paine.

To 'friend Mary,' therefore, I went on the twenty-sixth of October last, with friend Charley's paper in my pocket. I found her in a lodging in a back-room up one pair of stairs. I knew that I had no common cunning to set my wit against. I began with all the art that I was master of. I had got a prodigiously broad-brimmed hat on. I patted a little child that she had sitting beside her; I called her *friend;* and played all the awkward tricks of an undisciplined wheedler. But I was compelled to come quickly to *business.* She asked, ' What's thy name, friend?' and the moment I said *William Cobbett,* up went her mouth as *tight* as a purse! Sack-making appeared to be her occupation; and that I might not extract through her eyes that which she was resolved I should not get out of her mouth, she went and took up a sack and began to sew; and not another look or glance could I get from her.

However, I took out my paper, read it, and stopping at several points, asked her if it was *true.* Talk of the *Jesuits,* indeed! The whole tribe of Loyola, who had shaken so many kingdoms to their base, never possessed a millionth part of the cunning of this drab-colored little woman, whose face simplicity and innocence seemed to have chosen as the place of their triumph! She shuffled; she evaded; she equivocated; she warded off; she affected not to understand me, not to understand the paper, not to remember: and all this with so much seeming simplicity and single-heartedness, and in a voice so mild, so soft, and so sweet, that if the devil had been sitting where I was, he would certainly have jumped up and hugged her to his bosom.

The result was: that it was *so long ago,* that she could not speak *positively* to any part of the matter: that she *would not say that any part of the paper was true:* that she had *never seen the paper;* and that she had never given ' friend Charley' (for so she called him) authority to say *anything about the matter in her name.* I pushed her closely upon the subject of the '*unhappy French female.*' Asked her whether she should *know her* again.—' Oh, no! friend; I tell thee that I have *no recollection* of any person or thing that I saw at Thomas Paine's house.' The truth is, that the cunning little thing knew that the French lady was at hand; and that *detection* was easy, if she had said that she should know her upon sight!

I had now nothing to do but to bring friend Charley's nose to the grindstone. But Charley, who is a grocer, living in Cherry street, near Pearl street, though so pious a man, and doubtless in great haste to get to everlasting bliss, had *moved out of the city for fear of the fever,* not liking, apparently, to go off to the next world in a yellow skin. And thus he escaped me, who sailed from New York in four days afterward: or Charley should have found, that there was something else on this side the grave, pretty nearly as troublesome and as dreadful as the yellow fever.

This is, I think, a pretty good instance of the length to which hypocrisy will go. The whole, as far as relates to recantation, and to the '*unhappy French female,*' is a lie from the beginning to the end. Mr. Paine declares in his last will, that he retains all his publicly expressed opinions as to religion. His executors, and many other gentlemen of undoubted veracity, had the same declaration from his dying lips. Mr. Willet Hicks visited him till nearly the last. This gentleman says, that there was no change of opinion intimated *to him:* and will any man believe that Paine would have withheld from Mr. Hicks, that which he was so forward to communicate to Mr. Hicks' *servant-girl?*

Observe, reader, that in this tissue of falsehoods, is included a most foul and venomous slander on a woman of virtue and of spotless honor. But hypocrites will stick at nothing. Calumny is their weapon, and a base press is the hand to wield it. Mr. Bourke, of Norwich, will not insert this article, nor will he acknowledge his error. He knows that the calumny which he has circulated, has done what he intended it to do; and he and the '*gentleman*' for whose character he *pledges* himself, will wholly disregard good men's contempt, so long as it does not diminish their gains.

This is not at all a question of *religion.* It is a question of *moral truth.* Whether Mr. Paine's opinions were correct or erroneous, has nothing to do with this matter.

WILLIAM COBBETT.

We have not yet done with this subject. By a curious coincidence we have become acquainted with a Mr. J. W.

Lockwood, of New York. This gentleman had a sister, a member of the FRIENDS, who died about two-and-twenty years ago. On her death, Mary Hinsdale, who was known to the family, stated to them that she should come to the funeral, for that she had met Mary Lockwood a short time before her death; and that she (Mary Lockwood) had said to her: "Mary [Hinsdale], I do not expect to live long; my views are changed; I wish thee to come to my funeral, and make this declaration to my friends then assembled," and that consequently she should come. The relatives of the deceased, who were *Hicksite** *quakers*, or friends, knew the falseness of this statement. Those who had sat by her bed-side, and heard her continued and last declarations on religious subjects (for she was emphatically a religious young woman), knew that no change had taken place. Her brother, our informant, had heard her express her opinions with great satisfaction. He and her other relatives therefore said so to Mary Hinsdale, but invited her to attend the funeral. Mary Hinsdale did not attend. The falsehood was notorious and occasioned a good deal of loud conversation; and this Mr. Lockwood supposes deterred this orthodox friend from appearing among them.

We recently published the above account in the Beacon, and referred to Mr. Cobbett's account, which we had formerly published. On this publication Mr. Collins, frequently named above, called on us, not to complain of our remarks, but to assure us that his *conscience* could not suffer the Beacon to be left at his house, to be forwarded to a friend in the West Indies, as formerly. To this we made no objection; but finding Mr. C. Collins in our house, and knowing the importance of his testimony, we at once asked him what induced him to publish the account of Mary Hinsdale. He assured us he then thought it true. He believed that she had seen Mr. Paine, and that Mr. Paine might confess to her, a girl, when he would not to Willet Hicks. He knew that many of their most respected *friends* did not believe the account. He knew that Mr. W. Hicks did not, whom he highly respected; but

---

* Followers of Elias Hicks, not orthodox, or believers in the common scheme of salvation by the atonement.

yet he thought it *might* be true. We asked Mr. C. Collins what he thought of the character of Mary Hinsdale now ? He replied, that some of our *friends* believe she indulges in opiates, and do not give her credit for truth. We asked, and do you believe they are justified in their opinions ? He replied, " O yes, I believe they speak the truth" (Mr. Lockwood had given us the same opinion), but C., added " This does not affect her testimony when a young woman ; she *might* then have spoken the truth." Such is the testimony of Charles Collins, in relation to Mary Hinsdale, whom he assisted in publishing her fabrication of Mr. Paine's death-bed scenes, based on her *wish* to see Mr. Paine, and which fabrication has been echoed from pulpit to pulpit, and from press to press, in this country and England, and sanctioned by thousands of pious people who *wished* the account true.

There is one more subject to which our attention has been drawn, and to which Cheetham refers, Mr. Paine's alleged ingratitude to Mr. Monroe. We have seen in the body of this work that Mr. Monroe took upon himself to declare Mr. Paine a citizen of the United States, and to presume that Washington, then president, must feel an interest in him. It is evident that Mr. Monroe did all he could in the *absence* of *direct instructions* from his government about Mr. Paine, which he does not appear to have possessed. And we have seen, when Mr. Paine finally left the prison, that he went by invitation to Mr. Monroe's house, and that he remained there above a year. We hear nothing of any engagement, and we cannot conceive that Mr. Monroe, as plenipotentiary at Paris, would take boarders, or that Mr. Paine would stay at his house uninvited, or one moment beyond an apparent welcome. Mr. Paine's company before, and at this time, was sought by many as an honor. He afterward resided with Mr. Bonneville, either with or without an engagement for board ; but in that case we know, when Bonneville was ruined by Bonaparte, for publishing a republican paper, that Mr. Paine, finding on his return here the means of hospitality, generously invited the whole family to share his comforts. We cannot, therefore, perceive in Mr. Paine a natural ingratitude. Cheetham states, and others have repeated it, that Mr. Monroe afterward became poor, and applied to Mr. Paine, whom he said was then rich, to *pay for his board*, while residing with the consul at Paris, and that Mr. Paine took no notice of the demand, and was therefore ungrateful. If this really occurred, and we think it likely, all we can say is that Mr. Monroe at this period must have become penurious. He was at that time looking forward to the presidency, which he afterward obtained; and if, while in this situation, he made a demand as a boarding-house keeper, while acting as minister in France, and that to a distinguished individual whom he had invited to his house, and with whom he had made no such engagement, for none is even pretended, he must have forgotten the dignity of an American consul in France, as well as a presumptive successor to the presidency. We are perfectly aware that men, when they become old, frequently become parsimonious; Mr. Paine did, in part; and that others, who are both just and generous, on particular occasions, are constitutionally parsimonious. This was the case with Franklin. We have therefore made some inquiry as to Mr. Monroe, and we find that he was not unmindful of his interest. While acting as minister at Paris, Mr. Jefferson, then president, gave him a commission to transact some business in a neighboring country, intending an appropriation to Mr. Monroe for this service, but to save to the country the *outfit* of an especial minister or consul, which we believe is about *nine thousand* dollars. This outfit Mr. Monroe, we find, afterward claimed and recovered, and hence we think it possible that he might have made the charge upon Mr. Paine before stated; but unless Mr. Paine had agreed to such a charge, which does not appear from Mr. Monroe's alleged letter, we think the affair rather to the discredit of the latter than to Mr. Paine; and if Mr. Paine treated the subject in the manner alleged, he probably considered as we do, that the demand never ought to have been made.

We shall now conclude with the will of Mr. Paine. This falsifies at once, one part of Mary Hinsdale's relation, viz, Mr. Paine's poverty; and one part being shown to be false we can have no belief in the rest, which depends on the same authority. The fact is, she is now living, and is known as a silly lying woman, disgraced in the eyes of some of her former religious connexions for this very crime.

THE WILL OF MR. THOMAS PAINE.

"*The People of the State of New York, by the Grace of God, Free and Independent, to all to whom these presents shall come or may concern,*   *Send Greeting :*

Know ye, That the annexed is a true copy of the will of THOMAS PAINE, deceased, as recorded in the office of our surrogate, in and for the city and county of New York. In testimony whereof, we have caused the seal of office of our said surrogate to be hereunto affixed. Witness, Silvanus Miller, Esq., surrogate of said county, at the city of New York, the twelfth day of July, in the year of our Lord one thousand eight hundred and nine, and of our Independence the thirty-fourth.
                                                SILVANUS MILLER.

The last will and testament of me, the subscriber, THOMAS PAINE, reposing confidence in my Creator God, and in no other being, for I know of no other, nor believe in any other, I Thomas Paine, of the state of New York, author of the work entitled 'Common Sense,' written in Philadelphia, in 1775, and published in that city the beginning of January, 1776, which awaked America to a Declaration of Independence, on the fourth of July following, which was as fast as the work could spread through such an extensive country; author also of the several numbers of the 'American Crisis' 'thirteen in all,' published occasionally during the progress of the revolutionary war—the last is on the peace; author also of the 'Rights of Man,' parts the first and second, written and published in London, in 1791 and '92; author also of a work on religion, 'Age of Reason,' parts the first and second. 'N. B. I have a third part by me in manuscript and an answer to the Bishop of Landaff;' author also of a work, lately published, entitled 'Examination of the passages in the New Testament quoted from the Old, and called prophesies concerning Jesus Christ,' and showing there are no prophecies of any such person; author also of several other works not here enumerated, Dissertations on the first Principles of Government,'—'Decline and Fall of the English System of Finance'—'Agrarian Justice,' &c., &c., make this my last will and testament, that is to say: I give and bequeath to my executors hereinafter appointed, Walter Morton and Thomas Addis Emmet, thirty shares I hold in the New York Phœnix Insurance Company, which cost me 1470 dollars, they are worth now upward of 1500 dollars, and all my moveable effects, and also the money that may be in my trunk or elsewhere at the time of my decease, paying thereout the expenses of my funeral, in trust as to the said shares, moveables, and money, for Margaret

Brazier Bonneville, wife of Nicholas Bonneville, of Paris, for her own sole and separate use, and at her own disposal, notwithstanding her coverture. As to my farm in New Rochelle, I give, devise, and bequeath the same to my said executors, Walter Morton and Thomas Addis Emmet, and to the survivor of them, his heirs and assigns for ever, in trust, nevertheless, to sell and dispose of the north side thereof, now in the occupation of Andrew A. Dean, beginning at the west end of the orchard and running in a line with the land sold to —— Coles, to the end of the farm, and to apply the money arising from such sale as hereinafter directed. I give to my friends Walter Morton, of the New York Phœnix Insurance company, and Thomas Addis Emmet, counsellor-at-law, late of Ireland, two hundred dollars each, and one hundred dollars to Mrs. Palmer, widow of Elihu Palmer, late of New York, to be paid out of the money arising from said sale, and I give the remainder of the money arising from that sale, one half thereof to Clio Rickman, of High or Upper Mary-la-bone street, London, and the other half to Nicholas Bonneville, of Paris, husband of Margaret B. Bonneville aforesaid: and as to the south part of the said farm, containing upward of one hundred acres, in trust, to rent out the same or otherwise put it to profit, as shall be found most advisable, and to pay the rents and profits thereof to the said Margaret B. Bonneville, in trust for her children, Benjamin Bonneville and Thomas Bonneville, their education and maintenance, until they come to the age of twenty-one years, in order that she may bring them well up, give them good and useful learning, and instruct them in their duty to God, and the practice of morality, the rent of the land or the interest of the money for which it may be sold, as hereinafter mentioned, to be employed in their education. And after the youngest of the said children shall have arrived at the age of twenty-one years, in further trust to convey the same to the said children share and share alike in fee simple. But if it shall be thought advisable by my executors and executrix, or the survivor or survivors of them, at any time before the youngest of the said children shall come of age, to sell and dispose of the said south side of the said farm, in that case I hereby authorize and empower my said executors to sell and dispose of the same, and I direct that the money arising from such sale be put into stock, either in the United States bank stock or New York Phœnix Insurance company stock, the interest or dividends thereof to be applied as is already directed, for the education and maintenance of the said children; and the principal to be transferred to the said children or the survivor of them on his or their coming of age. I know not if the society of people called quakers admit a person to be buried in their burying-ground, who does not belong to their society, but if they do or will admit me, I would prefer being buried there, my father belonged to that profession, and I was partly brought up in it. But if it is not consistent with their rules to do this, I desire to be buried on my farm at New Rochelle. The place where I am to be buried to be a square of twelve feet, to be enclosed with rows of trees, and a stone or post and railed fence, with a head-stone with my name and age engraved upon it, author of 'Common Sense.' I nominate, constitute, and appoint, Walter Morton, of the New York Phœnix Insurance company, and Thomas Addis Emmet, counsellor-at-law, late of Ireland, and Margaret B. Bonneville, executors and executrix to this my last will and testament, requesting them the said Walter Morton and Thomas Addis Emmet, that they will give what assistance they conveniently can to Mrs. Bonneville, and see that the children be well brought up. Thus placing confidence in their friendship, I herewith take my final leave of them and of the world. I have lived an honest and useful life to mankind; my time has been spent in doing good; and I die in perfect composure and resignation to the will of my Creator God. Dated this eighteenth day of January, in the year one thousand eight hundred and nine, and I have also signed my name to the other sheet of this will in testimony of its being a part thereof.

THOMAS PAINE. (L. S.)

Signed, sealed, published and declared by the testator, in our presence, who, at his request, and in the presence of each other, have set our names as witnesses thereto, the words 'published and declared' first interlined.

WILLIAM KEESE,
JAMES ANGEVINE,
CORNELIUS RYDER."

MONUMENT TO THOMAS PAINE.

ON the fourth of July, 1837, we visited the tomb, or place of burial, of Thomas Paine, near New Rochelle, and in the Beacon of July 15, 1837, thus described it (see Beacon, Vol. I. page 331):—

"The tomb is close by the road side, but over a stone fence, and now consists of a low, broken, rough, dry stone wall, of oblong shape, of about eight by four feet, with loose stones, grass, and earth, in the centre; the upright slab, simply marked with

'THOMAS PAINE, AUTHOR OF COMMON SENSE,'

no longer exists. After Cobbett violated the grave, and removed the bones from the remains of Mr. Paine, the headstone was broken, and pieces successively removed by different visiters: one large fragment was preserved by a lady in an opposite cottage, in which Mr. Paine had sometimes boarded, and in which Mr. and Madame Bonneville afterward boarded; but this fragment gradually suffered diminution, as successive visiters begged a piece of what they could no longer steal. To preserve the last remnant, this lady has had it plastered up in a wall.

'We discovered that the lady mentioned, the nearest neighbor to the tomb, would be favorable to the repair of the tomb, and we learned that she believed that such repairs would be popular among the neighbors; and on this understanding, in which we have not been deceived, we determined to commence a subscription to repair the tomb, or put up a monument; and before we left the village we obtained from Mr. James, who had then marble saw-mills in New Rochelle, a promise to be at the expense of putting up a heavy block of marble, instead of a head-stone, if purchased by subscription; subsequently Mr. Frazee, an eminent architect, offered in conjunction with some friends to give the work on a monument, if the materials were procured, and other expenses paid. This has now been accomplished, and paid for. The monument stands on the Paine farm, at the head of the grave, on twenty feet square, enclosed by a substantial wall on three sides, and an iron railing in front (not yet up, March 1841). It is built of the marble of the country, and is valued at about thirteen hundred dollars. The accompanying cut is a faint representation, and the following extract from a letter from the architect will best describe the monument and the feelings of the neighborhood, which is two miles from the village of New Rochelle."—G. V.

"NEW YORK, Nov. 12, 1839.

To MR. VALE:

Will you please to inform our friends that the monument to Thomas Paine is erected? On Friday last I took with me a rigger and went up to the quarries, and on that day we got the marble to the spot with the machinery and other apparatus necessary to the work.—At an early hour on Saturday morning, we mustered all hands at the grave, and commenced the erection of the monument in good earnest, and in good spirits. Everything worked well, and at three o'clock, P. M., the crown piece was on, and the erection complete.—No person was hurt, nor any part of the work broken or injured.—The people up there say it is a chaste and beautiful structure. Its purely Grecian character and simplicity of form, render its general effect truly impressive and interesting.—The summit is twelve and a half feet above the level of the road at that point.

Paine's monument.

I was much pleased to find that among the number of fifty persons and more, that were assembled to witness our labors, not an unkind look was seen, nor an unfriendly expression heard, during the time. All looked and spake as though their hearts were glad at seeing such marked regard—such noble and lasting honor paid to the GREAT PATRIOT of our revolution and the defender of the rights of man.

I have a little trimming to do yet on the head, which will occupy me the best part of a day; this I will endeavor to accomplish this week when the monument will be completed.

Very truly yours,
JOHN FRAZEE."

NOTE.—The manuscript of the life of Mr. Paine, for want of surplus funds, lay by us for four years, and in the interim some changes have necessarily taken place, which we believe we have noticed in the body of the work; but aware of this delay (not unfavorable to accuracy) and willing to secure the *living* testimony then in being, and which, from the age of some of the parties, was of uncertain tenure, we published in the Beacon from time to time, such evidences as we procured, with all the circumstances, and thus secured, while living, the sanction of some who have since died.—G. V.

Thomas Paine, whatever may have been his errors in his estimate of the teachings, life & character of Jesus Christ, — was a friend to the rights of man. So was Jesus. Yet Paine's friendliness to the rights of man, — by the so called christian church, was counted infidelity; & so was anti-slavery, in the U.S. untill after it's abolition. Surely the prophecy of Jesus has been fulfilled, wherein he said that Antichrist should come in his name — saying "I go sir" but going not; while others should say, "I go not sir", but go. "If the righteous scarcely be saved, — where shall the unrighteous appear?"

Printed in Dunstable, United Kingdom

82209104R00112